DONALD MacINTOSH

TRAVELS IN
GALLOWAY

Foreword by Tom Pow

NEIL WILSON PUBLISHING · GLASGOW · SCOTLAND

To my brother Neil

a Gallovidian through and through

and to my sister Christina

who started it all

ACKNOWLEDGEMENTS

The following publications are due my thanks for having first published material used in some of the chapters of this book. The relevant chapters are listed against each publication: *Verbatim* – Chapter 1; A Nyatterin' o' Nyaffs. *Waterlog* – Chapter 12, Gentlemen of the Shadows. *Scottish Memories* – Chapter 19, Doing Porridge in Africa and Galloway. *The Countryman* – Chapter 20, Spectral Woods. *Yesterday* – Chapter 20, Spectral Woods.

I should also like to thank the following for their help with chapters 15 and 18 respectively: the Parton Games Committee; Philip Atkins, curator of the National Rail Museum;

I am grateful to the following Gallovidians for their help and advice in the chapters listed: *Alex Houston* – Chapter 5, Salt Winds. *Jean Austin* – Chapter 5, Salt Winds and chapter 14, The Worthies. *Margaret McCreath* – Chapter 8, Waifs in the Wilderness. *Tom McCreath* – Chapter 4, The Secret Life of Ditches and chapter 14, The Worthies.

And to my many Wigtownshire friends, past and present, who have given me so much fun over the years.

Lang mey yer lum reek – wi' ither folk's coal, av coorse!

First published by
Neil Wilson Publishing
303a The Pentagon Centre
36 Washington Street
GLASGOW G3 8AZ
Tel: 0141-221-1117
Fax: 0141-221-5363
E-mail: nwp@cqm.co.uk
http://www.nwp.co.uk/

ISBN 1-897784-92-9
Typeset in Joanna
Designed by Mark Blackadder
Printed by WSOY, Finland

CONTENTS

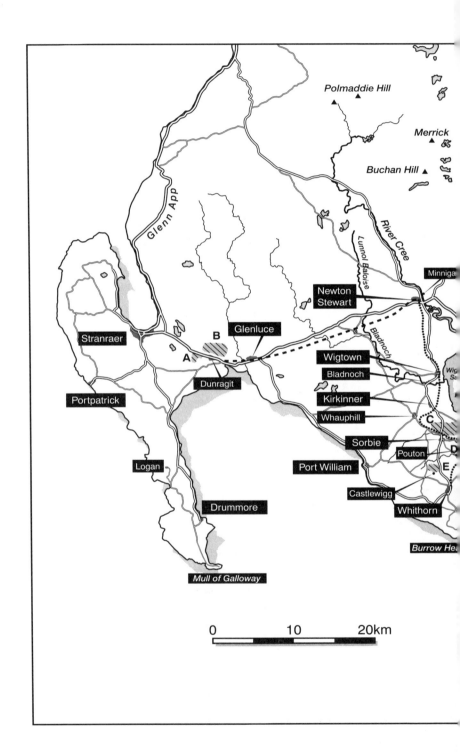

Polmaddie Hill ▲

Merrick ▲

Buchan Hill ▲

Glenn App

River Cree

Lunnol Baloise

Minniga

Newton Stewart

Bladnoch

Stranraer

Glenluce

B

A

Wigtown

Dunragit

Bladnoch

Wig Sa

Kirkinner

Portpatrick

Whauphill

C

Sorbie

D

Pouton

E

Logan

Port William

Drummore

Castlewigg

Whithorn

Burrow Hea

Mull of Galloway

0   10   20km

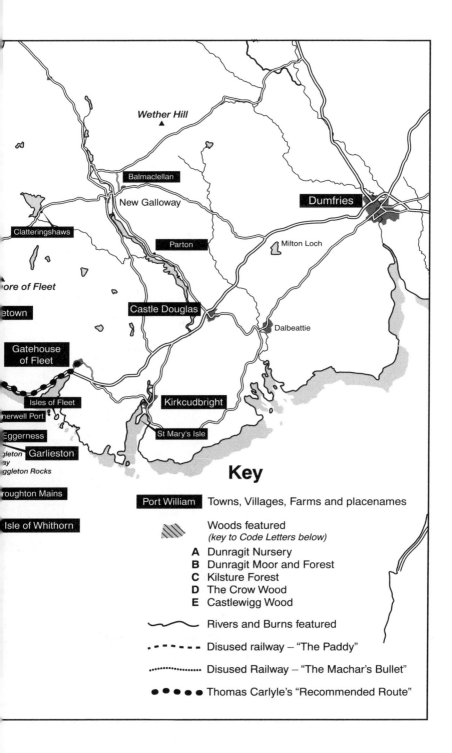

Wether Hill ▲

Balmaclellan

New Galloway

Dumfries

Clatteringshaws

Parton

Milton Loch

ore of Fleet

etown

Castle Douglas

Dalbeattie

Gatehouse
of Fleet

Isles of Fleet

nerwell Port

Kirkcudbright

Eggerness

St Mary's Isle

gleton Garlieston
ay
ggleton Rocks

roughton Mains

Isle of Whithorn

Key

| Port William | Towns, Villages, Farms and placenames |

Woods featured
(key to Code Letters below)
A Dunragit Nursery
B Dunragit Moor and Forest
C Kilsture Forest
D The Crow Wood
E Castlewigg Wood

Rivers and Burns featured

- - - - - - Disused railway – "The Paddy"

.... Disused Railway – "The Machar's Bullet"

● ● ● ● ● Thomas Carlyle's "Recommended Route"

TRAVELS IN
GALLOWAY

Land o' birk and rowan tree
Land o' fell and forest free
Land that's aye sae dear tae me –
Bonnie Gallowa'

Tom Pow

FOREWORD

As I write this Donald MacIntosh's first book, *Travels In The White Man's Grave* is contending for a major travel book award. Here are two short but characteristic extracts from it:

> *The gaboon viper's fangs are hollow and resemble curved hypodermic syringes. They are very long – a skull I found many years ago in Sapoba, Nigeria, had fangs measuring two inches. It has a very large volume of venom compared to the cobra, but its venom is less concentrated. Nevertheless, the enormous quantity it injects, combined with the power of its strike and the depth to which it buries its fangs in its victim, can make treatment very difficult indeed.*

And the second:

> *Though admittedly sorely tempted in later years at times, I have not, so far, got round to testing the toxicity of sasswood poison on any human being, and I have never, alas, been in a situation so erotic that experiments with ozouga bark might have been beneficial to me.*

What is striking here is the clarity of the writing in the first extract and, in the second, the tone – the familiarity he has with his material which allows the unforced humour. It is obvious also that the learning, so unostentatiously displayed, is derived, not from the library, but from his own lived experience. It many ways this sets his book apart; for, like any genre that has become popular, travel writing has been invaded by gimmickry; we now have books about humphing a fridge around Ireland or being humphed by an elephant around India. Perhaps, as Scots, we shouldn't complain about this trend as one of our greatest travel writers initiated the genre by travelling through the Cevennes on a donkey. Scholars have also noted the extent to which Stevenson relied on the library to flesh out the bones of his narrative upon his return.

Whatever, Donald MacIntosh is not that kind of writer and, because his relationship to his subject matter is not circumstantial or haphazard, you will find *Travels In Galloway* is more than a one-dimensional travel book. You will encounter the same clarity and easy learning that characterises his first book – the voice of the learned companion; who can make the humble earthworm as interesting to us as the gaboon viper:

> If [the worm] *escapes drought and drowning and predatory blackbirds and moles and little boys with bent pins, the earthworm stands a good chance of living to the ripe old age of six years, doing so mainly on a diet of dead vegetation and, occasionally, dead animals and even, I am told, on us.* "The worms crawl in and the worms crawl out; they play pinochle in your snout..." *goes an old drinking song.*

However, MacIntosh's interests in these travels aren't so much with the geography of Galloway as with its recent historical past. With the recall of those whose noses were always perforce in their own community, and in the immediacy of the natural world which surrounded them, before our collective attentions were fractured by television, MacIntosh's time travels teem with characters, anecdotes and incidents from his Galloway boyhood. There is certainly delight here and some understandable nostalgia, but also a sense of elegy springing from his determination to give us the richness of the world he knew – the fishermen, the sportsmen, the land girls, the forestry workers... For Donald is aware – at the turn of this century – of what has changed and what has remained the same. His historical sense ensures that he does not judge the moment, yet his Galloway is one that is in many ways vanishing or vanished. In this always engaging gallimaufry of a book – part-guide book, part-memoir, part-collection of essays – we travel through it one more time. We could not have a more delightful guide or a better reason for making the journey – it will make our present more interesting for us.

And incidentally, it makes the best case for hand-picking your own rasps you could hope to read.

Tom Pow, Dumfries, July 1999

Chapter 1
A NYATTERIN' O' NYAFFS

'Any fool can write a book, but it takes a man to herd the Merrick.'
Old Galloway saying

There is an old and much told story that Queen Victoria, in conversation with the historian Thomas Carlyle, asked him what he considered to be the loveliest road in all of Britain. 'The road from Creetown to Gatehouse of Fleet,' he informed her without hesitation. Knowing that Carlyle hailed from that part of the world, and suspecting that there may have been an element of bias in his answer, the monarch asked him what then did he consider to be the second loveliest road in the whole kingdom. 'The road from Gatehouse of Fleet to Creetown,' was the uncompromising reply from that discerning man of letters.

Carlyle was not the only scholar to have a good knowledge of Galloway, or indeed, of Gatehouse of Fleet. Robert Burns arrived there one night in a filthy mood, having ridden his pony 20 miles through a violent storm from Kenmure Castle. His newly purchased and highly expensive pair of English leather boots had disintegrated in the downpour en route and tradition has it that, looking for someone to savage on his arrival at Gatehouse, he had thought about his boots and, naturally enough, selected the English as the target for his grievances. Armed with a tumbler of whisky, a quill pen and a notebook, he sat down to write *Scots Wha Hae*.

Were either Burns or Her Imperial Majesty able to travel the main Gatehouse to Creetown road today, their ponies would get the fright of their lives. It is a real state-of-the-art highway nowadays, and it sears its way across Galloway from the River Nith to Stranraer. Great juggernauts thunder daily along this route at fantastic speeds and in enormous numbers, heading to and from the Irish ferry. Drivers of these metal monsters are rarely interested in the scenery around them: they are too intent upon getting to their destination as fast as possible and in avoiding collision with all the other nutters on the road. For them, Galloway is only one of the many places they have to pass through, and there is nothing more to it than that. Few of them would know anything of the history and the beauty of the place, and fewer still would believe you if you tried to tell them.

Which is a shame, for this is a corner of Scotland that is steeped in history and it has places of beauty to rival any. 'See the Waters o' Minnoch on a clear day,' eulogized an old Newton Stewart friend to me over a pint or three, 'an' ye'll nivver want tae see the Tadge MacCall again.' The publicity department of the Scottish Tourist Board could not have phrased it better.

In ethnological and theological terms, Galloway goes right back to the beginning of civilized (and not so civilized) time in Scotland. The dark little Picts were here, and indeed some legends would have it that the last known members of their race expired here. (Others, less kind perhaps, would have it that they are still alive and well in some of the more remote parts.) A very old poem tells the story of 'Trost of the Long Knife', whose family members were the traditional custodians of the secret recipe for Heather Ale:

> From the bonny bells of heather,
> They brewed a drink lang-syne,
> Twas sweeter far than honey
> And stronger far than wine...

Trost and his young son, the only ones left in possession of the recipe, were cornered by enemies at the southern tip of Wigtownshire's Rhinns peninsula and there they were threatened with torture if they refused to divulge the secret. Trost pushed his son over the cliff to his death, for – as so eloquently declaimed in the poem – while he, being of mature years, knew that he could never buckle under any kind of torture, he did not have quite the same degree of faith in the younger generation.

Evidence of ancient settlements is to be found wherever you go in Galloway, for the climate was mellow and the grazing was good. The remains of protective brochs and crannogs dating back to 5,000 BC would appear to indicate that the reception they received was not always as mellow as the climate. These early settlers left behind them no written records, and the relics that can be seen with the naked eye today are as mysterious as the people who created them. Huge flat standing stones jut upward from the green sward in the loneliest of places, and cup-and-ring markings chiselled into the boulders in similar spots leave one with the indelible impression of a race of hermits with a masochistic sense of humour. Had they nothing better to do with their time than to haul colossal slabs of stone upright and dig them into the ground, and to painstakingly chip meaningless designs into solid rock for no other reason than to have future generations scratching their heads and arguing with each other as to their meanings? Crannogs such as the one on Milton Loch, Kirkcudbright, are easier to explain. These man-made islands not only protected one's family from the squalling of the next-door neighbour's weans; they also helped protect one's livestock from wolves and other creatures of the night, both four-legged and two-legged.

Most of the modern speculation about the origins and lifestyle of the people responsible for these constructions is just that: sheer speculation. As usual, it was left to the scholastic missionaries to create some order out of the mysteries surrounding the origins and way of life of our forebears by keeping records, scanty though these may have been in the beginning. Although few of the early manuscripts survived, some of their buildings and relics did, and these tell their own story.

'St Ninian came to Galloway to teach Christianity to the Catholics,' wrote a Stranraer child in an essay competition, 'and he succeeded with some of the Whithorn savages.' The missionary Ninian is credited with having been the founder of Christianity in Scotland, establishing his bishopric and mission at Whithorn early in the 5th century. The 'Whithorn Dig' has produced many spectacular artefacts, including a beautiful 12th-century crozier, and the small museum at the site of the ancient priory is well worth a visit.

These early missionaries were sincere and dedicated men. Their good qualities were many, but tolerance could not be claimed to have been high among their virtues. They were the first of the genuine male chauvinists. The arch-chauvinist was Columba, the celebrated founder of the Iona mission. (Ninian pre-dated him in Galloway, but Columba obviously had the better PR.) In Columba's Hebrides, tending milch-cows had always been the traditional task of the women, and, as Columba was very much against the distaff side of the human race, he would allow neither cows nor women on Iona. Some of his younger and friskier priests attempted to put pressure upon him, trying to point out the benefits to be gained from the addition of milk and butter to the spartan mission diet. The worldly-wise Columba, deducing instantly – and perhaps correctly – that their concerns were more of a prurient than a dietary nature replied austerely in Gaelic:

'Far am bi bò bithidh bean, is far am bi bean bithidh molluchadh!'
('Where there is a cow there is a woman, and where there is a woman there is mischief!')

It was a saying that I heard quite frequently in the Mull of my youth whenever husband and wife fell out.

Religion, alas, brought another kind of intolerance over the centuries throughout Scotland. Galloway did not escape the brutality meted out to the Covenanters. Presbyterians were rounded up and shot or hacked to death wherever they gathered in secret prayer, and the barbaric end to the Wigtown Martyrs is now part of the folklore of Scotland. Two women, Margaret Wilson, aged 18, and Margaret MacLachlan, aged 63, were tied to stakes and drowned by the rising tide on the Wigtown Sands in 1685 for refusing to renounce their

Covenanter beliefs. (The graves of the two women, along with those of male martyrs who were hanged, can be seen in the old kirkyard at Wigtown, while the approximate site of the women's drowning is marked by a monument.) Corpses were often left to rot on the moors where they had been massacred, with friends and relatives forbidden to move them. Not all had headstones to mark their passing, but memorials to these victims can still be found here and there throughout Galloway and a local rhyme reveals much:

A grave – a grave is by the sea – in a place of ancient tombs –
A restless murmuring of waves, for ever o'er it comes –
A pleasant sound in summer tide – a requiem low and clear
But oh! when storms are on the hill – it hath a voice of fear

Someone once said that the greater the human tragedies, the greater the beauty of the land. It certainly applies to Galloway.

It is a land of natural – and sometimes surprising – beauty. Thanks to the warming effect of the Gulf Stream, near-tropical plants can be found growing in the cultivated splendour of the Logan Botanical Gardens to the south of Stranraer, and the wild and scenic grandeur of the Southern Upland Way, a 220-mile long trail across the south of Scotland, has its beginning at Portpatrick. Go where you will in Galloway and you will be confronted by burn and lochan and seascape, rugged coastline and placid sandy beaches, heather-clad hills and whin-covered knowes, brackeny birch woods and emerald pastureland, all combining to make this rather forgotten part of Scotland a joy to the visitor who still hankers for places that have not yet succumbed to the call of the hamburger and the caterwauling of the Spice Girls.

The modern highway that slices Galloway in two nowadays knows nothing of these quiet places, nor does it wish to know anything about them. But people of discernment who care to drift just a few miles to the north or to the south of this roaring motorway will find a way of life that is balm to the weary soul. Industry does exist, but it is small and never intrusive. Creameries cater for what is still, in the main, a pastoral way of life, even though (due to this modern obsession with 'centralization') they are admittedly thinner on the ground now than they used to be. Bladnoch, the most southerly distillery in Scotland has been closed for a number of years, but rumour hath it that it is scheduled to reopen at about the same time as London's great Millennium Dome is due to open its doors to an eager public. One lives in hope that this is so, and that the clean, pure air of Bladnoch will soon be rendered even cleaner and purer by that fragrance familiar to lovers of all that is good about Scotland. There can be few more distressing sights on God's green earth than a silent distillery.

Small businesses abound, but you have to search for them. Some surprises will be in store for the successful seeker: Creetown's Gem Rock Museum contains precious stones from all over the world and is considered to be one of the finest of its kind in Britain, while Wigtown's elevation to Book Town status in 1998 produced a rash of bookshops of quite astonishing variety in the old county town. Add to this the fact that excellent dining places are plentiful even in rural areas during the summer months, and it can be seen that tourism is considered a vital boost to the local economy.

The famous dry-stane dykes of Galloway can be seen everywhere. They, fortunately, have not succumbed to progress. Nor has the craftsman who builds them. Using the simplest of tools, like all the generations before him, the dry-stane dyker still plies his age-old trade through fields and by roadsides and over upland slopes. A dry-stane dyke built by a master of his craft is truly a thing of rare beauty, and it is a craft that, thank God, one can never envisage being 'improved' by the drab uniformity of computerization.

The lonely, whitewashed houses of the 'herds' are also still to be found scattered among the sheltered corries on far-off hills, for, like the dry-stane dyker, the Galloway herd, one hopes, will always be needed. The bleakest moors and the rugged sides of Cairnsmore and the Merrick are home to the blackface sheep, a breed as hardy as the men who tend them. Like their herds, the blackface will survive where others would perish. The freezing rain and the blizzards of winter hold few terrors for this hardy beast; it is well insulated against Galloway's winter storms for it has the thickest of coats, and lives happily on a diet of heather shoots and wiry hill grass. Even when the snow lies deep on the ground it will scrape its way down to reach its food supply. The blackface ram is a splendid looking chap, with great spiralling horns reminiscent of the Bighorn of the Canadian Rockies. The largest of Britain's hill breeds, he has a most imperious look about him, with the long face and the long nose and the cold, supercilious gaze one associates with Britain's ruling classes. The blackface sheep of the Galloway hills look tough and their looks do not deceive: lamb flesh is excellent and tender, but that from a ram who has roamed the frozen crags and screes for many a long and arduous winter is meant to be tackled only by the masticating powers and metal-dissolving digestive juices of one of the larger carnivorous reptiles of the late Cretaceous period.

There are occasional downsides of course, as there are in any area of outstanding natural beauty. The sombre bottle-green of the coniferous forests that blanket vast stretches of hill and moorland is not to everyone's liking. Nor is the way in which felled areas are left an unsightly bourach: jagged stumps and piles of broken branches, a scene reminiscent of the Somme in the Great War and a fitting reminder of modern man's shoddy workmanship. 'The mess will soon get buried by the undergrowth,' is the airy claim of the commercial tree extractor and, for good measure, the old cliché is added: 'After all, there's only one week's difference between a bad haircut and a good one.'

The starkness and sheer ugliness of the massive concrete dams built in the past by the hydroelectric people intrude less now than they used to, mainly because they are hidden from the view of the casual visitor, but also because they are popular attractions for fishermen and others who indulge in other, more energetic, water sports. High-powered boats screaming up and down those waters towing water-skiers is certainly not everyone's idea of rural tranquillity even in this frenetic age, and the dams were decidedly unpopular with the early environmentalists. The Galloway poet WGM Dobie wrote:

> This is our land of Galloway
> Where, in a more heroic day,
> The Bruce contrived to trap and slay
> An army of invaders.
> A raider comes today who kills
> The glories of our glens and hills
> With unheroic Acts and Bills
> And 'private legislation';
> The company promoter's pen
> Will dam the Deugh and dam the Ken
> And dam the Dee – oh, damn the men
> Who plan such desecration!

But it is not the occasional irritation that the visitor to Galloway remembers as he speeds along the motorway on his way back to the dreariness of his urban life. It is the beauty that he remembers. It matters not that it occasionally rains in Galloway. One day of sunshine over the glorious Galloway coastline and all is forgiven. Just one day free from the rain and the midges and the whole holiday has been a resounding success. It is always the beauty of the place and the friendliness of the people that will stick most in the mind of the departing guest.

Perhaps not quite: what he will remember more – and remember even unto his dying day – will be the Galloway dialect.

Some years ago I was a passenger in a car travelling along the shoreline of Luce Bay. The driver was an old friend and he was a small-time entrepreneur who took on such petty contracts around the county as would bring him some beer money and keep him out of jail. My friend was waxing eloquent about the village we were approaching – a village which, in view of the following story, had better remain nameless. He had recently been severely defrauded over a job of work which he had completed in the village and, as a result, he had declared a personal and very bitter jihad against all its inhabitants. As we trundled slowly along the street we espied in front of us a group of youths gathered at what has, from time immemorial, been the focal point for gossip in all Wigtownshire seaside villages – the brig by the shore. As we passed them, four of the youths, obviously recognizing my companion, raised an ironic cheer and made obscene gestures at us. 'Friends of yours, Andy?' I asked ironically. He looked at me sourly. 'Nay bliddy freends o' mine,' he remarked savagely and continued: 'Ye mind when we were at schule and we had tae learn a' these group names for animals and burds? Like "a flock o' sheep" and "a herd o' coos" and "a gaggle o' geese" and things like that?'

'Aye,' I replied, mystified. 'What of it?'

'Weel,' said he morosely, 'that bunch o' eejits is what ye would ca' a nyatterin' o' nyaffs.'

The Galloway dialect is unique. To one brought up with it – as I was – it is music to the ears when spoken by an old Gallovidian. But there is no doubt that, to the stranger, it can be as incomprehensible as Tocharian. We are told by some etymologists that it is a mixture of many languages and dialects and that may or may not be so, for Galloway has been reluctant host to many different races. But the earlier inhabitants, the shy Mesolithic tribes and the mysterious Picts, vanished forever into the moorland mists before the invaders. With them, they took their language.

The Roman came and went, leaving not so much as a place name behind him. Indeed, had not his Latin been adopted by the scholastic monks of the day, little would have remained to show that he had ever been there in the first place. 'Veni, vidi, vici,' he crowed smugly. 'And then,' as a historian friend so succinctly put it, 'he just buggered off.'

The Celt brought religion and the Gaelic. Unlike the Roman, the Celt left his mark in the many place names of Gaelic origin one can find throughout Galloway to this day. Stranraer, the largest town in Wigtownshire, is one such. Its name means, literally, 'fat peninsula', from the Gaelic *sròn reamhar*.

9

Gaelic was the mother tongue in much of Galloway for 12 centuries, but little trace of it remains in the spoken language of today. It was the pervasive Anglo-Saxon who set the foundation for the dialect spoken by today's generation in much of Kirkcudbright. But, while the Anglo-Saxon had a massive influence also in Wigtownshire, it is with nearby Ulster that its inhabitants had the greatest affinity. Indeed, to this day they call themselves and their dialect 'Gallowa'-Irish'.

It is as good a description as any. Although it is a form of English that they speak, the stranger would be hard put to believe it when he or she first hears them in full flow. It is a lingo that has little in common with either the slow, precise enunciation of the Highlander or the clipped phraseology of Nöel Coward. It is a thick macédoine of broad Scots and Ulster English, and it can have a most uncompromising rasp to it, especially if you don't understand a word that is being said to you.

Which, it might be added, is often the case if you happen to be a newcomer to that part of the world. Simple phrases like 'I wish to dismantle it' become 'Ah'm gaan tae tak' it sinnery', and even simpler words like 'foolish' become 'glaikit', so that by the end of your first day you are desperately searching for strong drink and the services of a good interpreter.

The 'Gallowa'-Irish' are a people of humour. There can, admittedly, be a cynically schadenfreude quality to some of it, for theirs has always been a hard life. But, more often than not, it is their Irish sense of fun that surfaces. Occasionally – and especially for those not accustomed to the dialect – their pronunciation of certain words can lead to embarrassing misunderstandings, as the following tale from my youth may illustrate.

Aul' Wullie was a smallholder. His only interest in life was his wee farm, and he had laboured long and hard among the stones and the whins to wrest a living of sorts from the reluctant soil. It was a way of life that would have crippled a lesser man, but Wullie was a tough old bird: when the day of his 100th birthday dawned he was still maintaining a keen interest in the daily running of his little place.

The old man would have been content to allow the occasion of his centenary to pass unremarked, but his extensive family had other ideas. They arranged a mighty soirée for the great day, and they invited a reporter from one of the county's newspapers to the event to record it for posterity. The reporter – a rather prim young product of singularly devout parents – was not only on her first such assignment, but, to make things even more difficult for her, she was completely new to Galloway.

Aul' Wullie was not his usual cheerful self. He seemed preoccupied, and he sat in his chair by the hearth sipping moodily at his whisky. The reporter's interview was not going well. In desperation, the girl asked him if there was anything she could do for him to make his day a happy one. A spark of life glimmered in the old man's rheumy eyes. 'Aye, lassie, there is that,' he replied with sudden interest, '…ye could gie me some sex.'

She recoiled in shock. When she had recovered somewhat, her messianic zeal boiled over and she reminded him that, at his advanced age, he should be more concerned with thoughts of the afterlife than with the prurient temptations of this one. She would probably have pursued this subject at some length had not the old man interrupted her.

'Mebbee ye're richt, lassie,' he said doubtfully, 'but ah still need the sex. Ye see, ah've got foarty-fower hunnerwecht o' tatties oot there ahint the byre, an' ah've nae sex tae pit them in.'

It is not, however, a dialect that travels well, and in a lifetime of working in a variety of countries overseas I cannot say that I have ever heard it spoken among Scots in everyday conversation. However, two Wigtownshire acquaintances of mine claimed to have heard it spoken in the most unlikely of places and by the most unlikely of sources.

The two of them were standing, drinks in hand, at the edge of the compound of an expatriate club in darkest Africa. It was just before sundown and the view before them was stunning – a great panorama of green plain stretching from the foot of the hill far below them to the shores of the Gulf of Guinea. They were talking animatedly in

1 1

'Gallowa'-Irish' about the beauty of it all. Near to them was a solitary African, also obviously enjoying the view. He was one of those Africans one comes across now and again whose coloration was so dark as to be almost blue-black, and, as he was rather humbly dressed, they assumed him to be a club steward or garden labourer. One of them spoke to him: 'Beautiful view, isn't it!'

The African smiled at them and replied in the broadest of Wigtownshire: 'Aye, it's no' bad ava'. But it's no' half as nice as the yin across the watter tae the Cairnsmore fae the Baltersan strecht!'

He had, so the story goes, been brought up in the Newton Stewart area before graduating as a medical doctor and returning to practice in his own country.

*   *   *

I had one moment of fun myself in darkest England with the dialect of Galloway. For reasons that need not detain us here, some years ago I happened to be in the translation section of a large publishing company in Hertfordshire, and I became involved in conversation with one of the employees, a charming young French translator. The subject of regional dialects in our respective countries came up. Being very new to Britain and having, so far, only encountered 'school English', she found it difficult to believe that dialectal variation could be so great in this tight little island of ours, and that so much of it could be so unintelligible to the uninitiated. We were interrupted in our discussion by the arrival of a worker clad in a boiler suit of some antiquity. I could not recall having seen him before, but I would have recognized the type anywhere. He was a raw-boned, sallow little chap with sunken eyes and lived-in features such as might have been found aplenty in bygone days while walking out mean-looking whippets in the thin grey mists of gloaming around the moorland tracks of Mossdale and Carsphairn. At that moment I would have bet my very soul that he hailed from Galloway, and the first words he uttered showed the intuition inherited from my mystic Hebridean forebears to be firing on all cylinders.

'Huv ye seen ma gaffer, Jim?' he queried. I sneaked a sidelong look at my companion and a glow of the purest contentment spread slowly through me. She was about to get her first lesson, and I could feel in my bones that it was going to be a good one.

'I don't think I know your boss,' I hedged craftily. 'What does he look like?'

The little man took off his bunnet. He removed a squashed cigarette from somewhere inside it and lit it carefully with the minute, barely smouldering stump of the old one. He drew with deep satisfaction on his reefer and exhaled a cloud of acrid blue smoke around us. He glanced at her, the world-weary eyes of old Scotia and the prelapsarian ingenuousness of Young Picardie's meeting in a fleeting look that spanned the ages. He coughed harshly and spat copiously on the ground. Then he let her have it with both barrels:

'Och,' he intoned with Bren-gun rapidity, 'he's jeest a greetin' wee gomeril wi' a skelly cack e'e an' a manky broony-kinna gansey.'

When he had gone, my young French friend asked me in understandable bewilderment: 'What sort of language was that?'

'English,' I replied innocently.

'ENGLISH??'

'Well, yes, sort of...'

'Oh my God!' she exclaimed, appalled. 'And I am supposed to be a translator! What on earth was he saying?'

I thought carefully for a moment or two before committing myself: 'He intimated that, in his humble opinion, his overseer is a diminutive malcontent of a somewhat devious and dissentient bent, that he is afflicted with a strabismus of the sinistral optical member, and is currently attired in a rather noisome woollen torsal garment of an indeterminate off-chocolate hue.'

She stood before me like a stricken stirk, her eyes glazed and her mouth agape. Then her teeth clicked shut and she lanced me with a look of frosted French steel. 'I theenk you are taking the meeckey out of me,' she ground out savagely. And off she flounced.

It was 1945. The Russians had entered Berlin and the war in Europe was drawing to a close. I was eavesdropping on a conversation between two forestry workers. They were cynics, as most old countrymen tend to be, and neither was convinced that the war just ending would be the war to end all wars. One of them, a Home Guard veteran, was particularly emphatic on the matter:

'Tak' heed o' whut ah tell ye, Erchie,' warned the sage, 'They'll be anither waar yet, so there wull. Wi' the Rooshans. An' whun it dis stert, ah wud wudger ma wumman an' weans agin yours that it'll be a faar waar waar th'n th' last waar wur.'

Indeed it may. But the invader had better come prepared if he dares to venture west of the Nith. He is in for a long, hard slog in the wind and the rain and the sleet if he wishes to master the 'Gallowa'-Irish'.

Chapter 2
THE CRUGGLETON ROCKS

The unlikely combination of Adolf Hitler and a Hebridean inshore fisherman almost put paid to my burgeoning interest in the sea before it had properly begun. It was, I vividly recall, a glorious summer in Mull, and I had spent much of it out on the water with a variety of 'uncles', either fishing for pollack and mackerel or cutting up dogfish for lobster bait.

It was I who spotted the mine first. Nothing looked more like the cartoonist's idea of what a mine should look like, with its long, horny projections chillingly visible as it undulated lethargically on the placid ocean surface, like a giant sea urchin floating in glycerine. But there was nothing funny about it to me. It was big and it was black and it was downright evil-looking. If it had had a bright-red swastika plastered on it, it could not have looked more sinister to me. All I craved at that moment was to get myself out of there, and right quickly at that.

But uncle Neil was made of sterner stuff. He was not for turning. To my absolute horror he rowed right up to the mine and began to push at it with his oar. 'There's usually a ring on them,' he nonchalantly informed me as I tried to make myself invisible among the fish gurry at the bottom of the boat. 'If we can find it, we can tie a rope to her to make her safe.'

'I feel sick,' I croaked, '...and I want to go home.'

'Be sick in the sea,' he said callously, 'and then grab one of these horns. Then see if you can turn the pugger over and catch hold of the pluddy ring.' He gave the mine another couple of violent prods, the oar clunking dully and threateningly against the metal casing.

I went green. 'For the love of Jesus, uncle Neil, let's get out of here,' I implored, 'You're might be old and not care if you die, but I'm only fourteen and I want to stay alive.'

Uncle Neil, who must have been 30 if he was a day, looked irked. He gave the mine another hefty poke. 'Man, but you are timid, timid,' he muttered reproachfully. 'No wonder those Sassenach hoors beat us at Culloden, with you pluddy MacIntoshes on our side.' He manoeuvred the dinghy round until he was next to the mine and grasping two of its horns, he flipped it over.

His knowledge of mines would have earned him the highest commendation from Admiral Karl Dönitz. There was, indeed, a large iron ring attached to the underside of it. Neil gazed at it in triumph. 'There!' he exclaimed. 'What did I tell you! Now, if you'll chust be patient while I light my pipe, we'll tie our rope to her and anchor her down with some of this pig iron ballast until the mines' officials come and blow her up.'

Later that night, by the cottage fire, as Neil puffed contentedly on his pipe, he pondered on the day's events. 'But it's myself that wouldn't care for that mine disposal chob. Man, they must have nerves of steel, these poys, to be working with these damt things aal the time.' He took the pipe from the corner of his mouth and spat fluidly into the fire. The gob of phlegm sizzled gruesomely somewhere in the heart of the peat flames.

'Mines,' he cautioned, 'can be aaful delicate things. Don't you effer be tempted to play with them. It needs a man with the finest of touches to be handling them. I've often been told that I'd be chust ideal for the chob myself, but ach! I don't know, somehow I kind of doubt that I'd have the courage for it at aal.'

*   *   *

But once you have been bitten by the sea bug, it takes a lot more than a Nazi megalomaniac and his weapons of war to cure you. Since those days, I have fished for cod off Newfoundland's wild and windswept shores and I have had barracuda and moray eel on the end of my line in equatorial waters. The guarantee of excitement was the common factor when setting off on a day's fishing in any of those places. There was the thrill of the uncertainty about what surprises the day might have in store for you, and — perhaps because I was at an impressionable age then — it was always a similar surge of excitement that gripped me whenever I was about to set off on a fishing trip around my beloved Hebrides, even without the mines. Nowhere else but in those three parts of the world have I ever experienced that heart-thumping, blood-racing joie de vivre that would take over my whole being at the beginning of a fishing trip. They were special places, each with their own special memories. But for sheer, indolent tranquillity, the sea-fishing days I remember best nowadays were those Sundays of long ago, before the advent of World War II, that I spent with my father and brother on the rocky shores of Cruggleton, near Garlieston in Wigtownshire.

It was not that I remember us ever catching much that was worth taking home on many of those expeditions. We would, of course, get the usual collection of bony little wrasse, the very occasional rock cod and once, even, a large coalfish, but more often than not we caught nothing at all. It could not be said that the Old Man was even much of a sea-fishing enthusiast — although he loved fishing on burn and river and was well-equipped for it. He possessed neither the proper rod nor the tackle for sea-fishing. Looking back on that period of his life now, I rather think that this was his escape from reality; an escape for 12 glorious hours from the sheer starkness of a life in which he was expected to provide for a growing family on Dickensian wages in those bleak years leading up to the war. It was the sort of escape that only the broad scope of the seascape and the openness of the ocean could provide. On the burn bank he was hemmed in by trees or bushes or whins or cows or sheep or something or other; but sitting on a bare rock with nothing but the sound of the waves and the gulls and with the wind and the salt spray on his face, a man had space – the space and the time to think or not to think as the fancy took him...

The seas that shape the Cruggleton rocks are a long way south of those patrolled by my eccentric Uncle Neil in those long-gone days. Between them lies the great industrial waterway of the Clyde and, going south from there, the long, narrow beaches of Largs and Troon and Ayr, traditional haunts of bucket and spade trippers from Glasgow who came 'doon the watter' before the coming of the motor car. Aeons of culture, language differences and geographical turmoil separate those coastlines and there would, on superficial examination, appear to be little that might tie the one to the other.

But there are similarities. The Gael was here, too, around Cruggleton, a long time ago, for the Gael was ever a lover of wild and lonely places. Today, the Gael has gone from Wigtownshire but the wild and lonely places remain in the craggy coastline that fringes much of that country. It is, admittedly, a coastline that may lack something of the intimidating grandeur of the Western Highlands, but this is still 'Caledonia stern and wild'. In from the coast, the land may have a more civilized, more cultivated look about it these days, but once you are out of sight of the farms and down on the black rocks that face the sea you don't need too vivid an imagination to find yourself transported back to a time when Celt and Pict grubbled for mussels and limpets among the bladderwrack beneath them.

It was always Sunday when we set off to the rocks to fish, and not just any old Sunday at that. My father had to be in the mood for it, and, equally importantly, the tides had to be right. The weather mattered little to him: wind, rain or sunshine, if the humour was upon him, he always did what he wanted to do. The problem was, when he wanted to go rock fishing, his plans always included us, the heirs to his misfortunes. My brother George and I spent days not fit for a dog, perched on some slippery prominence jutting out to sea, simply because the Old Man happened to be in the mood to commune with nature in the raw.

Tide times were important. The tide had to be out early so that we could dig up our lugworm bait at first light on the Garlieston foreshore, and we had to be out of there and on our way to the rocks by the time it had started to come back in. It was about three miles by cycle and foot from Garlieston village to 'our' section of the Cruggleton rocks, and we had to cut our rods of fresh green ash by the roadside en route.

Digging up the lugworm was the only hard part of the whole day. Even then, the Old Man would do most of it: we children simply did the gathering of the beasties. We would arrive on the Garlieston shore shortly after dawn, the little harbour before us dark in shadow and the early morning sun glowing prettily pink on the walls of the sleeping houses along the seafront behind us. Neither the crow of a rooster nor the bark of a dog could be heard from the village as the Old Man toiled and sweated over the heavy black silt, and even the gulls lined up on the Eggerness shore across the bay would be silent, fatly somnolent and pristine white as they squatted, shoulders hunched, awaiting the return of the tide later that morning.

The Garlieston lugworm were of particularly good quality. Nine inches long and as thick as a man's finger, their skin shone with that greenish-black patina that all health-conscious lugworms strive to acquire. But, like many a good thing in life, they could be very hard to come by. Their distinctive casts could be seen a-plenty on the surface, all right, but at the first vibration of footsteps on the surface above them they would be off, digging like gophers in order to keep that necessary couple of wriggles ahead of the Old Man's spade. It usually took us a good hour and a half to fill a large Lyle's Golden Syrup tin with them, and by that time even the Old Man would have had enough. Out we would trudge to where we had left our bicycles against the sea wall and we would ride them in silence out through the village, the Old Man looking neither to right of him or to left of him as he passed the quiescent houses. It was only when we were well out of Garlieston that his sombre mood would lighten somewhat. We had two pubs to cycle past in the village, and there must surely have been no more depressing a sight for a Scotsman with a drouth on him after a hard shift at the lugworm, than a couple of Scottish pubs, still as the grave and locked up like jails, at eight o'clock of a Sunday morning.

Our next port of call would be the narrow strip of scrub woodland on the Shabby Braes, a mile or so to the west of our final destination. It was here that we always selected our rods for our day at the fishing. Some years previously the Old Man had felled the trees on this strip, and he knew that many of the old ash stumps had since thrown up long, straight suckers. The traditional flexibility of green ash made it ideal for our use and they had the advantage of being easily cut. A pole twelve feet long by about by about two inches thick at the butt end would be the Old Man's choice, while ours would be less than half that size. Thirty yards of strong brown cod-line, to which was attached a cod-hook, a cork and a lump of lead, completed the tackle for each of us, and after that it required but an easy stroll over the farm fields to reach the rocks.

The safety-conscious parents of today would have had apoplexy over the Old Man's casual approach to the responsibilities that came with parenthood. Having chosen his favourite rock, he would tell us to go and find our own rock for our fishing, and never dare to bother him again for the rest of the day except in dire emergency. 'And by "dire emergency",' he would add, 'take it to mean that you have found a crate of whisky washed ashore, or something like that.' Then he would give each of us a pocketful of lugworm and leave us to it. We children who had managed to survive the first decade of our lives in that day and age were expected to accept certain responsibilities, too, and one of them was that we should be able to take care of ourselves.

Sometimes my brother and I fished; often, we didn't bother. It was much more fun to be just exploring. Far upshore from us we could see the silhouette of the Old Man against the sky, perched on his bare shelf of rock with his rod in his hand, motionless as a cormorant with smoke wisping from his clay pipe, lost in his own world, as we guddled for crabs, sea slaters and sand-hoppers in the wet crevices and little rock pools left by the last tide. Orange, yellow and green lichens plastered tightly to the rocks just above the high water level were a constant attraction, and efforts to scrape them from the rocks and transfer them with colour intact to our home at the end of the day were never very successful, as the colours always faded to a uniform dingy grey by the time we got them home.

In the spring of the year the banks above the rocks could be extraordinarily beautiful, with the golden fire of the whin blossom mantling the bottle-green density of its spiky foliage, while the delicate pink of the thrift added a touch of virginal class to the coarse sea grass. Along the brow that separated farmland from the shoreline below, the glaucous bloom of the fat blue sloes would already be evident, and the heavy tang of the sea would fill our lungs with every breath.

There were rarely moments of real high drama on fishing expeditions to the Cruggleton rocks. Here we were safe from Uncle Neil and his ilk, and in any case Hitler, while he must certainly have already begun to think about his plans for the future conquest of Europe, had probably not yet included Wigtownshire in his campaign plans, far less given any thought to dumping mines around her coasts. The nearest we got to a bit of excitement was when my brother rather carelessly left his line set when we went off on one of our exploratory sessions, jamming the butt of his rod into a cleft in the rock to hold it fast. We returned in time to see the rod flying out of the cleft and into the sea. When last seen it was speeding over the surface of the water at a rate of knots in the direction of the Isle of Man, towed, no doubt, by some subaquatic kraken probably unknown to the world of marine biology even to this day.

On another occasion, for some now long-forgotten reason, my brother and I had been sent on our own to the Shabby Braes wood to cut our rods on the evening before our scheduled fishing trip. The evening shadows were creeping over the wood by the time we got there, and local legends about ghosts and ghouls that supposedly haunted it after dark were not too far from our minds as we entered it. We had cut our rods and were hastening out to the roadside in the fast diminishing light when a rabbit crossing the path in front of us attracted our attention. It vanished into a large clump of dead bracken, followed by a sizeable stone hurled with considerable venom by my sibling. A loud and horrifying groan from the depths of the bracken in the wake of the dull thud of the stone turned our knees to jelly. Uncoiling his long and lanky frame from the undergrowth, like Mephistopheles ascending from the Underworld, rose Snib Scott, the local tramp, all six hairy, flea-bitten feet of him. We instantly metamorphosed into blocks of ice as this giant, eyes glowing madly through the thickets of jet-black hair that covered his face, slowly unwound himself, stretching higher and higher and higher before our eyes. It was only when he took one lumbering step towards us, rumbling throaty imprecations as he did so, that the spell was broken. Rods were dropped and we were out of that wood and over the roadside gate like squirrels, and never had children's legs moved faster up the long, long gradient to our home than did ours in the gloaming of that evening.

*   *   *

With the benefit of hindsight spanning six decades, I realise now that it was not so much the fishing that attracted the Old Man when he was sallying forth to the rocks on those Sunday mornings. Not really. The Old Man was – to employ a modern euphemism – simply chilling out. At no more cost to his physical and mental wellbeing than the effort required to dig up a can of lugworm, he could spend a whole day away from it all, doing nothing more stressful than watching a cork bob up and down on the water.

The Old Man had it all worked out. Today, people pay the sun and the moon and the stars to visit psychiatrists and to book themselves into 'health farms' when the pressures of life become a bit too much for them. Even if those supports had been available to him then for nothing, the Old Man would have scorned them. He had no need of any of them.

After all, he had his own private rock at Cruggleton.

Chapter 3
THE GENTLE ART OF CROW FISHING

'Frogs and snails and puppy dogs' tails — that's what little boys are made of.'

Whoever wrote that particular nursery rhyme must have been an urban dweller. He — or she — had to be. No country-bred poet would have failed to include the most essential ingredient of all in the make-up of every active little boy's character. Worms. Ordinary earthworms. Life for schoolboys everywhere would be much more dull without those most primitive — and probably least-loved — of all the world's creepy-crawlies. Especially for boys born with the love of fishing in their veins, and this (unless things have changed dramatically since my boyhood) includes a very high proportion of Galloway boys.

Lumbricus terrestris. The common earthworm. There can be few of us whose passion for angling has not had as its genesis this humble creature. The combination of children, bent pins and worms has been with us since long before some now-forgotten cartoonist featured them together for the first time.

The earthworm. An interesting beastie. It has been around for about 600 million years in one form or another, considerably longer than *homo sapiens* has, and it is likely to be around for a long time after we, the superior race, have succeeded in destroying ourselves. For this, if for no other reason, it deserves a closer study than the casual glance we generally give it when we turn it up in our gardens in the spring of the year, or as we thread it onto our hook when the night run of sea trout has begun.

Wherever a reasonable amount of moisture and organic material is to be found in soil, and that soil is not too acid, there you will find the earthworm. Worldwide, there are over 1,800 species of them, and they range in size from the incredibly small (1mm long) to the incredibly large (3.3m or 11ft in length). Even within the British Isles, their coloration can vary considerably, ranging from grey, red, brown, bluish and olive-green to a banded red and yellow. They cannot stand extremes of drought or wet: there is an Asian species – cross my heart and hope to die – that even shins up trees to escape the monsoon flooding.

If it escapes drought and drowning and predatory blackbirds and moles and little boys with bent pins, the earthworm stands a good chance of living to the ripe old age of six years, doing so mainly on a diet of dead vegetation and, occasionally, dead animals and even, I am told, on us. 'The worms crawl in and the worms crawl out; they play pinochle in your snout…' goes an old drinking song. The earthworm will break down most things it may encounter and consider edible on its constant journey through the earth, creating a better, more fertile soil by virtue of its passing.

It is admirably equipped for its peculiar way of life. Although it has no eyes or ears, it is very sensitive to heat, light and touch. It has a mouth, a brain and five pairs of hearts to circulate the blood around a body that consists of a tube of muscle organized in two layers, one layer arranged lengthways and the other wrapped like a corset around it. Tightening this 'corset' forces the worm's head forward, similar to the way in which toothpaste is forced from a tube. The contraction shudders down the body, squeezing more worm up the tunnel, until the long muscles take over to drag the tail forward. And so on, ad infinitum. So well-greased is the worm with mucus that it can move easily through all but the most compact of soils.

It is largely an underground operator, generally emerging at the surface only at night. Daylight is fatal to it – its skin is so thin that it provides no protection against the sun. On warm, rainy nights it will emerge from its subterranean chamber to mate, and even in this act it is peculiar in that each worm has both male and female organs. It cannot fertilize itself, however. It needs another worm in order to exchange genetic material, in much the same way as flowers cross-pollinate each other. Enveloped in slime, they mate head to tail in the *soixante-neuf* position so fervently advocated by aficionados of the erotic in France. A strange and messy business, even in the world of worms.

Contrary to popular legend, a worm cut in half will not grow into two worms. But should either end be snapped off – even the head – it will, in time, grow a replacement. I am furthermore relieved to report that I have never known the earthworm to feature on the menus of any of the tribes with whom I have enjoyed social intercourse during a lifetime of wandering through some of the more remote forests of this world, but no doubt there are, somewhere, hardy souls who do eat and enjoy them. I have, however, known them to be swallowed alive for wagers at drunken parties in 'civilized' societies, and I have been reliably informed that the trick in such situations is to shut one's eyes, place the unfortunate creature firmly on the back of one's tongue, think of Bannockburn and Robert the Bruce, and swallow quickly. A moment's hesitation and all is lost. Worse still, one little mistake, one involuntary rictal spasm, and you are left with two frantically squirming half worms, a mouthful of the gritty stuff, and an unforgettable flavour of decomposing corpses that will linger with you long after the normal hangover horrors of the following day have departed.

Many of us harbour an ingrained aversion towards this perfectly harmless invertebrate. The wriggliness...the sliminess...its association with death and with the soil that will eventually claim us... Boys overcome their repugnance to a certain extent through having to handle worms constantly for such vital purposes as the baiting of hooks, putting them in teacher's desk, and dropping them down the dresses of little girls. But still, deep down inside even the toughest of little boys, there is that secret revulsion, and it is a revulsion that never quite leaves them.

I shall never forget my first encounter with the great granddaddy of them all, the West African earthworm. It was six feet long and moving past me down a flooded path in the middle of the forest, foot after gruesome foot of it. I knew it to be as harmless as it was blind, but I would no sooner have thought of touching it than I would have thought of putting my hand on a live gaboon viper.

British worms, fortunately, come in much more respectable sizes. In any case, even at six inches long they are generally discarded as being too long and too coarse by the boy angler who 'knows his stuff'. The Galloway boy certainly knows his stuff, and he knows worms like he knows the backs of his grubby little hands. He knows what's good for trout and what ain't. He is aware from experience that Galloway trout 'know their stuff' too. The Galloway trout is, in fact, a bit of a gourmet in its own piscine way. There is no point in trying to fob it off with second-best: only the very best will do. Not for the Galloway trout the pallid, grey, common worm of the garden, no matter its size. Quality, rather than size, is the motto. The fat little worm with the rich red colouration dug up from undisturbed loams at the corner of some field or found under a flat stone by the side of the burn – that is what this aristocrat among trout really desires.

And, in the way that human connoisseurs have a fondness for the smellier cheeses at the end of a meal, so, too, does the Galloway trout favour the evil-smelling red and yellow banded dung worms encountered only in farmyard middens, a point appreciated more by the little boys who dig for them than the mothers whose job it is to sanitize their offspring afterwards. But worms, whatever their denomination, have to be affixed to hooks before fishing can begin, and this is what finally separates the boys from whatever are left of the girls at this point.

The wild brown trout of Galloway burns are as wily as ptarmigan. Lures have to be good to have much hope of fooling them. This is particularly so when the water is like glass and the sun is shining directly upon it. When the burn is in spate and the waters are a roiling brown flood, a worm fixed practically any old how on a hook will do. The trout's senses are dulled by the conditions, and in the feeding frenzy it snatches blindly at any food that may come its way. It has to, or the morsel has gone from it forever. But not when the burn is low. Then, in the clear waters, the trout has the time and the opportunity to study the menu. If it doesn't like the look of what is on offer, it will go elsewhere. To stand the slightest chance of attracting the wary trout's attention in such conditions, the whole of the hook, barb and shaft, must be covered.

The hook is inserted into the head end of the worm and very carefully pushed through its body, right through the tiny little mouth and its tiny little brain and its five tiny little hearts – being careful to ensure that the barb does not re-emerge through the skin – until the shaft of the hook is completely covered. It is not as easy as it sounds, at least until one has got the hang of it, for the worm protesteth much while all this is going on. But, once done, that, in a nutshell, is that. The wormer is ready for action.

Like most embryo anglers, I was an avid wormer in those early years. The 'bent pin' phase of my angling career – if it ever existed – could not have lasted long, for I do not remember it. My earliest memories are of worm hooks. Plain, single-barb number three hooks, if memory serves me correctly, and sharp as needles. They were my choice for serious worm fishing, and always remained so.

The hooks, an inch long at the end of a five-inch coil of gut, were sold singly in packets of cellophane at Crozier's little store in Garlieston. I cannot remember how much they cost, but they must have been very cheap, for I never seemed to be without at least a couple of them about my person throughout my primary school years. This, combined with my penchant for daydreaming in class, could lead to complications.

Our headmaster, a retired Royal Navy officer, was a strict disciplinarian. We were all rather terrified of him. He ruled by virtue of the tawse – a leather belt much in vogue in Scottish schools in those dark ages, and which, given the slightest provocation, he had no hesitation in using. His arm, toughened no doubt by years of splicing mainbraces, was strong and tireless.

Prize-giving day was the major event in the school calendar, and one such will live forever in my memory. This annual event, eagerly anticipated by proud mothers whose offspring were due to receive even the most piffling award for proficiency of any form during the school year, was also a cause for some celebration by we, the pupils, but only because of the fact that it brought to a close the long, dreary spring term and signalled the beginning of the summer holidays. This, however, was a time of the year when our headmaster could be expected to be especially cranky. On the particular day of which I write, the impending visit of a gaggle of local dignitaries had made him even more waspish than usual. During morning prayers his kestrel eye spotted my hand straying absent-mindedly towards my jacket pocket in pursuit – he wrongly suspected – of illicit pleasures contained with. He pounced, and thrust his hand triumphantly deep down into my pocket...

The resultant beating was accepted by me with reasonable stoicism. The glow that comes through being unexpectedly elevated – albeit temporarily – to the status of school hero helped ease my physical pain somewhat. There was also the balm of knowing that even greater pain had been inflicted upon the headmaster. Large worm hooks are neither easily nor quietly removed from the thumbs of choleric Royal Navy officers at the best of times, and this was certainly the case in that day and age when local anaesthetics were virtually unheard of. Apart from having a well-earned reputation as being a bit of a butcher, the doctor who had been given the job of extracting the two hooks had crossed swords with our headmaster on more than one occasion, and it is likely that he felt under no obligation to make the operation as painless as possible.

*　　　　*　　　　*

We were lucky as children. We had a father who enjoyed burn fishing as much as we did. He taught us many ways to take fish, some of them even legal. And it was he who taught us the art of the set line.

The burn in which we practised out burgeoning skills was the Pouton Burn, a peaceful little stream that had its origins in the moorland some miles to the west of us, from there meandering its sleepy way through green and pleasant farmland to the lovely little seaside village of Garlieston. It was really quite an unremarkable burn as burns go, and its trout would have been – for those insatiable trophy hunters to whom size seems all-important – considered equally unremarkable. For ordinary mortals, however, a ten-inch specimen taken from the Pouton Burn would have been hailed as a very satisfactory trout indeed, and a catch of five or six half-pounders in the bag at the end of one's day, a good day's fishing. To we children, of course, the burn was the closest to paradise we were ever likely to get. It flowed past our cottage, and we knew every pool, every eddy, for half a mile or more upstream and downstream from our home. We knew where the bigger trout were liable to be lurking when the burn was in spate, and we fished for them at such times with poles of tough, flexible ash cut from the wet hollow across the burn from our garden. Whatever their size, each trout was a thing of beauty, with the vivid carmine spots along their flanks that seemed to be the hallmark of all wild Galloway trout, and they had a taste to them that no modern-day trout reared in those dreadful fish farms can ever hope to emulate.

It was, however, a burn of moods. When in spate, fishing was invariably excellent, if the correct method of catching them was employed. When the clouds were hanging low and heavy overhead and the water was scurrying caramel-coloured towards the Solway Firth, only the worm held any attraction for the Pouton trout. When the rain had eased and the spate had fined off to the colour of weak tea, both worm and fly had their advocates, but the clearer the water became, the more the balance tipped in favour of the fly fisher. During dry spells, however, when the water was low and it seemed as though nothing short of dynamite could have roused the trout from their torpor, that was when we line-setters came into our own.

For the children of poor and ever-hungry families, the set-line had the advantage of being both simple and inexpensive. All that was required was a long length of strong, brown cod-line, a supply of ordinary worm hooks, and a can of worms. Deep pools which had been noted to contain suitably large trout would be targeted, and one line set in each pool. A flat stone would be tied to the line to act as a sinker a yard or so up from the bait and the other end of the line fixed to some immovable anchor – a protruding underwater root was ideal, for when it was submerged for its whole length the brown line was almost impossible to detect, even in the clearest of water.

Strangely enough, most of the fish caught by this method were of good size. As our budgets restricted us to the setting of not more than half a dozen lines at any one time, around two trout from the six lines were about as much as we could expect during any one night, and there was also, of course, the occasional trauma of finding a large eel wrapped in a seemingly inextricable ball of gunge around the line when we arrived to check our traps in the morning, thus rendering it quite unusable again. But, for the most part, it was trout we caught, and at least we were catching – and eating – when 'proper' fishermen were unable to get a rise. In our house, where financial crises were a constant companion, I never heard anyone complain about the monotony of the fish diet. A frying pan, a lump of dripping, and some oatmeal in which to roll your trout, and you had a meal fit for a king.

A quarter of a mile from our house the burn flanked the western perimeter of the Crow Wood, and it was within the shadows of its trees that we set most of our lines. The Crow Wood consisted of just a few acres of rather unkempt woodland, but to us it was a vast and primaeval wilderness of indescribable enchantment. Within its sombre shadows we played, and here, occasionally, we even cooked our catch. The word 'cook' is a euphemism: much more appropriate would be the word 'scorch'. By virtue of his superior cunning, my younger brother usually managed to purloin matches from somewhere, and with these we lit fires from dead pine roots. The fish would be gutted and thrown onto the embers. We ate them half-raw like the little savages that we were, and, even though we had no experience of haute cuisine, they tasted like something no master chef labouring in the bowels of a Michelin-rated restaurant could produce.

In the spring of each year the southern end of the Crow Wood was a seething, black mass of rooks. Here they built their unattractive – but surprisingly functional – nests of both dead and green sticks in the tall tops of the elms. They were the most raucously vociferous of parents, reminding me now of those Glasgow housewives of the old days leaning out of their high tenement windows endlessly yakking at their neighbours and squawking at their offspring. They were, too, rather sloppy housekeepers. A domestic dispute would send sticks flying and the distinctive brown-spotted, greeny-grey eggs tumbling to the ground. Nestlings would be found all over the place on the woodland floor under the trees, huddled disconsolately, left to starve to death or be eaten by foxes.

Sometimes Old Jimmy, the farm handyman, would lean over the dyke to talk rubbish to us. He was the only human being we ever saw there. The Crow Wood was, to all intents and purposes, ours, our very own private nature reserve. But it was in this Eden that we were to find ourselves confronted by what was to become known as The Great Crow Mystery. It was a mystery that we never solved.

Spring had arrived. On the first day of the trout season we headed with our lines, six in all, for the Crow Wood, and these we set in the deepest and most promising pools we could find. On the following morning, full of anticipation, we set off to check them. A dead rook floated on the surface of the first pool; a not unusual sight at this time of the year, with immature rooks quite often falling to their deaths from the high tops. What was unusual was the fact that, when we hauled our line in, the rook followed it in. The hook was firmly attached to its beak. Even more remarkable was the fact that, at the remaining five lines, precisely the same situation was encountered. Six lines and six crows. Agog with excitement we raced home with our story, to be greeted with the greatest derision and scepticism by the adult members of our family. The following day we bagged five more rooks and the day after that another full complement of three brace of the wretched birds, all in prime condition apart from being dead in the water when we reeled them in. For most of that summer we were plagued with rooks on our lines, all hooked by the beak. We still caught the occasional trout, all right, but the proportion of crows to trout was extremely high. That year, I was nearly put off fishing for life, not so much because of the constant nuisance of finding those black horrors on our lines each morning and the fact that I was starting to have nightmares about them, but more because of the perpetual jibes we had to endure from adults who should have had better things to do with their time. Nor were the jibes confined to our home: nothing spreads faster than bad news. We became known locally as the Crow Fishers, and it was a tag that was to haunt us until we moved from the area some years later.

The strange business ceased as abruptly and as mysteriously as it had begun, but not until we had made serious inroads into the county's rook population. While the mystery remained as just that with us, perhaps the mischievous glint that never seemed to be far from Old Jimmy's eyes ought to have provided us with a clue, had we been older and a bit wiser to the wicked ways of the world. Several times, in later life, I was to meet him by chance on the street of Whithorn, where he was living out his retirement years, and on each occasion it was on the tip of my tongue to bring up the subject. But, somehow the words would not come. By the time I finally got round to mentioning that incident of long ago, it was too late to get any sense out of him. Senile dementia had taken one of her sons to her bosom.

*   *   *

Love affairs end. Mine with the worm ended abruptly. I had called at Crozier's for a supply of worm hooks when I spotted a small selection of artificial flies on casts of gut behind the glass shelf on the counter. They glittered like tinsel on a Christmas tree and I was seduced. One fly in particular stood out. It was garbed in black, the most beautiful black I had ever seen in my life, with a flash of scarlet adorning it so alluring that it would have won the heart of Genghis

Khan. 'What do you call that one?' I asked Mr Crozier. 'That, son,' replied the proprietor, 'is a Bloody Butcher.'

There was no turning back. It was not only the beauty of the fly that had hooked me: its name now gave me the excuse for using a hitherto forbidden word. I forgot all about my worm hooks and blew all of my pocket money on the fly cast. Later that day, fishing the pool below our house, I landed a monster after a protracted struggle. It was a brown trout in perfect condition, and it must have weighed nearly a pound. I removed the Bloody Butcher reverently from the lip of the fish. I gazed alternately at the glistening beauty of my capture and at the sable-and-scarlet glory of the tiny fly that had caught it for me. Such is the fickle nature of the human male that I had no further use for the humble worm that had landed so many fine trout for me in the past. I was ten years of age, and hopelessly smitten by a love that was new and held infinitely more promise of excitement than the old. At that moment I turned my back on worms.

It is, after all, a very masculine trait. While one never quite forgets one's first love, it is nevertheless a cruel fact of life that when something more gaudily plumaged catches the eye, somehow things are never quite the same again.

Chapter 4
THE SECRET LIFE OF DITCHES

There are few things so guaranteed to concentrate the mind as that of finding yourself the object of an Ayrshire bull's wrath when you are in the middle of a large field in early morning and equidistant from each boundary wall or hedge or river, or whatever. In a trice, a mind which has been befogged through lack of sleep and the excesses of the previous night becomes as clear as Waterford crystal, with only one thought to occupy it – reaching the sanctuary of that boundary before the animal reaches you…

I had been spending a few days with a woodcutter friend at his bothy in the Galloway hills. Woodcutting is a hungry business and, with the burn now a rollicking flood from the previous night's rain, I had sallied forth with a rod early on Sunday morning to see if I could tempt a sea trout from the lower reaches before the estate gamekeeper had finished his morning matins.

Following the burn's course downhill would have been the sensible approach, offering as it did the required element of concealment, for it was a tortuous route strewn with gorse and briers and clumps of hazel. But teenagers have rarely been blessed with much common sense, and teenagers of whatever generation have never been known to take the long and arduous route when a shortcut happened to be available. This was a case in point.

The burn's erratic course took it in a wide loop over a series of small but steep waterfalls until, inevitably, it was on the bottom lands, to begin at once a much more gentle course along the southern boundary of the field to my left for a couple of hundred yards before entering the deep, narrow cutting that heralded its approach to the Solway Firth, glinting in the sun far below me. The field, I noted with a casualness I was about to regret, contained a herd of cows grazing far out in the middle, and I saw that by making my way diagonally through them I would reach the big pool at the foot of the first waterfall with the minimum of fuss and effort. After a careful study of the landscape to ensure that there was no one else around to spoil my morning, I set off briskly across the field.

Whoever said that bulls always wait until you are in the exact centre of their territory before showing aggressive intent, sure spoke a mouthful, to employ an Americanism. Take it from me. I was not even aware of the brute's presence among the cows until I was almost upon him, mainly due to the fact that he had, until then, been cunningly concealing his identity by lying on the ground, placidly chewing the cud. It was only when he got to his feet that I realised that I was in deep trouble, and by then it was too late.

It is a curious fact that when a bull first makes your acquaintance, it invariably looks at you as though you owe him money. (I was to note this same disturbing tendency many years later in Africa when involved in similarly unscheduled encounters with forest buffalo.) This bull was no exception. His was a stern and unsmiling Presbyterian mien, and he had that look of lean and lanky athleticism about him that all Ayrshire bulls seem to have, a not-a-spare-ounce-of-fat sort of frame that would have warned even the legendary Mick the Miller to step aside sharpish or he'd find himself in danger of getting trampled underhoof, had it ever been possible to match the one against the other on the dog track.

Only the previous summer I had been awarded the sum of 12 shillings and sixpence at the Whauphill Sports for winning one of their top track events, and this had been recorded for posterity by the timeless prose of the sports desk of the *Galloway Gazette* with the words 'U/14's Race. 1st. D. MacIntosh' in the column entitled 'Village Sports

Roundup'. I could see at a glance that this competitor intended to test my turn of speed to the limit. His obscenely long horns, honed to perfection for just such encounters as this, gleamed sharply white in the morning sunshine. He had just begun his first long, terrifyingly loud BRAAAA...when I left him and his harem at top speed, heading downhill and never once daring to look back.

I dropped my rod when I was less than halfway down the hill, for it was interfering with that fluency of arm action so vital to we top sprinters. Above the whish and the whistle of the wind in my ears I could hear the drumming of hooves and I sensed that the creature was gaining on me. It was at this point that all the hours of training I had put in for the Whauphill Sports stood me in good stead, for it was undoubtedly that final burst of speed as I hit the flats at the bottom of the hill that allowed me to remain that necessary yard in front and reach the bank of the burn a split second before him. Even if I had wanted to stop at that point it would have been impossible, such was my momentum, and I didn't even try. An instant later I was among the sea trout in the middle of the big, swirling pool at the foot of the waterfall, while Buster stalked the burn bank roaring his message of triumph and hate...

The Creagan Burn was typical of many Galloway burns. What often started as a group of acid ditches a few miles away among the moors and the hills would become, in short order, healthy burns full of beautiful little trout as they passed through green and fertile fields on their way to the sea. Sometimes one would find the very occasional sea trout in them, while others (a much rarer occurrence) would have regular runs of them. The Creagan was one of the latter, and, as such, fishing on it was strictly prohibited to all but those invited to dine on a regular basis at the table of the owner of the estate.

The woodcutters had never been part of that social scene, and they made up for this oversight on the laird's part by dining freely on his rabbits, pheasants and partridges. This, understandably, was a source of constant irritation to the gamekeeper, who took umbrage at the fact that the woodcutters were, as a result, better fed than he was. The laird's possessiveness over the fishing rights to the Creagan Burn was less easy to understand, for there was really very little that was of any sporting value about it. No salmon ever went up it, and the sea trout were never very big. Besides, beyond the first waterfall and on up the hill to its source among the bogs, it was impossible to fish by any means other than foul, while a large proportion of the half-mile stretch downstream to the estuary from that same waterfall was taken up by the deep cutting that constituted the lower boundary of the field through which I had been forced to flee. This cutting, in any case, was so narrow and overgrown with thorns that fly-fishing was quite out of the question.

The cutting had been a hand-constructed ditch and most of the field now bounded by the burn had, at one time, been under water. After the end of the Great War the estate owner, with a workforce boosted by the large number of ex-servicemen returning to the area, decided to drain the loch, thus adding a substantial area of good alluvial land to his estate. The cutting was the result.

Other things benefited, too. With the creation of the ditch the quality of the soil surrounding the Creagan Burn had improved and, with it, the size of the trout. Moorland trout, while in my admittedly biased opinion the most beautiful of all native British trout, could never hope to achieve the sizes of those of their cousins in more fertile parts of the country. There was too little feeding in the acid peat soils. Now, fat trout of up to a foot long could be caught on those lower reaches and, as the gorse and the blackthorn had gradually filled in the steep sides of the ditch, even larger trout had gathered in the deeper pools under the permanent shadows far below.

The fish that chose to remain in the cutting were not easily caught, as might well be imagined. In times of spate, when the open part of the burn between the waterfall and the start of the cutting was running fast, good trout could be caught on both the worm and the wet fly, but allowing one's line to vanish into the dark mystery of the cutting was a recipe for disaster. During long dry spells, when it seemed as though every trout in the burn had retreated to the coolness of the ditch, one could only stand high up on the bank, watching unreachable dimples on the water surface far down below through the tangle of thorns crowding the sides, futilely exercising the mind with delusions about the hidden giants that might be creating those ripples in the deep, dark, pools down below.

Gaining access to that quarry was always a problem to we ditch fishers. Sometimes it would turn out to be insurmountable, but that was what made it all such an adventure. There was both mental and physical stimulus to be derived from ditch fishing: not only did you have to figure out a way to work your lure down through the vegetal morass to the water below without getting it irretrievably snagged, but once you had hooked your trout you had to work out a way to get him out of there. The canal fisher of England could afford to sit back on his little chair with can of lager in hand, dreaming of Manchester United and the woman next door, but the true ditch fisher could never have that luxury. His mind had to be totally focussed on the job to hand. This, unfortunately, was what ruled out the Creagan Burn for the illicit angler. With an irate gamekeeper liable to explode upon one at any given moment, concentration was, of necessity, divided, and it was just not worth the hassle. It was not, therefore, on Kirkcudbright's Creagan Burn that I had my introduction to the pleasures of ditch fishing. This had taken place some years previously when, on the promontory across the water from where the Creagan emptied itself into the sea, I had, as a child, taught myself the art.

The Black Ditch slices through the southern section of the farm of Broughton Mains, in the Machars of Wigtownshire. It is a narrow ditch, not much more that half a mile in length, and so overgrown with scrub that the stranger is in danger of plunging over the edge and into it before he is aware that it exists at all. As with the Creagan, this was a cutting designed to drain a loch for the dual purpose of land reclamation and land improvement. The Black Ditch has an intriguing history. Estate records show that it had its beginnings at the time of the Irish potato famine in 1846. Murray of Broughton, the proprietor of the estate on which the farm stood had, like many landowners of that era in the south of Scotland, interests over in Ireland, and it was from there that he obtained his labour for the construction of the ditch.

The soils of Galloway tended to be rather thin and acidic by nature, and wherever possible these were improved by dumping calcareous marl on them. This marl was often obtained through the draining of the numerous shallow lochans with which the land was then dotted. (Not too many parasangs to the east of the Creagan Burn, the Carlinwark Loch outside Castle Douglas had been drained around 1750 for the same purpose, revealing crannogs and many artefacts, including an iron forge used by the English Edward the First's men for shoeing their horses during his excursions north of the Border.) It was a long, laborious and expensive process, only to be undertaken when labour was cheap and plentiful.

Diggings around the loch at the southern extremity of the farm indicated the presence of abundant quantities of marl, and a decision was taken to drain it. This was to involve cutting a ditch which would, in places be 30 feet deep, through solid rock, to link the loch with the main Broughton Burn. The great famine over the water had left most of Ireland destitute, and there was little difficulty in persuading Irish families to come over to Wigtownshire to grab whatever work was on offer. At seven pence per week – later increased to one shilling per week to keep pace with inflation – and all the potatoes they could eat, there was no shortage of volunteers. The Black Ditch is their monument. Water passes between its great shelves of rock as freely today as when the Irish opened it 150 years ago. Ninety years after they opened it, during my time there, it had become an environmental paradise, albeit, for children, a highly dangerous and totally forbidden one.

In my youth the farmer was Harry McCreath, with whose son, Tom, I had gone to school. Tom had developed an early fascination for the Black Ditch, one that frequently evoked dire threats from his parents as to what he could expect from them if he ever attempted to go near it on his own. I quote from a recent letter to me:

'An early memory for me was the Great Snow of 1936, when I was seven years of age. After a night and a day of heavy snow, I slipped out of the house while the adults were busily engaged with snow clearing and, crossing the burn below the house, I headed through the whins for the Black Ditch. I was spellbound. The Ditch was completely filled to the top with snow, even at its deepest part, and the dark waters rushed in a torrent from the cavern they had cut through the snow. I remember seeing the tracks of rabbits and hares where they had crossed over the Ditch and, looking over in the direction of the neighbouring farm half a mile away, I could see that the high march wall had vanished, completely buried in snow.

'The sequel to this was that we had a temporary thaw the following day, which caused the snow-fill to collapse completely into the Ditch. To the very considerable astonishment of my father and all the farm workers, a colossal Clydesdale horse belonging to the neighbouring farmer was found in our field, on our side of the Ditch. Neither my father nor the farmer to whom the animal belonged ever managed to figure out how it had got there. I, who knew the secret, which was that the horse had simply walked over the top of the march wall and the Ditch while they were covered with snow, dared not speak for fear of the retribution that would result from having disobeyed their instructions'

The Black Ditch was every child's dream. It was deep and it was dark and it was mysterious. It had a sort of arcanum about it, one that you can often sense about places that have had an unusual history to them, and it was a sense of the mysterious that did not lessen one bit for me as I grew older. But I never had the feeling that there was anything sinister about it, even when I walked its banks on the blackest of nights. For a time, I lived in a cottage on the neighbouring farm, quite close to where the Ditch met the main burn, and on occasions when I had nothing better to do I would take a stroll over the field in the moonlight to sit by the side of it. There I would watch the pulsing glow of the distant galaxies and listen to the night sounds around me, just looking and listening, hour after hour.

At times like these it seemed that I could hear the clank of steel picks on hard rock as those sturdy souls of long ago hacked their way out through this alien soil... almost hear the soft burrs of Armagh and beyond as they exchanged ribaldries while they sweated and toiled... hear the wild, sad Celtic airs as they gathered round their fires with their melodeons and tin whistles when the long day's grind was over...

The banks of the Ditch were near vertical. At its widest point it may have been 20 feet across, but not much more. Whins grew thick along the top of the bank and down the sides with clumps of blackthorn clinging to the screes of shale in many places, the whole interwoven with tangles of brier and dogrose. Here and there from the clefts in the bare rock down the sides, clumps of hawthorn and ash sprouted willy-nilly to add to the Ditch's general aura of impenetrability.

The edges of the Ditch and its surroundings were vibrant with life. Rabbits were everywhere, the close-cropped grass and the small knolls sprinkled with their droppings. The resident foxes were the fattest foxes in all of Galloway and they shared, when they had to, accommodation with a badger on one of the more inaccessible parts of the Ditch. Curlew and lapwing patrolled low overhead, filling the air with their plaintive cries, while somewhere up in the heavens the lark sang his glorious melody. Rose-breasted linnets nested in the whins and goldfinches glittered like jewels as they balanced on the purple knapweed. On top of the tall hawthorn the yellow hammer, resplendent in his waistcoat of brightest yellow and coat of richest chestnut, sang the best known – albeit the most repetitive – song in the United Kingdom, while the grating KAR-OWIK...KAR-OWIK... call of the handsome partridge filled the evening air from his lookout point on the knoll top. In the dark depths of the Ditch cruised schools of voracious fish, feeding on the caterpillars, beetles, flies, grubs – anything at all that happened to drop down from the overhanging vegetation to wriggle on the surface of the water.

Black Ditch trout ran to very respectable sizes. Nothing, of course, that would have been considered very remarkable in the chalk streams of southern England, but in these cold northern waters where a 14-ounce trout would have been cause for mild celebration, Black Ditch trout were looked upon as being a fair bit better than average. There was only one problem – how to extract them from their water fortress.

There was, in fact, only one way. Forget all this Izaak Walton stuff; sportsmanship was out of the question. At best, attempting to play a trout in the traditional manner would lead to the loss of both fish and expensive tackle, and, at worst, it could lead to a broken rod. At times when cattle came to drink in the shallows beyond the southern end of the Ditch, thus turning the water muddy brown with their activities, a worm could create havoc in the few easily accessible points on the Ditch. But this was too easy to be much fun and, in any case, once the water had become clear again the trout would simply vanish back into the dark recesses of the Ditch. Much more fun was a fly presented on the end of a light cast in places where the trout would least expect danger.

The banks were so steep and so high and so thick with greenery that the angler was almost always out of sight of his quarry. Indeed, because of this blanket of green between him and the water, the water was usually hidden from the angler himself. The trick was to choose a spot where he could see just enough of the water to be able to follow the slow and careful descent of the fly all the way down through the branches and the leaves and the thorns and the vines to the surface of the water. Once the fly had settled on the surface, that was as far as it was safe to let it go. He could never, under any circumstances, allow it to drift off with the slow movement of the current under the thorns. The angler had to hold it right there where he could see it, eyes glued to it, ready for the take.

It was seldom long in coming. Black Ditch trout were much less suspicious than those in more open waters, especially when they were hidden from view in their own secret part of the Ditch. What happened next would have made the great fly-fishers of yesteryear turn in their graves. The moment the trout took the fly it was hoicked up instantly through the tangle of thorns and onto the bank, to lie gasping on the rubble of slate beside its captor, wondering what the hell had hit it.

It was much more exciting than it sounds in the telling. For every fish caught, half a dozen were lost, either because the angler struck too soon or too late, or because he mucked about while the hooked fish was still in the water. It needed a steady hand, the keenest of eyes, and the concentration of a chess champion. The slightest bestirring of wind, the faintest of zephyrs as one was lowering the fly down through the thorns, could lead to total disaster. It was a sport for the very young, though. While older people undoubtedly had the patience for it, the reflexes and the lynx-eyed vision that are the prerogative of youth were absolute necessities in ditch fishing. By the time the ditch fisherman had bid farewell to his teenage years, he was already past it.

But good baskets of trout could be caught by this method, once you had got the hang of it. There were plenty of occasions when I walked proudly homeward from the Black Ditch with half a dozen of the nicest trout you could possibly hope to see anywhere. At times like these, the true ditch connoisseur would not have exchanged his patch for the very finest that the Spey could offer. Why should he have, after all? He was one of a very select breed and proud of it. He had every right to be proud, too. What Spey fisherman could have caught a trout in the conditions in which he had to catch them?

*   *   *

I went back there a few years ago. The Black Ditch looked even wilder, even more unkempt, than I remembered it. A few robins and wrens flitted through the undergrowth and a rabbit hopped lethargically along the bank, sending slivers of blue slate skittering down into the abyss. But I neither saw nor heard the yellow hammer, and the waters below me – what little I could see of them – were black and still.

I did not stay long, for I had far to walk before I reached my destination. There did not seem to be a lot worth hanging around for, in any case. There was nothing to see or hear in this place to remind me of my youth. Nothing. There were no chords to stir the memory or the imagination, no hint of ghostly Celtic laughter in the still air around me...nothing at all.

The sun was shining but I felt cold and depressed. I stood up and shrugged my haversack over my shoulders. What did I expect, anyway? The Ditch had always been for the young, for youthful dreamers. I was too old now, and its spirits were no longer in tune with me.

I climbed over the dry-stane dyke and into the neighbouring farm. I was halfway across the field when I stopped, conscious of a strange vibration in the still air. It was a strangely disturbing sensation, a feeling of déjà vu, and it was one that was becoming more disturbing as the seconds ticked by and the vibrations became an almost tangible throbbing. Suddenly, the throbbing had become a loud drumming sound that was more than a little familiar. My thoughts flashed back to that day of long ago by the Creagan Burn, and every instinct screamed at me to start running. But there was nowhere to run this time, and besides, half a century had elapsed since that famous victory at the Whauphill Sports. The sleekness of sinew and fluency of movement that had inspired such eloquence from the sports desk of the *Galloway Gazette* had gone. I hunkered down behind a clump of whins and hoped for the best. Seconds later, a herd of frisky young bullocks thundered by me without so much as a glance in my direction. Within moments, the drumming of their hooves had receded into nothingness.

I rose and stretched myself thankfully. I adjusted the straps of my haversack and strode briskly over the field towards the east, never once looking back at the Black Ditch, leaving its wild and magical splendour to enchant a new generation of children, just as it had once enchanted me.

Chapter 5
SALT WINDS

The story of Galloway is as much a story of the sea as it is a story of the land. Indeed, up to the middle of the 19th century the two were inseparable commercially, for the bulk of the trade with the outside world was conducted by sea. It was by far the quickest and, often, the only way.

The sea meant everything to the early Gallovidians, but it meant other things, too. The people and the sea were joined together inextricably, even those people who had never set foot on a boat and had no intention of ever doing so. The strictly agrarian families who worked the acidic soils inland depended on the sea for their fertilizers and much of their domestic day-to-day necessities. Seaweed was the main source of fertilizer and it was gathered by the cartload from the foreshore to dump on the land. Salt was extracted from saltpans and the odd whale washed ashore provided oil for lamps.

The seashore provided a lot of their food, too. Between the high-water and low-water marks there was always an abundance of shellfish among the wet, black stones. Nor were the shells themselves wasted: they were burned in kilns to produce lime and mortar for building purposes. Many old Galloway fortifications held together with those primitive materials have lasted for many centuries, something one cannot say of too many modern constructions. I was discussing this peculiarity recently with a man who had been given the task of restoring a 700-year-old fort which was, at last, showing signs of wear and tear. He told me that it had been discovered that the original mortar had been mixed with human urine, and, wishing to adhere as closely as possible to the original formula, they had experimented with large quantities of urine extracted – voluntarily, in most cases – from their workers on site. Subsequent scientific tests, however, revealed that none of the mortar produced by this process had anything like the tenacious binding properties of the original. 'It just goes to show,' he remarked sadly, 'nowadays they don't even make piss like they used to!'

The earliest Galloway seamen undoubtedly used light coracle-style boats of willow framing and leather, which were ideal for inshore fishing on calm seas and easy to carry up the shore to safety when storms threatened. As bigger and bigger vessels evolved knowledge of the coastline and its sheltered havens became of crucial importance. Any crew caught out in a storm with nowhere to hide was in very serious trouble indeed. The Galloway coast is an incredible mixture of calm inlets and storm-lashed rocks and cliffs, of sweeping stretches of golden sand, bleak tussocky dunes, and rank marshland. There are plenty of caves, too, if you know where to look for them, and wherever you find sea caves in remote areas you can be sure that the smugglers of old would have made full use of them.

Smuggling was rife in Galloway in the first half of the 18th century. Until the Act of Union with England in 1707 there was little in the way of law enforcement insofar as the smugglers were concerned. Even after this date, when the London-based regime enforced customs dues upon a startled populace and revenue cutters began to patrol the Galloway coastal waters, the gaugers had little success. Escape routes and hidey-holes were just too numerous, and few true Gallovidians were interested in grassing on the smugglers to excisemen, most of whom were either outsiders, or were hired to undertake each job. A further problem for the authorities was that it was not until 1760 that uniform custom dues were extended to the Isle of Man, just over the horizon. Illicit trade between Man and Wigtownshire was therefore quite brisk and locally smugglers were referred to simply as Manxmen, such was their reputation. Brandy, tea, silks and tobacco were the main commodities on the shopping list of the smugglers, but anything that would turn a groat for them would be considered. Even after the imposition of custom dues on the Isle of Man good profits could still be made through goods illegally landed there and then reshipped to Galloway.

Most of the contraband was carried by luggers and small coastal vessels, but a few were fast, heavily armed brigs. The revenue men stood no chance against them. An old story tells of a shore-based exciseman accompanied by 25 soldiers of the Crown challenging one such vessel as it was about to land its cargo at Port William. The captain of the brig told the exciseman in somewhat peremptory fashion to go away or he would dismantle his tin pot detachment with a 22-gun salute and send his own 100-man crew ashore to dismember those who might still be alive. Eventually a deal was struck which allowed the relieved government troops to march smartly out of sight over the horizon, where they waited until the coast was clear before returning to collect the 30 barrels of spirits set aside for their own consumption by the accommodating and estimable smuggler.

It happens to this day in the highest of society.

But not, of course, in Galloway. Nowadays an evening spent in a Port William pub is enough to convince even the most hardened of we old sceptics that the good people there are far too law-abiding to have even top-of-the-range liquor forced upon them at anything less than the prices decreed by our revered leaders at Westminster. There are some things, even in this day and age, that are just not on.

*   *   *

The Galloway seas produced two people whose names will forever be part of Scotland's folklore. Rear Admiral Sir John Ross was born at Barsalloch, near Stranraer, in June 1777. He first made his mark at the tender age of nine when he joined the Royal Navy. By the age of 39 he was a commander, married, and had started to build a house in Stranraer. One year later he had accepted an invitation from the

Admiralty to command an expedition in search of the elusive Northwest Passage from the Atlantic to the Pacific. The passage remained that way for nearly 100 years until Roald Amundsen traversed it between 1903 and 1906, but Ross added greatly to the world of marine science with many discoveries. (His nephew, James Clark Ross, who sailed with him as a midshipman gained even greater fame with his discovery of the North magnetic pole in 1831 and the Antarctic sea which he discovered between 1839 and 1843 and which bears his name.)

Of even more exalted status – and of decidedly more controversial habit – was a certain John Paul Jones. Born the son of a gardener at Arbigland near Kirkbean in 1747, his early youth was fraught with what might charitably be termed youthful high jinks, culminating in him being pitched into Kircudbright Tollbooth on charges of murder. Springing himself somehow or other from this rat-infested pen, he then spent a few uneventful years in mercantile shipping before accepting a commission in 1775 with the revolutionary American navy on the outbreak of hostilities against Britain.

From then on the diminutive commander was regarded by Britain as a mere pirate and the antipathy of the British towards him grew rapidly and in direct proportion to the considerable number of her ships that he sank – both in American and British waters. He created a sensation when he had the audacity to invade the Cumberland port of Whitehaven on 22 April 1778, a feat which had not been attempted on British soil for over a hundred years. But he had another side too. Five days later he landed on the other side of the Solway at Kirkcudbright with the intention of taking the Earl of Selkirk hostage to exchange for American prisoners-of-war. On entering the earl's home on St Mary's Isle he discovered that he was not 'at home' and promptly took possession of the family silver and made off. Doubtless with an eye to the future Jones did not let the matter rest and after the war, he personally handed the silver back to Selkirk. The earl, for his part, is not at all remembered for his unwitting part in this curious escapade but rather as the Selkirk after which Robert Burns penned his famous 'Selkirk Grace' on a visit to St Mary's Isle. You can't say the old boy didn't keep interesting company.

Jones had his most famous victory of all in 1779 off Flamborough Head when his ship *Bon Homme Richard* Jones defeated the British frigate *Serapis* in a fierce battle lasting four hours. At one point when his ship appeared to be sinking beneath him Jones responded to a call from his British counterpart to surrender with the immortal words which I feel have been mouthed in one form or another by every super-confident, cornered, pint-sized pugilist since then: 'I have not yet begun to fight.'

He subsequently became a rear admiral in the Russian Navy and fought in the Baltic Sea against the Turks. Today, he is regarded as being the 'Father' of both the American and Russian navies, and he is buried in the US Naval Academy in Annapolis, Maryland. A wee man with a big life.

Like all seas, those around Galloway can display moments of treachery. The Irish Sea, with its bottle-neck of a passage between Antrim and the high cliffs of the Rhinns of Wigtownshire, can be especially vindictive. So, too, can the cliffs. They are spectacular, but they are best avoided by those suffering either from crapulence or vertigo. Long ago an unfortunate nursemaid walking along the cliff-top path near Portpatrick with her lady's child in her arms, had a dizzy spell. Faced with the prospect of plunging to her death along with the child as her legs gave way under her, or dropping her precious bundle and grabbing at a convenient rowan bush growing out of the very edge of the cliff, she did what seemed to her to be the sensible thing at the time. She clung to the rowan bush gratefully while the child plummeted to the rocks far below. Local history does not record whether she was disciplined for her momentary lapse in concentration. Perhaps not: good nursemaids, after all, were hard to come by in those days of full employment.

The narrow river of sea beyond the cliffs has claimed countless lives over the aeons, for there has always been very heavy traffic between Northern Ireland and Galloway from the time the first coracle put to sea. But the most remembered disaster – and certainly the most horrific – in this part of Galloway in modern times occurred on 31 January 1953, when the Stranraer to Larne ferry, the *Princess Victoria*, foundered in a terrible storm with the loss of 133 lives. A memorial to the dead can be seen in Agnew Park, Stranraer.

To the south and round the corner from the western seaboard of the Rhinns, the great bay of the Solway may give the impression of innocence, especially if seen for the first time on a calm day when the waters are barely moving, like a vat of liquid lead. But looks are deceptive: the Solway has claimed its share of lives, and those who 'daur meddle' with it do so at their peril. Even when it appears to be on its best behaviour, it is best to remain on your guard. The vast stretches of open flats one often sees when the tide is so far out it can barely be seen, for example Wigtown Sands, may look inviting enough to make you want to go for a long hike on them with your dog. But the tide can come in with quite astonishing speed, not just in a long, straight line towards you as civilized tides ought to do, but far off on the flanks where you cannot see it. Then after meeting behind you, it wraps itself around you cutting off all means of escape. The story that the Solway tide comes in quicker than a galloping horse is not one to be laughed at in these parts. There is also the problem of quicksands, from which, once you get bogged down to the knees in them, you will find it virtually impossible to extricate yourself unless you have someone near at hand to help you out. There are many awful stories about cattle, horses and – even – human beings finding themselves being slowly and remorselessly sucked under as the tide marched inexorably towards them. Once taken, these poor souls are never given up.

But few reports of accidental drowning can have been more freakish and more poignant than the one reported in *The Gallovidian* almost a century ago.

On 14 November 1862 the *Comet*, a coal wherry bound for the Isle of Whithorn took shelter from a storm in Garlieston harbour. It was high tide when she got in, and, as the tide receded she settled on a sandbank on the verge of the Pouton Burn which ran along the harbour wall at that point. The Garlieston tides were traditionally uncertain, and Captain Brodie, master and owner of the vessel, was only too aware that unless he did something fast, he could be stuck in Garlieston for several weeks until another suitable tide came along. He decided to have the sand dug away from the side of the vessel nearest the burn so that she would have a deeper channel in which to float out on the incoming tide. The half-dozen locals he hired for the job did their task only too well: the vessel began to heel over on its side. All except one of the men managed to scramble out from under her as she tipped over. Young Wullie Loch just failed to make it, and the bilge-log of the craft pinned his legs into the sand. Wullie was quite hopelessly trapped, lying on his back on the mud with the tide already on its way in. Block and tackle and wedges were put into use in an endeavour to ease the wherry off him, and shovels, spades, picks and till-irons were employed in a frantic attempt to free his legs by digging the sand from under them. It was all to no avail: the wherry, heavy enough when empty, was still loaded with her cargo of 60 tons of coal. Within the hour Wullie Loch had drowned in little more that two feet of water. James F Cannon of *The Gallovidian* reported:

> Ere yet the last faint hope had given way to a despair that was awful in its stillness, the Rev Thomas Young, pastor of the little Independent Church in the village, took his place beside the prostrated form of the young man, and, with his characteristic earnestness, administered to him the blessed hopes and consolation of the gospel, standing by him in the water till it was all over. The grief-stricken mother and some other relatives of the youth also attended him till the last – his mother holding his trembling hand in hers until his spirit had taken its flight.

*   *   *

The sea was the lifeblood of the coastal Gallovidians. In the early days the fishing fleet at a typical village would consist of only a few rowing boats, fishing with hand lines and set lines for cod, lythe and mackerel. Small-scale drift netting for herring took place, but only on a seasonal basis and on a very small scale. (In the days before the modern 'echo-sounder', shoals would be located by towing a long length of piano wire with a heavy weight attached to the end. One of the crew would hold the wire until he could report that he could feel the vibrations of the fish hitting it, upon which the net would be shot.)

Gradually, fishing boats got bigger and were able to fish further off-shore for fish such as skate and plaice. This involved a method called 'otter-trawling', in which a net heavily weighted on the bottom would be towed along the seabed. These boats were all powered by sail.

Larger sailing boats, – Annan and Morecombe Bay smacks – came into fashion between the two world wars. These had a much deeper draft, carried more sail, and were partly decked. Built initially as sailing boats, most of them eventually had small engines installed. They had very little freeboard aft, allowing the net to be pulled aboard easily.

Lobster fishing was an important industry, too, the bulk of them – and indeed of all the fish caught – being sent to markets in London, Glasgow, Leeds and Manchester. In the 1960s there came a big boom in scallop fishing – or, more specifically, 'queenies', or queen scallops. The great fishing ground for these was just to the south of Burrowhead, at the southern extremity of the Machars peninsula of Wigtownshire. Boats from Campbeltown, Maryport and Northern Ireland homed in on this seafood El Dorado, and as many as 20 boats were habitually landing catches of 2,000 bags in Garlieston harbour. The village had never seen anything like it. The catches were initially transported by road to factories in Irvine, Fraserburgh and Campbeltown, until latterly a shellfish factory was opened in Kircudbright.

Closer to land, stake netting for salmon was an annual business. Long oaken poles were embedded in the sand on the approach to river estuaries and nets hung upon them in the hope of syphoning off a few of the migrating salmon as they headed for their favourite rivers to spawn. There were good years and some very bad years at this business, depending mainly upon the vagaries of the Galloway climate and the generosity of the local seal population. Many villages had their own traditional fishing families, and generation succeeded generation in following the profession. In my time and in 'my' village of Garlieston, it was the Houston family. God knows how many of them there were, but there seemed to be Houstons in constant traffic to and from the pier any time I happened to go down there during my schooldays. They fished the Solway from the Machars of Wigtownshire to the Isles of Fleet away over on the Kirkcudbright coastline. They fished far beyond that, too, but as this is a story of Galloway we shall leave it at that. They were sailors through and through and you could smell the tang of the sea on them when you were at one end of the village and they were at the other. I admired them immensely, one and all.

Today the Solway fishing – as is the case just about everywhere else – is in serious decline. In my opinion over-fishing out on the high seas by massive vessels equipped with incredibly sophisticated technology is largely responsible for the decline. It has become easier and easier to catch greater and greater quantities and the fish have no real chance of escape; they are being hounded to extinction. Like my own beloved African primeval forests, the ocean is buckling under the strain. It is revealing at last that it is not a limitless resource. As our rainforests vanished before the onslaught of modern technology, so too, will those vast shoals that once roamed the seas in such profusion. It is inevitable.

*   *   *

On my last visit home, I sat with Alex Houston in his beautiful house overlooking Garlieston harbour. Alex is the last of the fisherman Houstons, having had to sell his vessel *Westering Home* and retire from fishing in 1985 after undergoing open-heart surgery. His interest in fishing remains undiminished. We talked about practically nothing else during my short visit.

I asked him if his son Cameron had any interest in following the great Houston tradition. His eyes lit up with pride. 'Oh, he's mad about boats, all right,' he replied, 'but he's only interested in painting them.'

'Painting them?'

'Aye,' said Alex, 'like that.' He indicated a painting of a fishing vessel hanging on the wall. One of Alex's old fishing boats. It was an expertly crafted painting and he showed me some others, equally good. A young man of obvious talent, like his forebears, I reflected. It was just that the talents of his forebears lay in a different direction, in their expertise with boats and their knowledge of the sea far out there across the bay where the salt winds blew.

I walked to the window and looked out, out over the harbour to where young Wullie Loch had lost his life in this sea a hundred years ago. Alex spoke again behind me. 'If it wasnae for this heart problem…' His voice trailed off into silence.

The sun had gone behind a cloud. The tide was out and the face of the pier wall was a dull loden colour. A gull flew disconsolately overhead. In the shadow cast by the cloud the lumpy sand in the harbour had assumed a dingy donkey-grey hue.

I turned away from the window. 'Aye, Alex,' I said, 'I'm quite sure you would.'

Chapter 6
ARCADIAN FIELDS

Broughton Mains is typical of lowland Galloway farms in that it consists of rolling expanses of good arable land interspersed with whin-covered knowes and the odd bit of boggy ground. It would look, I suppose, a rather ordinary sort of farm to the stranger who might travel the country road that bisects it. But there is nothing ordinary about it to me.

Broughton Mains was my youthful Elysium. Here I had played as a youngster, and here I had earned my first pay-packet as a man. It was, for a long time, a second home to me. When I was recently tempted to venture into my past I accepted the opportunity with alacrity, partly out of curiosity, I admit, but mainly because I wanted to write about my findings. So it was only natural that I should start my journey here.

The 'Big Hoose' looked much as I remembered it, a rather classy looking edifice of stone sheltered from the prevailing winds by a little grove of trees. Harry McCreath had been the farmer in my time. He was a gentleman of the old school, one of those all-too-rare human beings about whom it was quite impossible to imagine anyone having a bad word to say. After the horrors of the Great War – where he served as a machinegun officer in Belgium with the Royal Scots Fusiliers under Winston Churchill – he had married and settled here at Broughton Mains.

In my time the farm had had a large herd of dairy cows. Dougie the dairyman took care of the milking, assisted by his wife and family. Quite often, I would help out in the evenings; the oldest son and I were close friends, and the more hands there were the sooner Steve would be free to join me for whatever youthful ploys we had in mind for later on.

I was never trusted with the actual milking. Quite correctly, Dougie soon figured out that milking machines were far too complicated and technical for my antediluvian brain. He therefore assigned me to the job best suited to my limited talents – the shovelling and barrowing of dung from the byre to the midden outside. And, for those readers who will never be privileged to become members of our small but elite club of dung-barrowers, let me assure them that this is an art in itself. A barrow laden to overflowing with gloppy dung is incredibly heavy and awkward to manoeuvre, and on icy winter evenings the plank up which it had to be pushed to reach its offloading point above the midden could become extremely treacherous. I lived in constant dread of the time when my feet might slip and I would find myself plunging face down into the stinking effluent. It never happened to me, thank God, though I know of one or two who did suffer that fate.

To this day, I treasure Dougie McHarg's comment, delivered one dark winter night in the byre as he watched me at work: 'Donal', ye're the best shoveller o' coo shite ah hae seen in mony a lang day!' How many can claim to have received such an accolade from a genuine master of the art? Precious few, I warrant. If I could be assured that those words would one day be chiselled in Celtic script on to the Creetown granite of my tombstone, then I would die a proud and happy man indeed.

I followed the burn down. It meandered through the farm, flanking it here, traversing it there. Many's the good trout I had taken from it in my youth, but it had clearly been cleaned out at some time in the fairly recent past, and the deeper pools which I had known, traditional haunts of the larger trout, had gone. Now, the burn hurried on its way, with no fallen trees or boulders or banks of silt to block its progress.

I came to a dry-stane dyke. Before me a field of rape dazzled the eyes with its vulgarly effulgent yellow glare. This field had contained swedes – staple winter food for livestock – when I had last worked here. Thinning them had been an annual late-spring necessity then, and every available man, woman and child over the age of 12 took part in it. This work was referred to locally as 'turnip howin', though the 'howin' part was very much a euphemism insofar as we were concerned. While on a few farms 'hows', or hoes, were employed in singling the turnips, and were soon to become the standard in Broughton Mains, in my day the singling was done by hand. Literally. Hard, backbreaking work it was, too, crawling on hands and knees up and down the drills. Lengths of hessian sacking tied around our knees were our only protection from the stony soil; luxuries such as leather work-gloves were unheard of then and, in any case, would almost certainly have been scorned as being 'cissy' by we supremely macho boys. Deep and painful chaps on the hands soon callused over so thickly that the heel of one's hand became as hard as a horse's hoof. Nor was there any of today's obsession with hygiene. None of us cared that there was usually nowhere to wash our hands before tucking into our midday 'piece', or that the nearest clump of concealing whins had to act as the loo for man and woman alike.

The grieve at the farm was Bob McColm. We youngsters were all rather scared of Bob, for no particular reason other than that he possessed a certain gruffness of manner and a quite intimidating appearance. He was big and burly, with the sort of features that one tends to find on retired professional pugilists whose long and undistinguished ring careers had been spent in the mistaken belief that sturdy durability and the ability to mix it with far heavier and infinitely more talented opponents would stand them in better stead than evasive tactics and good old-fashioned common sense. Bob was a good worker and (I have no reason to doubt) also a good grieve. Provided you stuck at your task and did it to the best of your ability, you got no hassle at all from him. I certainly never had a problem with him. But, with Bob, work was work and play was play and that was that.

In this philosophy, he was totally at odds with my brother George. George was strongly of the belief that every single minute of every single day had been bequeathed to him by a benevolent God for the sole purpose of extracting from that minute as much fun as was humanly possible. It was this rather flippant approach to work that was to ensure that he only ever worked under Bob McColm for two hours and forty minutes, give or take a couple of minutes either way as you choose. George and I were both scheduled to work at the turnips on that fatal day. At 14 years of age I was already an old hand at the business and an established summer worker on the farm. My brother, one year younger than I, was on his first morning.

We were all assembled at the foot of the hill, ready to begin our day's work. There would be about ten of us, a mixture of boys and girls, men and women, some old, some young. Before us lay our day's task: row upon row of tiny seedlings, each row 100 to 200 yards long, stretching away up the hill towards the dry-stane dyke marking the boundary of the field. The seedlings had to be thinned to eight inches apart, the heel of the hand pushing the clod of earth containing the unwanted seedlings away from the 'hower', and, on the return journey, pulling the next clod back clear of the drill. Push-pull-push-pull-push-pull…an excruciatingly monotonous task. But good 'howers' could thin as fast as they could crawl.

Although my brother had never worked under Bob McColm before, the grieve was well aware of his reputation. He was equally aware that within his gang on this day there was a girl who knew my brother well. Worse still, he too knew that Big Jessie – let us call her that for propriety's sake – shared my brother's happy-go-lucky approach to life. The biblical exhortation, 'Lead us not into temptation,' fell on very stony ground insofar as Wee Geordie and Big Jessie were concerned. On their own, they were pests enough, but linked together they were bad news, and well did Bob McColm know it. So, wisely, he kept them well apart. He placed Wee Geordie far out on the end row next to a morose old Latter-day Saint, while he kept Big Jessie on the second row right next to himself where he could keep an eye on her.

The day began uneventfully. The long line of workers crawled slowly and silently up the hill. The rain of the previous night had turned the soil to porridge and the fitful sunshine was, as yet, making little impression on the general glaur of the conditions.

Halfway through the morning Wee Geordie, bored by his isolation and the taciturnity of the Latter-day Saint beside him, began to fall behind out of the grieve's direct line of vision. He glanced up and saw Big Jessie, still working away unenthusiastically on her hands and knees but now lagging slightly behind the overseer. She turned her head round and their eyes met in a brief but − ultimately − fateful glance. He made a face at her and she responded with a vulgar gesture of her hand before returning her attention to the task before her. Instantly, he scooped up a clod of earth and hurled it at her.

Out of the corner of her eye Big Jessie, with that inherent instinct most Whithorn lassies of that day and age had for aggressive intent, caught a glimpse of his swinging arm. She ducked instantly. The soggy missile, travelling at something just short of the speed of sound and spewing grit like Halley's comet, hit the grieve behind the right ear with the force of an exploding shell, sending him base over apex among the turnips.

The grieve struggled to his knees in the mud like a mortally wounded buffalo, giving tongue lustily and trying to unscramble his befuddled brains while his rotating vision endeavoured to focus on his assailant. Wee Geordie, however, anticipating retribution with the intuitive intelligence of one who had been through it all before, was already some distance down the hill and setting a brisk pace for the sanctuary of the wood at the far corner of the farm.

*   *   *

I meandered on over the land. The next field contained hay-time memories. This, in my opinion, was where global warming really began. Old Maisie's explosive flatuses would have punched a hole in the Jovian atmosphere, never mind the Earth's ozone layer. At the time we fell in love with each other, Maisie was 27 years old, which was positively ancient for a horse. Clydesdale carthorses are renowned for their docility, and Maisie was even more docile than most and because of my inexperience with horses, she had been given the job of towing me around on the hayrake.

The hayrake was an odd looking contraption bristling with tines, used for raking new-mown hay into lines to facilitate collection. On a metal seat above the main body of the machine sat the operator. This perch was a mite uncomfortable, but the discomfort was somewhat alleviated by the fact that it kept me just above Maisie's direct line of fire. Not that it made a lot of difference, mind you, for Maisie was one of the world's truly great farters. I read a book many years ago entitled *Le Petomane* about a Frenchman who, in the years between the two World Wars, had made an excellent living on stage through his remarkable farting abilities. Metaphorically speaking, he could not have held a candle to Maisie and physically, he wouldn't have dared try. Had there been a stage living to be made for horse farters, Maisie would never have had to tow another hayrake in her life. Her flatulence was on a Brobdingnagian scale, especially when she had been feeding on new clover. Each step she took produced a thunderous retort, and she expelled gases so thick you could almost see her vapour trail. Even perched as I was on my eyrie behind her, I could not escape the fallout. It was particularly bad on those long, still summer days, of which there seemed to be an inordinate number then. On days like those her bodily emissions seemed to settle in a cloud over the field. And not only over the field, either: Maisie's farts were wet farts, and they permeated my clothing and the pores of my skin with the efficacy of mustard gas. How I did not suffer permanent brain damage and skin cancer from this noxious effluvium in which I seemed to be permanently enveloped, I shall never know. One thing I do know, however, is that I was the only one during that long, hot month of haymaking to avoid the attentions of the bloodsucking clegs and horseflies that infested that hayfield. Maisie saw to that.

At one time or another I had helped with the harvesting in most of the fields through which I passed now. 'He that hath a good harvest may be content with some thistles,' is an ancient maxim. It is one that most farmers, of whatever generation, would go along with. But dedicated retrospectionists never remember the thistles. For we of certain vintage, everything was perfect in our harvest years.

If it ever rained during the harvests of my day, I choose not to remember the fact. This was a time of sunshine and sheaves and stooks, a time when harvests were real harvests, before cold mechanical economics arrived with the combine harvester. My memories of those days are many: helping old Jeck Aird with the scythe to prepare the way for the reaper while listening with avidity to his incredible tales; the jingle of harness and the clumping of huge hooves and the clatter of iron wheels over the stones of the road surface as Maisie plodded steadfastly homeward with her load of ripe corn; the farmer's daughter and her helpers, clad in their prettiest summer frocks, carrying baskets of scones over the fields to feed the hungry hordes...

Harvest time was a special time, the last golden fling of the year before the land settled down to prepare for the drabness of winter. It was a time when heaven and earth became one. There can be no place for the thistles of life when we dreamers of dreams are gathering the corn of our yesteryears.

*   *   *

I hopped over the march dyke and into the Pouton fields. The old stone bridge over the burn was still there, but now it was so rickety as to be downright dangerous looking. I stopped in the middle, gazing upstream. My memory was sharp and clear, as though I was back all those 60-odd years ago as a wee boy standing on this same bridge. I looked down over the edge. There used to be a beautiful little clump of harebells – the Scottish bluebell – which grew on the ledge below my feet, and I remembered how much I looked forward to the appearance of their delicate Wedgwood blue, like a cloudless sky at the beginning of spring, each year. Although this was now early summer, there was no sign of them. Did I really expect there to be after all this time? I think I probably did.

I walked up the track to the little cottage. This was where I had spent a most important part of my childhood. The original structure was still plainly recognizable, for the blue whinstone walls were still there. It had been modernized, of course, since my day, with what used to be two separate but adjoining cottages now obviously knocked into one. A couple of skylights now adorned the roof and a sun porch had been added to the front. It still looked good, though, and the memories came flooding back.

I had lived here from the age of five until I was ten. At five, my knowledge of the English language was scant, to say the least. But I learned fast, courtesy of a Galloway primary school education and my Wigtownshire peers who, while initially regarding me with the curiosity and suspicion that they might have accorded the arrival of a Cherokee Indian complete with a feathered head-dress in their midst, quite quickly accepted me as one of their own.

My grandfather had no problem with the English language, for the simple reason that he never bothered to try to learn it. But he knew his Gaelic, all right. Indeed, he had a total distrust of anyone who didn't know the language of God, and that included my father Geordie MacIntosh, who, being a Perthshire man, knew only a few words of the ancient language. Being an itinerant woodcutter, my father was away from home a lot in those days and thus Gaelic was the lingua franca among us while he was gone. My grandfather would listen politely enough while my mother translated for him the BBC news that came over our wireless from London, but he would believe not one single word of what he had heard until it had been confirmed by the Gaelic news – also from the BBC in London – later that night.

Each evening when I came home from school the old man would take me into the back room of this cottage before which I now stood, to give me my Gaelic lessons. The evening would be divided into three parts. The first part consisted of the reading of a piece from the Bible over and over again. This was, for me, the least interesting part of the whole evening, mainly because names like Nebuchadnezzar kept cropping up, and even the old man was stuck for adequate Gaelic translations for those. Nevertheless, he was a natural teacher, and he made that Bible come alive in a way that no professional preacher has ever been able to do for me.

Fairytale time came next, and Grandfather had an endless supply of those. He had many Gaelic books on them, and what he couldn't find in his books, he would unearth from the endless store of Hebridean mythology he had locked up in his mind. I remember some of them today, but I still regret that I was unable to tape-record the old man back then when he was in full flow.

The last part of the evening – and this was the best part of all – was the singing. I can see the scene now as I write: an old man and a wee boy sitting by the fire on a winter night with the rain slashing against the window, the old fellow with the big tackety boots on his feet and his favourite walking stick in his hand as together we gave it belters:

Thugaibh aran do na gillean
Leis a'bhrochan súghain,
Thugaibh aran do na gillean
Leis a'bhrochan súghain,
Thugaibh aran do...'

Neither of us were singers, and the row must have been awful. It would reach its crescendo with the chorus:

BROCHAN TANA, TANA, TANA,
BROCHAN LOM A'SÚGHAIN,
BROCHAN TANA, TANA, TANA...'

And the old man's tackety boots and walking stick would be pounding the stone floor and the paraffin lamp would be fairly jumping on the mantelpiece with the vibration and the racket. Then the bedroom door would open cautiously and my mother would peer into the room in some alarm and she would shake her head sadly and say: 'Old man, you'll soon have that child as daft as yourself!' We didn't need the Spice Girls for entertainment on winter nights at Pouton Farm back in those days.

I turned around and looked across the fields towards the east. In those fields my brother and I had, at the ages of seven and eight respectively, cut thistles and dockens with sickles for the magnificent sum of one shiny half-crown per week between us. Jimmy Bell, the farm handyman, generally joined us with his scythe to keep an eye on us. Jimmy had a marvellous rapport with children, for he was a very playful old boy, and his was a type of playfulness to which my brother George was, perhaps predictably, more than receptive. I remember a poem he taught my brother as we worked:

> 'Young Geordie an Aul' Geordie
> Went oot tae cut the grass;
> Young Geordie stuck his hyook
> Up Aul' Geordie's arse.'

It was a poem gleefully recited by my brother whenever he was in a situation most designed to shock those of more genteel upbringing.

The lady whose responsibility Pouton Farm was at that time was Miss Hannay, a reclusive but rather terrifying spinster who lived in the farmhouse a few hundred yards from our cottage. She kept a very large and noisy flock of guinea fowl which raised the most incredible hullabaloo whenever anyone approached the farmhouse. They could fly like partridge and they nested over what seemed to us like half the county. One of the tasks given to us by Miss Hannay was to try to track down their nesting sites. This was easier said than done: it was like trying to track down the nests of African plover in the vast expanses of the Tsavo National Park in Kenya. Out we would go with our baskets in early morning, often not returning until late afternoon when the pangs of hunger began to assail us, having, in the interim, roamed far from sight and sound of the farm buildings. But our baskets would generally be full of eggs and we invariably got a couple of dozen or so from Miss

Hannay for our efforts. They were not only good to eat, but they were also excellent for the baking.

In frosty weather the guinea fowl took to roosting in the tall trees of the adjacent Galloway House estate woodlands, to the massive fright and discombobulation of the local poachers, for the slightest crack of a twig as the poachers were creeping through the woods at night would trigger the wretched birds off into a most hellish chorus that was probably heard across the water in Kirkcudbright.

*   *   *

I sauntered on down the road towards the beautiful seaside village of Garlieston. Ash trees still lined my way, but they seemed smaller and more gnarled than I remembered. Most were heavily cankered and dying. The chaffinches singing in the leafy crowns sounded much the same, though, and the placid waters of the burn alongside the road looked every bit as dark and mysterious as they had done 60 years before when my siblings and I had walked this same road to school together.

A worming angler, hunched by the side of the burn, attracted my attention. He showed me his catch: two fine fat trout. 'Lovely, aren't they, granddad!' he remarked cockily. 'Easy when you know how, eh?' He was young and his accent was very English. Probably a visitor to the area, I guessed. I took the fish from him and admired them, just as I had done so many times in the past. I handed them back. 'Aye, they're no' bad lookin' son,' I agreed dismissively, with my best Wigtownshire accent and then, climbing up the bank I turned to him again and said, 'Kinna wee, though. In my day, we only kept the big yins!'

I stepped down on the other side of the bank and left him. I was walking briskly now, hugely satisfied with myself. Nostomania, I was reflecting smugly, may be the refuge of the ageing, but there is surely no harm in spicing it up when circumstances demand with some modern one-upmanship.

Chapter 7
THE WOODMEN

When I first set eyes on this wood as a mere boy of 10 years of age, its tall trees resounded to the songs of birds. It was springtime and the very air throbbed with the joy of it all. Rabbits stood on their hindlegs, ears stretched high, to stare pop-eyed at me, as though they were witnessing their first ever human being, and red squirrels scampered friskily in front of me, pausing to turn and look back cheekily at me every few yards.

The sky was cloudless. Long shafts of sunlight, dust-laden, speared through the trees, highlighting the blue and pink of the hyacinth and campion that carpeted the woodland floor, and vivifying the verdancy of the leaves and nut clusters on the hazel bushes. There was a great variety of tree species in this wood and the warmth of the sun released fragrances of many kinds: the distinctive cedar-scent of the Douglas Firs as their resin blisters popped in the heat; the strong turpentine aroma from the bark and buds of Scots Pines and Silver Firs; the fruity orange scent wafting downward from the needles of the four colossal Giant Firs that stood tall and proud above all the other trees at the far corner of the wood. The whole woodland, in fact, was a vast perfumery of fragrances on this day, and the great Gabrielle Coco Chanel herself could not have hoped to produce anything to match their exquisite delicacy.

Five years later I returned to the wood. I jumped over the dyke and crossed the fields to the scene of my previous visit. Only the tree stumps remained on a silent, barren landscape. Already, the green, shrouding moss was creeping all over them, claiming them, as though trying to obliterate from the view of man and God the shame of their passing. A piece of ancient, windblown newspaper rustled and flapped its way over the stumps. It was the only moving thing to be seen.

The day was cold and grey. There was a dampness, a hint of rain, in the air. Not a living creature was to be seen. Somewhere in the far distance the mournful cry of a curlew echoed plaintively over the drab and empty spaces.

*   *   *

The years of World War II were good for the timber barons of Scotland. Suddenly, an industry that had largely been forgotten since the end of World War I in 1918 found itself in demand all over again. All at once, the smallest of timber enterprises assumed an importance they could never hitherto have dreamed of. Every factory, every sawmill in the land wanted timber, and they wanted it badly. Almost every single species of tree was considered to have a value, even those that would have been discarded as rubbish previously. All had a use in this most pressing of national emergencies. Larch, beech, oak and ash timbers went to the shipyards of the Clyde, the lightweight spruces and firs to the aircraft factories in England, poplar and elm to the railways and mines for wagon decking, and sycamore for flooring just about everywhere. Just to prove that some things seldom changed, even in wartime, the best cuts of oak and walnut were still earmarked for the furnishing of flagships, staff limousines and even the occasional stately home. The commoners got the scraps for firewood, providing, of course, they paid for them.

Galloway did not escape. Estates were plundered for their timbers, including those that had managed to escape being looted in the previous European caper. While even the most dedicated of environmentalists – of which there were precious few anywhere in those days, in any case – could not have argued against the necessity of wholesale felling during the exigencies of global conflict, it did signal the beginning of the end of the great estates of the past, and it meant the end of the glorious sylvan beauty brought to our countryside through this mixture of species, native and exotic, planted with such loving, far-sighted care by our forebears in past centuries.

But the trees had to be felled, and someone had to do the felling. My father was a foreman woodcutter, initially with Jones of Larbert, then finally with Callander of Minnigaff. When I was about ten years of age he began to take me with him to the woods on my school holidays. It was the consummation of a love affair that has lasted to this day. I had always been in love with the woods, and from as early as I could remember I had had close associations with trees. Up until I was five years of age we lived in a cottage on the southern fringe of Kilsture Forest, and the great expanses of woodland behind our house were both my playground and my haven. There were no houses anywhere near us and my contacts with the human race were very limited as a result. Thus, the rare and unexpected appearance of a stranger at our door could not have been viewed with greater alarm by me had the visitor been a Martian. A district nurse from Garlieston who paid an official monthly visit to check that all was well with we children – there were three of us then – hardly ever got near enough to me to speak to me. Even when she did manage to catch sight of me, it was usually only the briefest of glimpses as I vanished into the thickets. Many years later, when I was a grown man, that delightful nurse McCrae was to tell me that, while she had a very good idea of what my backside looked like when I was a child, she had only the vaguest notion as to my visage.

God alone knows how we escaped serious injury in those halcyon years before we went to school. My brother and I could climb like squirrels and we had no fear at all of heights. Any tree that was climbable, we climbed it to the topmost branch. In addition, Kilsture Forest was alive with adders during the summer months, and the fact that none of us was fatally bitten by one of them was nothing short of miraculous.

Woodcutting was a relatively gentle and peaceful business in those wartime years. The era of the shrieking, noisome chainsaw had yet to come. The only sounds to disturb the peace while the woodcutters worked were the chinking of axes on wood, the soft rasp of a file on saw teeth, the metallic – but strangely soporific – swishing, wet sound of the big two-man crosscut saw in action, the crackling of bursting resin bubbles as branches were piled high on the fire, the muted roar of the fire itself as the flames soared higher and higher, and the occasional laugh at some witticism cracked by one of the younger members of the gang. And, of course, the tearing, splintering, crashing wallop as some giant tree fell to earth.

I was never brought to the woods by my father just to stand around looking pale and interesting, not even at the tender age of ten. Everyone in a woodcutting gang had to be able to contribute. The traditional boy's job was the burning of branches, and a most important task it was, too. Starting a fire, then being able to keep it going even in the wettest of conditions, was an art in itself.

The stump of a long-dead Scots pine, or 'Scotch-Fir', as it was often called, was the prospective fire-starter's dream. Chips from these were absolutely saturated with resin and would ignite fiercely even on the wettest morning. Old newspaper helped, too, but with those resinous chips available, newspaper was simply an unnecessary luxury. Dry twigs were piled wigwam-style over the chips, thicker and thicker dead twigs being added and mixed with green twigs as the blaze got stronger and stronger. Gradually and with care, the first leafy twigs and small branches would be added until a good-sized bonfire had got under way. Larger and larger branches were added until you had a fire going that would have roasted an ox. But this was the critical point, and this was where the boy who really knew his stuff came into his own. A roaring fire with flames shooting ten feet upwards had to be kept fed, or it would die down again with dramatic suddenness, and once in this state, it could be a damnable job to get it going again. The bigger the fire got, the hungrier it became and the more it needed to be fed. At this point it needed three workers to keep it going – two trailing branches to it and one on permanent duty in the searing ether surrounding it, heaving the branches on the fire. Even on the coldest winter day there was never any chance of hypothermia setting in; clothing often became as full of holes as a pepper-pot from the burning ash climbing in the torrid upstream above the pyre, before it was caught by the down-draught to descend swiftly and settle on one's head and shoulders.

The estate woodlands of those days were extraordinarily beautiful, and I feel a sense of sadness now that I was then, even in small part, responsible for their demise. But, as a child, there was no sense of sadness; there was only this wonderful sense of excitement at it all, the glamour of being part of a felling gang, a lumberjack. Tall, stately Noble and Silver and Douglas firs mingled with the velvet-leafed beech and graceful silver birch. Sturdy, moss-covered oaks rubbed shoulders with dark, saturnine elms on the higher ground, and in the wet peat hollows spruce and ash crowded each other for space. All would soon come under the axe, and I couldn't wait to be part of it.

'Laying-in' was the first and most important task in the felling of any tree. It was an art that very few axemen – even good axemen – ever succeeded in perfecting, and there was, in fact, a sort of arcanum surrounding it that few of the old axemen were prepared to reveal. It determined the direction in which the tree would fall and the way in which it would fall. It was also a guard against the tree splitting right up the middle as it fell. A badly laid-in tree could not only prove to be an embarrassing nuisance through falling in the wrong direction; it could prove to be downright dangerous, if not fatal. My father was an expert of the highest calibre, and he did all the laying-in for the gang.

A 'mouth' would be cut in the base of the tree with the axe, the size of the mouth depending to a great extent on the lean of the tree, wind strength, and the direction in which the tree had to fall. Great wedges would be cut out, first with an angled downward arc, followed by a horizontal sweep. The only sound to be heard then would be the solid 'thunk' of the Old Man's great felling axe and his explosive grunt as each stroke tolled its knell on the doomed tree. It was then that I first became aware of a curious phenomenon: even in the hiatus between swings of the Old Man's axe all the leaves in the crown would be aquiver. At such times I used to think: 'Can a tree really feel things? Does it know what's going to happen? If not, why does it tremble so?' It was a thought that was to come back to me many years later when I witnessed the same phenomenon during tree felling operations in Africa.

When the Old Man had finally satisfied himself that the laying-in process was complete, he and his regular felling colleague – at that time, my Uncle Neil – would buckle on their leather kneepads. Now was the time for the actual felling to begin. This was a job for men, not boys. And strong, fit men at that. It was a job for powerful arms and shoulders and thighs, because those long, cumbersome felling saws would have tested untried muscles beyond endurance. It was a job for men with back and stomach muscles so powerful you could have broken rocks on them. In short, it was a job for *real* men. It looked easy enough, but then experts at their trade always make their work look deceptively easy. But this was really hard work; in all of the woodman's tasks, this was the one job I never cared for. I loved axe work and eventually became good at it. But felling trees with those monstrous saws...

'PULL, never push!' the Old Man would order the tyro. The man on each end of the saw would pull on the wooden handle, drawing the saw across him as he knelt beside the tree. Immediately his companion on the other end would pull it back...

PULL...

...pull

PULL...

...pull

PULL...

...pull

Veins standing out on the neck...faces smeared with grimy sweat...shoulder muscles bunching and arms swinging smoothly and rhythmically as the saw sang tinnily and the great teeth sank quickly and deeply into trunk. Long streaming cords of wood fibre were stripped from its heart with each pull and the white, crisp, fragrant confetti sawdust piled higher in front of each man's knees.

Towards the end sawing would become more difficult as the tree began to settle back on the saw. The Old Man would call a halt and reach for the bag of wedges and the sledgehammer behind him. He would then mell a couple of heavy steel wedges into the slim opening left behind the blade and sawing would recommence. The end was near now. The deep-seated creaking would begin as the great tendons inside the tree began to shear. Suddenly, there would be one loud explosive crack and the whole tree would shiver and shake as it let out a groan while its executioners got up off their knees and calmly walked away. Slowly at first, then with gathering speed, the tree would arc over and thunder remorselessly down in a shower of leaves and twigs and other debris as its branches and limbs were coarsely broken before it thumped in to the earth with an almighty wallop, sending a thick cloud of dust whuffing upward from around the shattered crown. In the eerie aftermath a stillness would settle over the whole wood. The birdsong ceased and the forest became still, as though in mourning for the loss of an old friend.

Snedding came next. This consisted of removing all the branches from the fallen tree by axe. Branches were removed at their base, level with the surface of the bark of the tree, so smoothly that no rough splinters, no unpleasant snags, protruded from the bole. Real axemen prided themselves on leaving a surface as smooth as marble on the trunk of the tree, no matter how thick or how thin the branch removed might have been. The whole tree would then be measured and marked for crosscutting into the required lengths by the Old Man, and after this the individual logs would be measured and their volume entered into his notebook. Large branches considered unfit for processing into anything useful in the sawmill would be stacked at the edge of the clearing for future sale as firewood.

The midday 'piece-time' was hallowed, when weary bodies could rest a little and hungry bellies could recharge their batteries. It was the boy's job to ensure that the fire had been allowed to die down sufficiently to let the men get near enough to boil their billy-cans. 'Woodman's tea' will never, I suspect, reach the drawing rooms of the stately homes of England. It was certainly an acquired taste, but it was perfectly suited to the conditions. Flask tea would never, somehow, have been the same. Woodman's tea was cooked in a 'drum', which consisted of an old syrup tin with a wire handle laced through a couple of holes punched opposite each other, just below the rim. It was a very simple but effective method, and the drums were held over the glowing embers on the end of a long stick until the water in them began to boil. At this point a fistful of tea was thrown into each drum, which was then replaced on the fire and allowed to stew for a minute or two, according to individual taste. (There was an old woodman's belief that a small piece of twig placed in the boiling tea would keep the smoke out of it, but I never found this to make too much difference. Indeed, just as certain Scotch malt distilleries extol the smokiness of their whiskies, so I found that the woodland smokiness enhanced the flavour of Woodman's tea.) A couple of handfuls of sugar thrown into the jet-black brew and voila! tea was served. Milk was never added.

Great hunks of bread with thick slices of Sorbie cheese were a favourite accompaniment, as these could be toasted over the embers. They complemented the tea to perfection, and I can smell and taste this excellent fare even as I write.

There were downsides, of course, to this daily idyll, as there are with most pleasant experiences. In those wartime years environmental considerations just did not exist. Felling took place all the rear round. I remember my sadness when I picked up the nest of a chaffinch from the broken remnants of a newly felled sycamore. It was the most beautiful thing I had ever seen, an exquisitely crafted cup of green moss, silver lichen, brown grass and spiders' webs, lined with soft, white feathers. One of the four eggs was miraculously intact, a pale-creamy-white marvel of nature with deep purplish-red spots and streaks. I took the nest and its single egg out to the edge of the wood and placed it in a thick hawthorn bush, hoping for...what? I have no idea, but somehow it seemed less callous than just casting that wonderful creation aside to be trampled underfoot in the mud.

*   *   *

Most woodcutters had a poaching streak in them, and my father was no exception. He always had a dozen or so snares set around the perimeter of any wood in which his gang worked. These would often produce a pair of rabbits, and even – but only on the very rare occasion – a throttled cock pheasant. It could be a risky business, though, for estate gamekeepers regarded woodcutters as being no higher up the scale of morality than tinkers and just as liable to steal anything not nailed down. The arrival of a gang of woodcutters in their area had them on red alert and reaching for their nerve tonic. Snares had to be set as darkness fell and lifted again before the 'keeper got out and about on his rounds in the morning.

A rare – but most welcomed – benefit of the woodcutter's job was the finding of a colony of bees in a hole in a tree. If the colony was big enough, the hole would usually contain an absolute bonanza of honey. But it was never easy to get at, even after the tree had hit the ground. Bees, at the best of times, are highly protective of what is theirs by right, and their natural irascibility is rarely mellowed by the destruction of their homes. They would erupt in clouds, just looking for something to sting. Apart from the Old Man, all of us would retire with some haste far into the thickets and watch subsequent events from a safe distance. The Old Man seemed impervious to their stings, and he would plough through the dark, swarming mass like a bear, plunging his hands into the wreckage of the colony's home, scooping out masses of the rich, amber honey and filling his buckets with it. He would eventually emerge from the furious, swirling hordes, bees stuck all over him, even on his ginger moustache, but as pleased as a little boy who had successfully raided the minister's orchard. Most of the honey would be taken home by us, but some of it would be eaten there and then around the fire. It had a wild, bitter-sweet flavour to it, quite

7 4

unlike that of the honey obtained from domestic beehives, but it was truly excellent. The wax stuck, cloying, to the teeth and the roof of the mouth, and you had to keep a sharp lookout to ensure that no bees were buried inside the lump you were devouring.

As darkness approached in those wartime years, fires had to be completely extinguished. These were the regulations, put in force to ensure that no naked light should be visible to enemy planes. Our last task of the day, therefore, was to chuck buckets of water and clods of earth over the embers. Young though I was then, this struck me as being somewhat ludicrous. With London and Clydeside being pounded daily at that point of the war, I would have thought that Hermann Göring had quite enough on his plate without diverting his Luftwaffe to the bombing of the remote Galloway woodlands of Ravenstone and Castlewigg.

There was one moment of high drama, totally unconnected with the war, and for this story I am indebted to one of the Old Man's colleagues who claimed to have witnessed the event. They had been felling a strip of woodland to the north of Whauphill. As the Old Man was wending his way to the road for his bicycle at the end of the day's work, he was accosted by the local gamekeeper, who accused him of concealing a rabbit in his satchel. This was indignantly denied by the Old Man. Accusation and denial followed thick and fast, with the conversation becoming generally rancorous. They were standing on a steep bank of the Sheep Park burn at the time, a narrow but quite deep ditch that ran through a long peat bog. The gamekeeper made a grab at the satchel, and the truth of what happened next is shrouded in some uncertainty. The Old Man's subsequent version was that the 'keeper slipped on the edge of the bank'. Seeing that the poor fellow was about to tumble backwards into the burn, the Old Man solicitously put out a hand to help steady him. My informant's version differed somewhat: he said it was a straight right to the jaw, delivered with speed, power and accuracy. Whatever the truth of the matter, the 'keeper crashed backwards through the tangle of dogrose and brier and whins and blackthorn with which the sides of the bank were liberally covered, and down into the deepest part of the burn, where he wallowed in the black mud for some time before his senses had regained their equilibrium. Long before he had managed to crawl back up the bank, torn and bleeding and soused with the blackest peat water in all of Wigtownshire, my father had calmly pedalled off down the road for home. It is said that drinks on the house were his for the asking in at least two of the local pubs for a very long time afterwards, but that, of course, may well be another story.

Those early days of mine in the woods saw the end of the era of the old-fashioned carter. The carters were a tough and hard-drinking crew. They operated with horse and pole-waggon, the wheel axles being adjustable up or down the pole according to the length of logs they had to carry. Their horses were often bad-tempered brutes, and maybe they had good reason to be. The carters were seldom gentle with them, and the conditions in which they had to operate could be quite awful. Soft soil would turn into a mush after the lightest rain and the loads they had to tow, very heavy in the best of conditions, would become doubly so when the iron-banded wheels got bogged down in the glutinous ruts.

The carters themselves fared little better in the mud, and they would be thickly plastered in it long before they were loaded up and ready to move. But they were a cheerful bunch. There was one whose penchant for reading Wild West stories, coupled with a vivid imagination, made him believe that in some past life he had belonged to the open prairie. His rendering of Frankie Lane's song 'Mule Train' as he sat on top of his logs after a longish spell in the pub, while his team of horses slipped and skidded down the steep and icy Perth Brae in the middle of Newton Stewart on their way to the Minnigaff Sawmills, is still spoken of fondly by one or two old-timers to this day.

The woodcutter's job has always been a hazardous one. It is probably even more so today with the frightful chainsaws. In the old days a slip would generally mean, at worst, a most unpleasant cut. But it would usually be a 'clean' cut, an axe cut. Today, falling on top of a chainsaw just does not bear thinking about. But accidents did happen, even back then, and they could happen even to the most careful of woodmen. One of my father's colleagues, a most experienced tree feller, was killed when a tree fell back on him. A momentary lapse in concentration, an instant of carelessness, and you could be in deep trouble. It happened to me once. Although only in my early twenties I was already quite an experienced woodman and was clearing scrub oak at the Castle o' Park, outside Glenluce. I was walking down a steep and frozen slope with my axe over my shoulder, an incredibly foolish thing to do, when the inevitable happened. My feet flew from under me and I collapsed on the deck with the razor-sharp axe slicing through my thick clothing and deep into my back. The only wonder was that the damned thing hadn't chopped my head off. As it was, I had learned a very salutary lesson by the time the local nurse stitched me up.

Heart-stopping moments could occur in less physically painful ways, too. I was helping out in the felling of a wood near Castle Kennedy, just outside Stranraer, before I left for Africa. One of my fellow-workers was a most engaging Irishman who called himself Mickey-Son. Mickey-Son was in his mid-fifties, and he was the irrepressible, cheerful, prematurely wizened type of Irishman so often seen up and down the west coast of that country from Clare to Donegal. He was a simple soul, quite illiterate and deeply religious, and with a deeply ingrained dread of the unknown. He was as superstitious as a spae wife but he was a marvellous raconteur, the sort who, if the story he was telling appeared to be lacking in audience appeal somewhat, would soon remedy that with a droll Irish quip and a more than adequate punch line. He was a bit of a drifter, as most single woodcutters tended to be then. One evening after work we met in a Stranraer pub and he told me about the last job he had had, that of felling trees on a large estate in the region of Glen App, on the road to Ballantrae. The estate owner was an animal lover and collector, and she had travelled all over the world in her search for ever more exotic creatures. She was no believer in keeping animals cooped up in cages, either, and in the summer months some of the less dangerous would be allowed to roam the spacious gardens around her house.

She was generous to the workers and she often brought them scones and cakes when they had their midday break. She took a shine to Mickey-Son, he told me, and she had asked him if he would like a permanent job on the estate. 'I would have taken it, too,' he said wistfully, 'If it hadn't been for the bloody fright I got on me last day there. Still get nightmares over it.'

It had been a drowsy late-autumn day, and Mickey-Son was suffering somewhat from the effects of a convivial evening with friends the night before. But he was a conscientious worker and he kept plugging away until the midday break. During it, an urgent desire to obey the call of nature gave him the excuse he needed to be on his own for a while and clear his throbbing head. He slipped away from the rest of the workers into the concealing cover and the dark shade of a huge clump of tall rhododendrons at the edge of the wood. He squatted there, lit a cigarette and allowed himself to sink into a soothing, drink-induced dwalm while he waited for nature to take her inevitable course. It was while he was deep in this reflective torpor that his meditations were interrupted by a hoarse cough from behind.

Irishmen in their mid-50s who have been lifelong chain-smokers and who have partaken overmuch of the products of John Barleycorn from a young age, are not generally noted for their athleticism. But Mickey-Son was not your ordinary Irishman. He achieved the seemingly impossible by leaping vertically from his sitting position high in the air with his trousers and long johns around his ankles while, in the same movement, performing a beautifully balletic mid-air pirouette-cum-entrechat to confront the source of his discomfiture. He instantly wished devoutly that he hadn't, for staring at him with basilisk intensity in the gloom from a range of three feet was quite the most terrible vision Mickey-Son had ever seen, even in his worst dreams.

'The bloody thing,' he shuddered, 'was lookin' me straight in the eye. It had a most horrible long black face covered in hair and wit' a long white beard and jet-black horns and red, glowing eyes. I knew instantly that the Divvil himsilf had come for me and I shook off me trousers and drawers quick as a flash and I lep that boundary wall like a deer and I left that wood and himsilf behind me like I was Jesse Owens heading for gold at the Olympics. I never even went back to collect me pay and belongings.'

'What on earth could the thing have been, then?' I asked curiously. 'The Divvil, I'm telling you, man, it was the Divvil. It could have been none other. The woman tracked me down a week later in this very pub wit' me pay and things and she told me it was only one of her animiles that got lost in the woods. She said it was a ...' But here his memory failed him. He looked down into his pint and lifting it, drank deeply, licked his lips and then continued: 'One of her animiles, me left elbow! Dat bugger was no animile. He was taller nor mesilf and twicet as ugly. Dat bugger was no animile. Dat was Satan in disguise, dat's what it was. And not too heavily disguised, neither!'

Mickey-Son lifted his pint pot again. His face had an unusual pallor to it and his hand was shaking. I could see that he was deeply disturbed. I hurriedly bought him a large Bushmills. He drank it gratefully in one gulp.

'Sure,' he concluded vehemently, 'what did she mean, "only an animile"? Wasn't it me that saw the bloody thing, now? Not hur. I know what it was. And I have the best proof of all that it was Oul' Nick in disguise, for didn't the bastard cough at me in an English accent...'

They were unique, these old-timers. And they had a mental and physical toughness about them that one encounters but rarely these days. While I was overseas my father, well into his 70s by this time, ran his fingers through a circular saw while helping out a young friend with his firewood business. I am indebted for the account of what happened to those who had witnessed the accident, and I have no reason to doubt what I was told. The story goes like this.

With great gouts of blood spurting from him and eight miles to travel to the nearest doctor, the Old Man (a) insisted on searching amidst the sawdust for the missing digits in the belief that they might be sewn back on; (b) insisted on having his usual midday plate of soup before he travelled anywhere; and (c) insisted on stopping at a pub en route to the doctor for a good stiff dram. The Whithorn doctor could do very little for him other than patch him up before sending him on the long, long journey via his young friend's firewood truck to the Royal Infirmary, some 60 miles distant in Dumfries. At the hospital, pre-warned of his arrival, the nursing orderlies were waiting at the door with a wheelchair. The Old Man brushed them aside indignantly. 'Think I'm a bloody invalid or something?' he retorted as he strode into the hospital.

They don't make em' like that any more.

Chapter 8

WAIFS IN THE WILDERNESS

Chauvinism had always been alive and kicking in Britain before – and during – World War II. It still exists today, but the male of the species has to be more circumspect about his choice of words and the situation in which he utters them. No longer can he say openly, as Kipling once wrote: 'A woman is only a woman, but a good cigar is a smoke.' Or even, as Churchill is once reputed to have replied when asked what he foresaw to be the future role of woman: 'The same as it has always been since the time of Adam and Eve.' For a husband to even whisper such ineffable tosh within earshot of his nearest and dearest would be to risk being arraigned before a coven of feminists and have his marital rights withheld for the foreseeable future, if not, indeed, forever.

There were two distinctly different tiers of chauvinism in Britain in those early wartime years and neither reflected too well upon the male of the species. Firstly, there was the upper-crust, Home Counties type, the condescending 'good-at-opening-village-fêtes-and-organizing-Conservative-tea-parties-but-nothing-else' sort of chauvinism that must have made many a genteel lady long to apply her riding crop to her consort. Alvar Lidell, the renowned wartime BBC newsreader, on being asked how he would feel about the possibility of a woman taking over his job, replied haughtily that there was no chance of this ever happening. 'She would burst into tears if she ever had to read bad news,' he explained. The boffins at the Ministry of

Supply believed that cosmetics were 'as essential to a woman's well-being as tobacco was to a man' and that in important wartime duties a woman would spend too much time powdering her nose to be of any practical use. At Whitehall Herbert Morrison promised that no woman would ever have to serve in any building infested with rats or mice, while one of London's broadsheets commented sniffily about lady ambulance drivers taking driving tests in Hyde Park and 'careering madly on and off the bridle paths swathed in silver fox and rattling with pearls and creating a jolly bad example for the underclasses'.

The chauvinism of the 'underclasses' was very much more down to earth. She was fit to be his cook, dish-washer and bed-warmer, but nothing more than that. The very idea that she should forsake these pleasures and go off to work in a munitions factory or join one of the services was enough to drive a man to drink. But the reasons for his sense of alarm at the prospect were quite different to those of the plutocracy. The son of the soil knew that, given half a chance, his soul mate might just prove herself to be as good in her new role as any man, or, indeed, even better, and then what would the harvest be? It did not bear thinking about.

There were a few men who would have been perfectly happy to have seen their wives off to serve king and country in some foreign field far, far away. One Gallovidian – who had best remain unnamed – was quoted as saying that his one regret in life was that his wife was too old to be called up for front line duty with the 8th Army. 'She would sort out Rommel in ten seconds flat,' he asserted patriotically. 'And besides,' he concluded wistfully, 'Africa's a helluva lang distance away fae Wigtownshire.'

My own father was by no means exempt from this deplorable lack of amatory sentiment. I remember one occasion when my mother, God rest her, had travelled to the Whithorn cinema to witness the American actor Douglas Fairbanks at his romantic best in some long-forgotten movie. She was most impressed by the fact that Mr Fairbanks never failed to greet his spouse with a tender kiss when he returned from work each evening. The trip back home from Whithorn to Sorbie in a dilapidated, draughty, evil-smelling old bus failed to dim the rosy hue of her dreams, and by the time she arrived at the door of the house wherein reposed the Love of her Life, she had already made up her mind that the time had come to add even more spice to the mad, erotic whirl of her marriage.

'Old Man,' she said as soon as she had hung up her coat, 'in future, I want you to be like Douglas Fairbanks. I want a kiss from you every day as soon as you come home from work.' Her Old Lochinvar did not even bother to look up from the *Galloway Gazette* he was reading. 'Do you think I'm a bloody sex maniac or something?' was his gallant riposte. Not much chance of nightingales singing in Berkeley Square about marriages such as those, one would have been tempted to think. Or even around Wigtown Square, for that matter.

A song popular of that era probably came closest to summing up the male attitude to women then. It described the antics of a couple of idle old Hebridean fishermen who had decided that, after a lifetime of carefree bachelorhood, the time had come to think about the many advantages to having a wife to look after them in their dotage. They eventually came to the conclusion that Mhairi Bhan from the clachan up on the hill had all the necessary attributes to make a suitable partner for one of them at least:

> *And Mhairi Bhan will pull the oars*
> *For she is big and strong,*
> *And we will sit down in the stern*
> *And sing a Gaelic song.*

There were more than a few outwardly docile Mhairi Bhans around then, and it must have proved to be something of a shock to the system when they showed to their men during World War II that they could be quite as efficient when serving their nation as when taking care of the needs of their Lord and Master in the home.

The arrival of the Land Girls and the evacuees in the early days of World War II hit rural Galloway with the force of a tsunami. It was a trauma from which some would never quite recover. Contrary to popular belief, the Women's Land Army did not first see the light of day during World War II. It was, in fact, founded in 1917 by Roland Prothero, the then Minister of Agriculture. I remember my father talking of seeing their members at work in the Perthshire fields around 1918 and they were, apparently, almost as great a curiosity as had been Buffalo Bill Cody's touring Wild West Show 20 years earlier. People came from far and near to gawp at these strange feminine creatures clothed in breeches and smoking cigarettes, and loud and virulent was the condemnation of their scandalous mode of dress and 'mannish behaviour' in kirk pulpits throughout the land.

In June 1939 the Women's Land Army was re-formed under its honorary director Lady Denham, OBE, who donated her own home, Balcombe Place, for use as its headquarters. The WLA was an extremely well-organized set-up. Wages, costs of training, uniform costs, hostel accommodation payment and travelling expenses all came under the jurisdiction of the Agricultural Wages Board, while requisitioning of hostels was the responsibility of the Ministry of Labour and Works.

Each county had its own organising committee and local representative. The representative was responsible for the welfare of the girls, for disciplining in the event of any indiscretions, and – perhaps most important of all – for lending a shoulder on which to cry for girls depressed and far from home. The uniform was smart and attractive. It consisted of beige coloured breeches, leaf-green jersey, white Aertex shirt, fawn overcoat and black wellington boots. The hat was of a style favoured by Miss Annie Oakley, crack pistol shot with the aforementioned Buffalo Bill circus. For the rougher work and the more inclement weather conditions, dungarees, tackety boots, sou-wester and oilskins were provided.

They came from all walks of life, those colourful girls, and many were unbelievably naive about their expectations of life on the farm. The first sight of a bull mounting a cow was enough to give the city born and bred girls a fit of the vapours – there was one reported case of a girl from England's stockbroker belt who fainted clean away at the horrid spectacle. When she emerged from her swoon she instantly resigned, cancelled her forthcoming marriage, and joined a convent of such cloistered seclusion that she would never see another male creature, animal or human, in her life again. Another, a preacher's daughter, could not bring herself to utter the vulgarity of the words 'belly-band' in respect to that part of a horse's harness. She insisted on calling it a 'tummy strap', to the intense amusement of the farmer (and probably the horse as well).

But surprisingly few packed it in. Most stuck it out to the bitter end. Eventually, by dint of sheer hard work, determination and grit – not to mention the speed at which they managed to acquire a commendable degree of skill – they succeeded in winning over all but the most sceptical and anti-feminist of their farmer employers. They worked in all weathers, in the rain and the wind and the sleet of winter and in the baking heat of mid-summer. They ate beetroot sandwiches until the red juice was practically squirting out of every orifice in their bodies, developing in the process a life-long aversion to this aptly named member of the *Beta vulgaris* family. In some hostels in Southern England a standard breakfast fare was prunes and cold, fat, bacon which had been fried the night before to save time. It is little wonder that this disgusting menu came high on most Land Girls' list of Meals-I-Can-Well-Do-Without.

But they were a cheery bunch and they were popular. They loved their Saturday nights off at the village 'hops' and they were a boon to lonely servicemen stationed far from home. Proximity to an American base was the posting most desired, for the Yanks were generous with their gifts of nylon stockings, chewing gum, cigarettes and chocolate. Galloway had a fair share of Land Girls during the years of World War II and, although the dialect never ceased to puzzle them, they coped well with the work and the weather. The lung-choking dust and the grime of the threshing mill work was universally detested, and their early attempts at milking cows and the building of hay rucks were risible. But they learned fast. There were few Yanks around them in Galloway to bribe them with nylons and chocolate, but the Poles at Burrowhead proved to be a surprisingly good substitute, while the 'Brylcreem Boys' at Baldoon's RAF base were no slouches either when it came to romance. Formidable competition to the Poles and the airmen was to come later with the arrival of the Italian prisoners of war; while completely indolent at work, they proved to be surprisingly active when pursuing matters of the flesh. In addition, for a nation so lacking in aggressive intent during war, they could be very determined in situations amatory. A girl finding herself inadvertently trapped in a remote hayshed on a wet day with one of Mussolini's Finest knew that she was in for the fight of her life if she hoped to emerge from that hayshed with virtue intact.

The Women's Timber Corps was an off-shoot of the Women's Land Army. Its members, too, came from all walks of life, and they had opted to work in the woods rather than in the open fields. Like their Land Army compatriots, most of them had arrived with a very romantic view of life in the wild woods but they soon found woodcutting to be hard, backbreaking work. Most, though, came to love it, and many became surprisingly proficient with their little $4^1/_2$-lb axes.

I have a vivid memory of one of their number. Ellen was an extremely pretty English girl who had been a secretary in London before the outbreak of war. She was madly in love with an airman from the Baldoon camp, and her 'piece-time' break was invariably taken up with daydreaming that was to come within a whisker of being the death of her.

I was snedding branches at the edge of a large clearing in the middle of a wood while, far across from me at the other end of the clearing, my father and his helpmate were felling a huge Silver Fir. I heard the first loud crack of the giant tree's heart fibres shearing and my father's obligatory warning 'halloo'. I looked up in time to see Ellen wandering aimlessly across the clearing, her mind obviously on another planet, oblivious to the fact that she was right in the path of the falling tree. Before our horrified eyes, she vanished under the mighty branches as the crown of the tree smashed down over her.

We set to work instantly with our axes, frantically clearing the branches from around the area where we had last seen her. To our relief and astonishment we found that the great trunk was fortuitously propped up off the ground by the two crossed logs over which it had fallen, the girl, by the greatest of good fortune having stumbled over one of the logs at the last vital second and fallen into the neat little cavity created beneath. Ellen was dazed and a bit scratched here and there but otherwise unhurt. Her huge blue eyes were open and she gazed up at my father's anxious features. A seraphic smile spread slowly over her lovely face. 'Geordie...' she murmured dreamily, '...you moved the earth for me.'

Her airman boyfriend could hardly have done it better.

The evacuees created an even greater stir than the Land Girls, and Margaret McCreath retains vivid memories of their stay at her father's farm in the Machars of Wigtownshire.

'Three days before war broke out my father came in and announced to my mother that she had better prepare. Because of the size of the farmhouse, the initial official assessment had been for 16 children and two helpers. There was no electricity, we had an old black range in the kitchen, and oil lamps and candles were used for lighting. Our sole domestic help was a local 17-year-old maid...'

Up until the beginning of the war years, coal came in bulk to the people of Sorbie by train, and it was collected at the station by horse and cart by the farmer's men on a regular basis. Tea was purchased in quantity twice a year from a representative and it, too, came to the farm via Sorbie Station. Flour, oatmeal and sugar were purchased by the sackful from Stranraer. Margaret McCreath writes:

'Water came from the well across the road from the house. There could be water shortages and then the fire in the range had to be put out to avoid blowing up the hot water system. One learnt to recognise when the water in the tank was boiling and take action quickly. The problem was not in the supply in the well, but in the amount of water required to drive the water wheel for the pump. The house was at the highest point of the farm, and the supply failed there first, especially if the cows were thirsty. When the range had to be put out of action, cooking was done on a two-burner paraffin stove. There was no quick way to boil a kettle...'

The ordering of sugar and tea in bulk stopped abruptly when war began. So did the drowsy pace of life on the farm. The evacuees were on the way. Instead of the original assessment of 16, the McCreaths found themselves stuck with 11 boys aged from 6 to 14 years. It was – they were soon to find out – quite enough. Most of the children came from Clydebank and the Gorbals and they were tough critters. They were also definitely not used to homes of such capacious splendour as the farmhouse in which they were now to be billeted. Mrs McCreath, a lady of much perspicacity, took one look at them and decided that certain house rules were necessary:

'Upstairs was declared out of bounds. So was the parlour, our family living-room. Meals would be taken in the large tiled kitchen at the long, scrubbed harvesting table which could seat 12 adults. There would be forms for the children. The largest room in the house, the drawing-room with three windows (complete with wooden shutters for blackout purposes) was cleared to make a dormitory. The dining-room opposite was also cleared to make a playroom. The old horsehair couch which was in our playroom went into the dining-room. The back door led to the kitchen, a centre of activity. We lost our own playroom, which led off to the kitchen, but there was not much time for play in any case...'

The preparations for the evacuees involved much packing away and storing of valued domestic goods and fittings. Carpets had to be rolled up and stored: experience elsewhere had shown that the less house-trained among the little guests soon discovered that, by lifting the edge of the carpet, they could with the minimum of inconvenience deposit underneath that which in more civilised society would be flushed down the loo. What was more, by the time the stench had revealed the dark deed, the culprit or culprits could lay the blame on just about everyone else.

'Rolled up carpets lay in the corridor upstairs. The Bechstein piano was moved to the sitting room. This required tremendous effort since it was iron framed and very heavy indeed. The other high Victorian piano went out altogether and I have no idea where it ended up. It had belonged to my grandmother. She was very musical and had, for a short time, taught the Reith boys, one of whom became Lord Reith of the BBC...'

Country life was a sensation to the evacuees. Everything was a mystery to them. Cows in particular floored them. They had never seen anything like them. 'Whit are thae things in the field wi' fur on them an' bags hangin' doon?' Margaret recalls that on receipt of the necessary information, they instantly went off milk.

Their propensity for relieving themselves under the carpet was not the only type of unpleasantness associated with the evacuees. Most of them had head lice on arrival and were quite ready to share them with others. Combing them out was a nightly chore. Every cut went septic and several had infectious skin diseases. A special house for those suffering from the latter ailments had been set up in the Isle of Whithorn and the victims were whisked off there to avoid infecting the others.

Most of the children were quite inadequately clothed and shod for the long walks to and from school in the often inclement Galloway weather. Local parents – often hard-pressed themselves to find the wherewithal to clothe their own children – joined forces to better equip the newcomers with that generosity of spirit that will always be a part of Galloway. The evacuees could not understand why there was no gang culture in Galloway similar to that which they had left behind in Glasgow, and the fact that Gallovidians appeared to regard razors as being implements to be used strictly for shaving and chains to be solely for use in propelling bicycles along the road was quite beyond their comprehension. Some of them speedily set about rectifying this deplorable situation via crash courses in hooliganism for the hitherto unsullied Galloway children. Soon, packs of embryo thugs were sprouting up all over the two counties until horrified parents got wind of the nefarious activities and instantly stamped them out of existence.

An interesting study of the comparison between city and country children was made by the resident teacher helping to look after the evacuees at the McCreaths' farm. To quote Margaret again:

'...the city ones reacted like quicksilver – they probably had to in their lives on the street and dodging stairhead fights and sets of china coming crashing down. (Both of these hazards were mentioned by the youngsters.) The country children, on the other hand, seemed much slower, but they had thought things through...'

There were many tears, Margaret recalls, when the evacuees eventually returned to their homes in Glasgow. One of them told her father that he wanted to write to him. 'Whit's yer close number?' asked the little fellow. A few wrote pathetic letters back saying that they were saving up to buy boots to walk back to Galloway from Glasgow. They could have paid no greater compliment to the people of Galloway who had adopted them and taken them into their hearts.

*   *   *

They came suddenly and they departed just as abruptly, those strangers. Looking back on those years now, it seemed to have been a period that had lasted no longer than the summer visit of the chiffchaff and the swallow. The ageing process in man tends to gradually – ever so gradually – condense time in the mind, just as the infinitesimal accumulation of tiny particles of dust and sand will gradually compress the layers beneath into the thinnest of sheets in the earth's strata. Surprisingly few of the strangers opted to remain in this land of Galloway to which they had contributed so much fun and so many memories. Certainly, one or two of the Land Girls stayed to marry and settle down. Some of the former evacuees returned as visitors many years later, mainly out of curiosity, and perhaps also to show off to their wives and families and girlfriends this quaint, forgotten corner of Scotland to which they had been so rudely and so unwillingly transported during those terrible years of war. They looked, they remembered, and then they drifted back to the noise and bustle and odours of their beloved cities.

But one thing could be guaranteed – they would never forget Galloway. And Galloway would never forget them.

Chapter 9
PRISONERS AT LARGE

World War II ended for Tony and Seppy in predictably inglorious fashion. They had deserted during the night and, at 9 o'clock in the morning, after a night of aimless wandering through the Libyan sands, they had surrendered to a startled and unarmed Desert Rat who was enjoying, simultaneously, a cigarette and the call of nature behind a sand dune.

The hearts of Tony and Seppy had never really been in this war. If any of the blood of Agrippa and Caesar ran in their veins, it did not run strongly. Indeed, had the Roman Empire been dependant upon the likes of Tony and Seppy during its heyday, it can safely be assumed that the citizens of Gaul would have had little to fear. These two were cowards through and through and proud of the fact. They hankered always for the easy life and the good life, and they would go to extraordinary lengths to achieve their aim. Getting shot at by hostile Australians and Highlanders most emphatically did not feature in their long-term plans, and, while their only contact with the enemy so far had been a long-range skirmish which had left no casualties on either side, enough, they felt, was enough. It was time, the intrepid two decided, to change digs.

Many years after the war the American President Lyndon Baines Johnson, when asked why he had retained his bête noir, the universally despised and feared J Edgar Hoover as head of the FBI, was to reply: 'Ah'd ruther have the bastard inside mah tent pissin' out than outside pissin' in.' It was much the same sort of philosophy that sparked off Tony and Seppy's move from the Italian Army. They were terrified of Montgomery's troops, and from what they had learned from their more experienced colleagues, they had every right to be terrified. There was going to be only one winner in this sordid desert campaign, they surmised, and it was not going to be the Italian Army. When the 8th Army won this nasty little war, Tony and Seppy intended to be part of their victory celebrations. Thus, it came to pass that Grade II Company Clerk Hamish Morrison from the Isle of Skye was to find himself the apprehensive guardian of two relieved Italian prisoners of war when he walked back to camp from his toilet that morning.

Tony and Seppy had never met before the war. But, from the moment a fickle fate had thrown them together on the ship transporting them to Africa they had become inseparable. Tony was the clever one. He had been to university and he spoke fluent English, French and German. He was also the good-looker of the two, and so devastating was his charisma and charm with the ladies that at least three fathers of winsome but impressionable maidens in his native Sicily were anxious to have a few words with him when his service in the cause of Il Duce came to an end. Tony was in no hurry to return.

Seppy could not have been more different in looks and in personality. The only characteristic he shared with Tony was the latter's horror of unpleasantness, and that included war. He was from the opposite end of Italy, from a tiny Alpine village to the north of Lake Maggiore. He was as ugly as an old and mouldy leather boot and his intelligence quotient was of such a humble rating that Mensa International – had that prestigious organization been in existence then – would have hesitated to employ him even as a night watchman. His English consisted of a very rudimentary form of pidgin, and he tended to remain silent most of the time, communicating only in primaeval grunts when spoken to. But Seppy was by far the nicer of the two. Tony was possessed with the ruthlessness that all selfish people have, and it was a ruthlessness that had no part in Seppy's simple and uncomplicated make-up. He revered Tony, though, and he would have done anything for him. It was a hero-worship that Tony exploited to the full.

Montgomery had never been in the habit of keeping Italian prisoners around to contaminate his front line troops. In a very short time indeed they were shovelled off to Cairo to await shipment to England, and in what seemed to be no time at all they found themselves working on a farm in the heart of Kirkcudbrightshire. The farmhouse was huge and the farmer and his wife were old. But they were friendly and easy going. They made the two prisoners as welcome as the restrictions of wartime life would allow. A major inconvenience was that the POW camp was some considerable distance away from the farm and much time was wasted in getting to and from work each day. Arrangements were made to have them billeted in the Big House annex during the working week.

It was an ideal situation. They had the freedom of the farm and few people bothered to check up on them, even in the initial stages of their stay. Escape was the last thing on their minds in any case, for that would have meant incarceration in a secure camp in the event of their recapture, or – far, far worse – a return to the horrors of war to defend their country in what were now, according to all news sources, increasingly desperate circumstances.

The nations of the Geneva Conventions never had two more contented prisoners of war than Tony and Seppy.

A huge cauldron sat on the wood-burning range of their annex. This came to be known as the Pot That Always Boiled. There was always something simmering in it, for Tony and Seppy were fond of food and they were forever on the lookout for something to put in it. They were never too fussy about what they ate, either, and some of their meals would have made the great gourmets of the day like Nubar Gulbenkian go green at the very thought of them. The farm had acres of marshland, and ditches had to be regularly maintained to keep the land from being waterlogged in winter. Neither Tony nor Seppy could ever have been accused of being overfond of work – indeed, the poet Coleridge's lines 'as idle as a painted ship upon a painted ocean' tended to come to mind when one was watching them at their place of work – but this was one job that they tackled with alacrity. The reason for their enthusiasm was that the ditches were full of eels and Tony and Seppy loved eels. Eels boiled, eels stewed, eels fried and eels baked – Tony and Seppy ate them all with gusto. Gallovidians in general are not fond of eels, and Tony and Seppy's culinary propensities were not viewed with much favour by the good country folk of Kirkcudbright. 'Durty buggers!' shuddered one local when he met them going home one evening bearing a sack full of the writhing, slimy creatures.

The good people of Kirkcudbright did not know the half of it. Had they but known of some of the ingredients that occasionally found their way into the Pot That Always Boiled, they would have been even less favourably disposed towards the pair. The farm, like most Galloway farms, was alive with sparrows, and in the spring of the year the rones and eaves of all the buildings would be full of their nests. This was a time of plenitude for Tony and Seppy and they made the most of it. Baby sparrows were a delicacy to them, and into the black cauldron went the tiny hatchlings by the hundred, as blind and naked and ungutted as they had been in their nests. Occasionally even legally obtained, civilized butcher meat would go into the pot, but only if there was nothing else available. Tony and Seppy seemed to prefer the wild flavour of things that they caught for themselves outdoors. Snares which they had set around the perimeter fences of the farm produced the periodic hare and rabbit and once or twice they were lucky enough to catch mallard in traps set in bogland around the farm. The farmer's lambs and poultry were a temptation which they had no trouble in resisting: old though the farmer and his wife were, they knew to the last chicken how much livestock they had and the slightest suspicion that their prisoners were stepping out of line would have meant a return to the discipline of the dreaded camps in double-quick time. Tony and Seppy knew when they were well off.

Tony was actually a very good cook by any standard. Like all good cooks, he was a great believer in the beneficial effect of the judicious use of herbs in cooking. There were wild herbs a-plenty in

Galloway if you knew where to look for them. A pinch of this and a pinch of that could spice up the most humdrum of meals. Even an elderly, very dead male hedgehog which they had found in a dry ditch one midsummer day – and which was already beginning to make its presence known to all and sundry in the shimmering heat – had been hailed a gastronomic success by the addition of goodly soupçons of the strongly flavoured wild mint and lavender and bog myrtle. Minced in the large, cast iron meat grinder bolted to the end of their rough deal-plank table, even the oldest and toughest of creatures could be rendered edible in their stews, and the elderly hedgehog had been voted such a success by them that they had demolished what was left of the animal cold for breakfast the following morning.

They had few visitors. The farmer's wife dropped in now and then to bring them scones (baking was not one of Tony's accomplishments) and to share a cigarette and a cup of tea with them. The farmyard moggy, named 'Hitler' by the farmer because of his crabbit nature, occasionally dropped in to scrounge food and milk from them. Hitler was old and fat and well past his sell-by date. The farm rats and mice had nothing to fear from him, for the chronic arthritis that had seized his bones up and contributed greatly to his irascibility had rendered him incapable of any other movement than a slow, laborious hirpling gait. He was hoaching with fleas but the Italians liked him. He, too, was an outcast and they empathised with him.

Hitler's end was, perhaps predictable. The two Italians came in from work one very wet, late-October day to find him curled up on the hearth in front of the fire. He was stone dead. The old, cantankerous heart of him had given up the ghost at long last. Seppy shed a little tear or two and stroked the lifeless fur gently. Even Tony seemed somewhat affected. Outside, the wind had risen and was making low moaning sounds in the chimney. A flare of lightning suddenly illuminated the darkness of the heavens and the first clatter of thunder rent the air.

'What should we do with Hitler?' enquired Seppy at last.

Tony drew slowly on his cigarette. He was obviously deep in thought. Finally, he stubbed out the cigarette and got up. He piled more wood on the fire and stood warming himself before it. He lifted the lid of the cauldron and peered inside. He picked up the wooden spurtle and absently began to stir the remnants of last night's stew. He put the spurtle down and returned to his chair.

Tony gazed at Hitler's corpse.

He looked at the Pot That Always Boiled.

He looked at the mincer.

Lastly, he looked at Seppy.

'Mama mia!' whispered Seppy, turning pale and crossing himself.

*   *   *

The arrival of the aristocratic Lady Wilkinshaw at the farm the following day was as sudden as it was unexpected. She had a habit of descending upon unfortunate farmers who had prisoners of war on strength, for she was on the executive committee of the Red Cross and it was her duty to check on prisoners' welfare. She was suitably impressed by the free and easy approach of the farmer and his wife to their Italians, and she could not help but be impressed by the conditions in which her charges lived. She was certainly very impressed with Tony. There was something about those swarthy Mediterranean types that made her matronly heart go bonkety-bonk, like a water wheel when the floodgates have suddenly opened.

She sipped her tea as she sat with them in their little room. Seppy was as silent and saturnine as ever, but Tony was laying on the charm. She revelled in it, and the pleasure he was giving her was evident in her eyes and in her manner.

The scent of exotic spices filled the room. Her Ladyship was feeling peckish. 'I hope I'm not keeping you two boys from your lunch?' she enquired coquettishly.

'Not at all, your Ladyship,' replied Tony courteously. 'Would you care to join us?' It's only a simple Italian dish – a stew with potatoes, I'm afraid.'

Another plate was found, and Tony carried it over to the Pot That Always Boiled...

'What do you call that dish?' asked Lady Wilkinshaw, leaning back contentedly. 'I've seldom enjoyed anything so much.'

'Pousse,' replied the quick-witted Tony. 'The French would call it "Pot-au-Feu", or "Hot-Pot". But I prefer to call it Farmyard Pousse. It's from an old and secret Sicilian recipe.'

'Well,' gushed Lady Wilkinshaw, 'It was absolutely fabulous. And I think you are a marvellous cook. Whoever you marry will be a very lucky lady.'

Tony took her hand in his. His dark eyes were unfathomable as they gazed deep into hers.

'When I am in the presence of a beautiful lady,' he replied with all the sincerity of one who was well practised in saying these things, 'I always aim to serve.'

Lady Wilkinshaw practically purred.

Chapter 10
COMMISSION CAPERS

There is a distinct masochism involved in the reminiscences of old men. Even the many horrors of the 'good old days' are recalled with something akin to pleasure, as though the relater had actually experienced joy from them at the time. An eminent publisher – not a native of this country – once told me that, at the end of World War II, he had found himself employed as a senior editor with a large publishing house in Glasgow. His office was in a huge old sandstone building in the centre of the city, one of those buildings that look so dignified and imposing from the outside but are as cold as morgues inside. In his case, however, there was nothing cold about them in the summer, for the radiators worked so efficiently through the warm weather that no one could turn them off. Exhausted, no doubt, by their sterling efforts during the hot months, they went on strike for the whole of the winter.

As a result, his circulation – not all that good at the best of times – gave him definite problems during the long, unforgiving Glasgow winter. His blood, he claimed, refused to venture south of his knees, wisely concentrating its activities on keeping his heart pumping. Thus, while by wearing two pairs of Harris tweed trousers, several cardigans and a sheepskin overcoat all day long at his desk he managed to avoid being stricken down by pneumonia or hypothermia, his feet, however, were constantly in the permafrost zone. He eventually solved this problem by adopting the novel approach of immersing his feet in a large pan of hot water conveniently located under his desk as soon as he got in each morning, and by employing a young girl whose sole task was to constantly check the temperature of the water with her finger and to keep topping it up from a kettle to ensure that it remained at the exact temperature required by her lord and master. The girl, he claimed, even dried his feet and put on his shoes and socks at the end of each day and he was so pleased with her that he awarded her a bonus of two shillings and sixpence at the end of the winter. 'Whoever she eventually married,' he remarked, 'should be eternally grateful to me. What wonderful training I gave her on how to properly look after a husband!'

I have never, regrettably, been in such a fortunate situation as to have young ladies attending to my material comforts in this way, nor do I ever expect to be so lucky. But I am always more than willing to regale the younger generation with stories of just how rough it was in my time, should they be unable to effect their escape before I get a grip of their sleeves.

There were, in truth, plenty of hard times during my early working years. But there was no scarcity of good times, either. My real working career began on the day I joined the Forestry Commission at Kilsture Forest, near Sorbie. I had worked summers on farms and with woodcutting gangs, but these had all been school holiday jobs. This, though, was to be the real thing. This was to be my life.

Kilsture Forest was cut in two by the main Sorbie to Kirkinner road. Every part of it to the east of this road had been planted in previous years, but the part to the west of it was a forbidding jungle of thorn and birch scrub, whins and the occasional elderly tree. This area, consisting of some few hundred acres, had to be cleared ready for planting, and, at 16 years of age, I was to be one of the motley crew engaged for the task.

I knew not a single one of the other workers. Most, like myself, had been newly recruited. There was one other lad of about my own age, but the others ranged from the fairly young to the not-so-young. There was also a smattering of women among them, two of whom were wearing Land Army uniform. The women had been working there for a few months and obviously considered themselves to be veterans of the show. They eyed we newcomers with suspicion and some hostility, well founded in at least some of our cases, it has to be admitted.

This, of course, was long before the era of mechanical tools. Everything had to be done by hand. Scrub had to be disposed of in bonfires as it was cleared, boggy areas had to be drained, and a perimeter fence had to be erected around the whole area to keep the local rabbit population at bay. It was a long and laborious process. Hands and wrists would be torn by briers and dogroses and various parts of the anatomy as full of thorns as pincushions long before the end of each day. But I loved every minute of it. Scrub clearing and tree felling were done by axe and Yorkshire billhook, the latter being a fearsome, double-edged weapon that would surely have won the favour of Robert the Bruce had a supply been available to him at Bannockburn. Shuggie and I, the two 'boys' in the squad, took turn about with the 'lassies' in the burning of the scrub and the tree branches. I even enjoyed this hot and tiresome work: the distinctively acrid smell of the blue wood smoke; the crackle of exploding leaves through the roar of the flames; the showers of gold and carmine sparks soaring upward into the autumn sky. But I preferred the axe and the billhook. I was already efficient with hand tools of this nature, far more so than most of the other workers, for I had received a good apprenticeship while working with my father in the woodcutting gangs. It was most satisfying work. There was something about the chinking sound of a razor sharp blade biting into wood that was clean and exhilarating, something about the jar that ran all the way up the hickory shaft to the shoulder that was exciting and invigorating, and there was something that was decidedly exotic about the highly individual scents from each species of tree or shrub when the axe cut released their fragrances to the clean fresh air of Galloway.

Different timbers had different degrees of hardness, too: holly, hawthorn and crab-apple were surprisingly hard, especially when they were old and gnarled, while birch, rowan and alder were very easy to deal with. Horse chestnut was as soft as butter.

Additions to our gang appeared from time to time, and they came from all walks of life. Some were with us for brief periods only, others for very much longer. One, a Canadian airman, looked a dead ringer for Randolph Scott, the cowboy film actor, and he was just about as taciturn. He was quiet, industrious and popular with everyone. We also acquired over the years an ex-RAF squadron leader, a Red Beret who had lost an eye at Arnhem, an ex-detective constable who bore a striking resemblance to another American actor, Broderick Crawford, and a devout English Latter-day Saint. A number of young lads, hellers all, arrived to swell our numbers, and we had the occasional girl student as well.

Joe, the Latter-day Saint, was extremely popular. His was the kindest and most gentle of natures. He did not speak often, probably on account of the fact that he was afflicted by a severe stammer. He never used bad language of any kind, not even the mildest of expletives, and the more rascally of we younger members of the gang would tease him cruelly in the hope of extracting even an innocent 'damn' from him. It was all in vain. Joe was one of those rare people who seem to be totally without a trace of bad temper. No matter the provocation, he would just smile benignly and continue with his work. Tormentor-in-chief was young Shuggie, and the usual response from old Joe would be: 'Shu..Shu..Shu..Shuggie, you're a tu..tu..tu..terrible bu..bu..ba..ba..baaa..bu..boy.'

Events reached a dramatic denouement one day when we were constructing the perimeter fence. Shuggie and I had been delegated to assist Joe. Shuggie, being a big, strong lad, had opted to be the one to manipulate the 16-lb mall, a massive sledgehammer used for driving stobs into the ground. Joe and I took turn about in holding the stobs steady while Shuggie battered them in. Shuggie was operating the mall in classic fashion – a round-armed swing of his wiry arms that had the hammer swinging in a 180° arc before it thumped on top of the stob. All was going well until about mid-morning when Joe, holding the stob, suddenly yawped at Shuggie. God knows what he was trying to say, but he could have chosen a better moment for it: Shuggie was in mid-swing when he caught a glimpse of Joe's mouth, open like that of a codfish on a marble slab as he tried in vain to get the words out. In that split second Shuggie's concentration had gone: he uttered a guffaw and the cast iron head of the mighty mall missed its target and grazed down the side of the stob, smashing Joe's thumb.

Joe sprang in the air like an impala, blood spouting from his thumb. His yell of anguish rang out over the adjoining fields. He leapt up and down before us, his face contorted in agony. Finally he stopped and glared venomously at Shuggie, his mouth working as he tried to get the words out. Finally, out they came: 'Shu..Shu..Shu..Shuggie, you're a cu..cu..cu...' We were riveted to the spot, appalled at the obvious severity of his injury but probably almost as appalled by the fact that this most gentle and devout of men had at last been goaded by us into uttering the foulest of expletives. Finally the sentence was completed in an explosion of breath that seemed to come from the very soul of him: '...cu..cu..confounded nuisance!'

From that day onward, we left Joe alone. Some campaigns are just not worth the hassle.

There was only one job connected with forestry that I thoroughly disliked and, needless to say, I found myself working at it for the whole of one long summer. This was the creosoting of stobs. In a small yard beside the road a large tank full of creosote had been installed. Into this tank the stobs were put each morning, a few hundred at a time, and they were firmly wedged in to prevent movement during treatment. The fire under the tank was then lit and the stobs slowly cooked in the creosote for the rest of the day. The job was by no means an arduous one: all I had to do was to keep the fire going and check the creosote temperature at regular intervals to ensure that it remained at a constant temperature. By about three o'clock in the afternoon it would be assumed that the stobs had absorbed sufficient creosote and the fire under the tank would be raked out. The following morning, when the creosote had cooled, the stobs would be fished out with hooks and the tank refilled with more stobs. And so on, ad infinitum and ad nauseum. There was little in the way of protective clothing for workers in those days and we certainly had no fancy face masks or goggles. The fumes scorched the lungs and soaked into the skin so that the body burned constantly. My colouring changed dramatically, and all of a sudden Stephen Foster's *Swanee River* became a popular air among the more witty of my colleagues.

*   *   *

By the time the scrub had been cleared and the fence had been erected the first frosts were upon us. Winter was the time for tree planting. Both conifers and broad-leaved species were planted in Kilsture, each individual species being planted in the soil conditions considered best suited to it by the foreman and forester in charge. The seedlings were planted in rows, the distance between each plant and each row also varying according to species: the slow-growing oak, for example, being planted at distances of three feet by three feet, while the fast-growing larch was planted at distances of five feet. It was hard work but it was most satisfying work, at least for idealists such as myself who could envisage those same seedlings growing to tall forest trees and being there long after we who had planted them had all gone.

With the arrival of spring came the process known as 'weeding'. New bracken, nettles and fireweed suddenly appeared, shooting upwards at a quite astonishing pace. This weed growth had to be kept in check, otherwise it would smother the seedlings. Our tools for this task were sickles, or 'grass hooks', as they were more commonly called locally. These were very sharp and they were most dangerous implements. We younger workers tended to be very casual in our handling of them and it is a wonder that none of us suffered really serious injury from them. The proximity to each other at which we worked was just asking for trouble. We moved up between the rows of plants, swinging our hooks as we scythed the rank growth down. It only needed one tiny lapse in concentration from yourself or the chap working beside you... It happened to me once, and I was entirely at fault. I was chattering to my colleague as we worked side by side, oblivious of the fact that I was edging ever closer to his swinging blade. The inevitable happened: the tip of his sickle went straight through my hand. The resultant five stitches inserted in me taught me a lesson in the necessity to exercise great care when handling sharp implements.

It was during this summer that I first came across a strange custom peculiar – so far as I am aware – to the British nation. It was one I was to encounter even during my working life overseas wherever young bloods of British extraction gathered at drinks parties. This was the custom known as 'debagging'. I had been called away to the forestry office for some reason or other, and on the way back to rejoin the gang I had taken a short cut through some young birch scrub. As I approached the end of the thicket I heard scuffling sounds in front of me. Thinking that it might be a couple of roe deer at play I moved forward with caution. At the edge of the scrub I stopped dead. On the grass beyond the scrub four of the younger members of the gang had one of the girl workers on the ground and were in the process of pulling her breeches and knickers down to her knees. Being a rather naive 16 years of age and a bit on the reserved side, it was without question the rudest shock I had ever had. I was rooted to the spot in incredulity and horror. The girl made no attempt at resisting and nothing further happened to her; having achieved their purpose in exposing her, the youths let her go, while she, giggling and slightly flushed of face but showing no outward sign of embarrassment, stood up and pulled her trousers back on. Indeed, she gave every appearance of being much less embarrassed by what had happened than I was as a witness to it. Probably it had happened to her before. In any event, by that same afternoon she and her assailants were laughing and joking together as always.

Today such incidents would correctly be labelled sexual assault, with the perpetrators ending up in court. Indeed, even in those less emancipated times, there is no doubt that had either of our supervisors found out about it, those involved would have been summarily dismissed. But these were more lax times, and no one ever complained about anything. While dubious pranks were a predominantly male thing, the women workers were not averse to perpetrating them either, as I was to find out for myself some time later...

*   *   *

Long hot springs and autumns are the bane of every forester's life. The fear of forest fires is never far from his mind. You don't often get protracted, completely dry periods at any time of the year in Galloway, but I have a vivid memory of one such period during my early years at Kilsture. I was walking up the main road with a colleague when we simultaneously noticed a plume of smoke rising from one of the older areas of plantation to the east of the road. Fire! We raced back to where the gang was working to raise the alarm, and from then on it was every man to the attack with fire brooms in an attempt to quench the blaze. By the time the first of the fire engines arrived on the scene, however, the forest was a roaring wall of flame, and it was getting near darkness by the time it was brought under control. By that time, none of us ever wanted to see a forest fire in our lives again. What had started off as one of the most exciting things ever to happen to we youngsters had become an exceedingly dirty, numbingly tiring exercise in utter tedium.

Many acres of beautiful woodland were turned to black ash and there was, inevitably, much loss of wildlife. A subsequent enquiry laid the blame squarely on the shoulders – or perhaps, more correctly, a part of the body to the south of his shoulders – of one of the workers, who having retired to the edge of a clump of larch to obey the call of nature, had lit a cigarette as he squatted among the dead, bone-dry bracken. Smoking was totally forbidden during such periods of fire hazard and the worker denied to the end that he had ever lit a cigarette. Despite his denials he was instantly sacked when the fire investigators discovered the stump of a cigarette at the very point where the fire had started, along with other, quite irrefutable, evidence of his having been there. 'If he didn't light that bloody cigarette,' remarked our acerbic forester Jack Slater afterwards, 'It must have been the sparks from his arse that did it!'

One event that generated much excitement among we workers was the annual deer shoot. Kilsture had a goodly population of roe deer and, as they could cause tremendous damage by browsing on seedlings and debarking young trees by rubbing against the stems to scrape the velvet off their new horns, culls were considered necessary after each breeding season was over. Local farmers, innkeepers, minor dignitaries such as vets, doctors and stationmasters – indeed, virtually anyone who possessed a firearm no matter what vintage it was and regardless of how much regard he had for the safe handling of it – would be invited to take part in the shoot, while we workers acted as beaters.

We would be lined up at one end of an area of plantation while the guns lined up at the other. A whistle would blow and we would move forward through the trees, the scrub, the briers and the heather, beating at the undergrowth with our sticks and shouting at the tops of our voices to drive the deer forward to where the guns were waiting. Three or four deer killed by the end of a day would be considered a good tally, and the occasional fox would meet his end, too. How none of we workers ever found ourselves included in the bag I shall never know, for some of those shooting should never have been let loose in a fairground shooting gallery. On several occasions I heard pellets smashing through the branches around me as I moved within range of the guns along with the other beaters.

I remember one particularly horrifying and poignant scene when a roe deer, trapped on top of a moraine of boulders, had its two hind legs shattered by shot. The wretched creature kept straining desperately to crawl forward by means of its forelegs while two young men, high on wine but low on ability, pumped shot after shot at it.

We workers always received our share of the venison. Some of the more fussy professed not to care very much for the dark and unattractive looking meat, but to we from poorer homes in those times of rationing, it was a real boon.

When our planting schedule at Kilsture had been completed we found ourselves being transported on a daily basis to the Kirkcudbright hills to work. This proved to be quite a different kettle of fish to the type of work and conditions we had experienced at Kilsture. Forestry at Kilsture was like an exercise in gardening compared to that into which we found ourselves catapulted among the dark, bleak mountains and glens of Glentrool and Clatteringshaws.

Winter planting in those places was a misery of freezing rain, blizzards of hail and snow, and wet peat bogs. We seemed to be permanently soaked to the skin, filthy with black peat mud, and frozen to the marrow. To add to our discomfort, this was the era of that spiky stranger from the wastes of Alaska, the Sitka spruce.

The Forestry Commission has come under heavy fire for the policy it had in those early post-war years of blanketing moorland and mountainside with mile after mile of Sitka spruce. The criticism, in my opinion, is perfectly valid. There can surely be a few less appealing trees on God's green earth. It is a policy that the commission have, by and large, now abandoned, but in those less enlightened years we must have planted millions of them around Galloway. Even now, my hands and forearms ache at the very thought of those jaggy little horrors. Protective gloves were not in common use in those days, so even those of us who were, like myself, blessed with a fairly tough hide, suffered badly from their needle-sharp prickles. As the green needles contained a sort of formic acid, to those with sensitive skin it was sheer agony – indeed, on two occasions known to me the sufferers ended up in hospital.

There were other forms of torture associated with Sitka spruce, too. I do not ever recall planting this species in decent weather. For successful planting, it seemed that climatic conditions had to be as near as possible to those of its native Alaska. Raging blizzards, howling gales and pouring rain seemed to be the order of each day as we stuck the wretched things into just about every lump of bogland from the Moss o'Cree to the furthest reaches of the Kirkcudbright interior.

It is not as though it is a terribly attractive species even in maturity, either. It is so funereal in aspect. The gloom under its thick canopy kills off everything in short order, from the prettiest of wild flowers to the most tenacious of weeds. Even the bracken and the rankest of hill grasses are unable to cope with its unforgiving shades. There is, too, a spookiness about its dark, silent chambers in maturity that tingles the base of the neck as you walk through them, a feeling that black-caped assassins might be lying in wait for you in the disquieting hush of its cold, dark woods.

But there is no doubt that this stranger from the tundra took to our land as to the manor born. It grew fast, and it could grow practically anywhere. It thrived particularly well in the raw acidity of our moorland soils, and there was a long period when every tree nursery in the land seemed to be full to overflowing with its spiky progeny. It responded well to even the most slapdash of planting techniques, and soon every acre not required for grouse shooting echoed to the roar of great mechanical ploughs ripping up the landscape. Almost overnight the delicate purples and lilacs and golds of heather and myrtle and asphodel were buried forever beneath the stark, blue-green shroud of this ubiquitous invader; vast, symmetrical blocks of trees that made no pretence at all of blending with their surroundings. It could not happen today, one hopes, but in those austere times ordinary people had more immediate and more personal things to worry about than environmental issues.

We were the usual very mixed bag of workers up in those hills. I was then approaching army age and, for a short period, I found myself as one of only two males in an otherwise all-female gang. Winter was over, and the planting season was drawing to a close. We were having our midday snack on a grassy knowe somewhere behind the Clatteringshaws dam, and it was an unusually warm and sunny early-April day.

My sole male colleague was Daft Allie, and he was obviously in a somewhat playful spring mood. Allie was a huge lad and, as he was regarded by all and sundry as being a bit of a simpleton, he tended to be the butt of much teasing by the others. However, he was a harmless big lad and we all liked him.

On this particular day the girls were winding him up about the fact that he had no girlfriend. Daft Allie was responding heroically, but he was no match for the sharp wit of his tormentors. I was only vaguely aware of the banter, because I was lying on my back in the grass some distance apart from them, drowsily watching a buzzard soaring high overhead. Suddenly, my drowsiness vanished when I heard Daft Allie's retort: 'Ye wudnae ken whut tae dae wi' a richt man even if ye fun' yin daft enough tae gaun wi' yis, the hale loat o' yis!' I just had time to say to myself 'Allie, my boy, you're in deep trouble!' when they pounced.

Daft Allie hadn't a hope of escape. He uttered one squawk of protest and then they swamped him. With an expertise obviously born of some previous practice they hauled his trousers and his drawers off. They paused a moment or two to admire what they had uncovered. Daft Allie may not have been 'the full shullun'' upstairs, but he was a good Scottish pound and a half downstairs. It was also becoming patently obvious that he was enjoying this assault just as much as his assailants. I waited no more. I slipped away quietly and stealthily as they knelt around him, performing God knows what iniquities upon the poor fellow. I slid round the side of the hill, heading for where the heather was tallest and thickest, intending to remain there, hidden from sight, until things had quietened down back there. Flushed with their success over Daft Allie, the women might be looking for another victim upon which to practise their undoubted skills and I intended that it should not be me. Private possessions, I had always felt, should not have any place in the public domain and, in any case, I had no wish to have them making unfavourable comparisons with what Daft Allie had to offer.

*   *   *

Some years later, having graduated from forestry school in Argyll, I was posted to a large Forestry Commission nursery near Stranraer.

It was only to be a brief stay, for I was soon due to leave for Africa. I disliked nursery work, but I got on well with the workers. They were, as I recall it now, some 80 in number, of which around half were female. The time soon came round for me to leave for good, and I was both touched and flattered when, on the morning of my last day, the female members of the squad presented me with a beautiful shaving case to mark my departure. They had never done this for any previous supervisor and, considering how very poorly they were paid, they must have really had to scrape to find the money. The presentation speech made on their behalf by one of their number was most complimentary.

Towards the end of the morning I emerged from the little portable toilet cabin at the far end of the nursery. Waiting for me outside, looking even more nervous than usual, was Melissa.

Melissa, rather like Daft Allie all these years before, was regarded by the others as being slightly unhinged, although I always found her to be pleasant and intelligent, albeit excruciatingly shy. I greeted her in some surprise: 'Looking for me, Melissa?'

'Aye,' she said. I waited, but she stood before me like an apprehensive stork, just looking at me, saying nothing.

'Well, Melissa,' I said patiently, 'What can I do for you?'

It all came out in a rush. 'Donal', they're gaun tae tak' yer troosers doon!'

'WHAT??'

'The lassies. They're gaun tae grab ye at piecetime an' tak' yer troosers doon! They want tae see whut ye've got afore ye gaan tae Africa.'

I stood transfixed. I was absolutely rooted to the spot, unable for a moment to speak. I was stunned by the treachery of it all. All the time they had been telling me at the presentation how much they were going to miss me, they had been plotting this foul scheme. Melissa continued:

'An' whut's mair, they're gaun tae pent it black. Wi' Kiwi polish,' she added descriptively but unnecessarily.

She turned to go. I shook myself out of my trance. 'Wait, Melissa,' I said, 'How many of them are involved in this?'

'Every single yin o' them,' she informed me.

Good God! There were 40 of the swine! I looked at my watch. It was 20 minutes to go to piecetime. Time for action stations.

'Dinnae tell them I warned ye,' pleaded Melissa, 'Or they'll tak' it oot on me.'

She walked away. 'Bye, Donal',' she called over her shoulder. She did not look back.

I walked down to where the women were working on their hands and knees among the drills of seedlings. I wandered innocently through their ranks, speaking to the odd one, whistling a little tune, proceeding slowly and casually past them down to the shed at the bottom of the hill where they would be having their midday snack. Once out of their sight behind the shed I shot inside, grabbed my satchel and my coat, closed the door behind me and raced towards the nursery boundary. I forded the perimeter burn like a deer and bounded out through the tall marsh grass beyond it, heading as though my life depended on it for the thick clump of whins at the far side of the bog. Once safely out of sight among them I settled down, panting more than somewhat. I glanced at my watch. In five minutes they would be down at the shed, expecting to find me there. I looked forward to hearing their cries of frustration...

That night I handed my books back to the village library. I would be leaving my lodgings for good the following morning. It was a terrible night, cold and simply pouring with rain. When I got back into the house an hour or so later my landlady told me that a young lady had called at the house. 'She had this parcel for you, all wrapped up in oilcloth to keep it dry,' she told me. 'She was drenched and very bedraggled. She said that she had cycled from Stranraer with it. I asked her to come in and warm herself by the fire but she refused. She just gave me the parcel and bolted.'

'Did she give any name?' I enquired, puzzled.

'Yes, she said her name was Melissa. And she looked a bit odd.'

I opened the parcel. It contained a hand-knitted pullover and a note. It said briefly: 'I didn't get to put money in for your present. But I had already knitted you this instead to take with you to Africa.'

I held it up before me. It was a muddy grey colour, with a weird black design across the front of it. The wool with which it had been made was as thick as binder twine and, as a thermal garment, it was a pullover that would have won the acclaim of Shackleton on any of his polar expeditions. In the boiling heat of equatorial Africa it would be a real sensation.

I looked out into the black night. The rain was hammering down and the light from the street lamps showed as a blurry orange wash through the river of water that ran down the window panes. I thought about Melissa. She had cycled the ten miles here from her home in Stranraer on this awful night to deliver to me a pullover that I would probably never wear in my life. She might be about halfway home by now if she was lucky. But perhaps not even as far as that, for she would be pedalling into the teeth of the wind.

I took the garment upstairs and packed it carefully into my case. Outside my little room I could hear the wind picking up and the cold Galloway rain slashing against the window with ever greater ferocity.

Chapter 11

THE MILESTONE INSPECTORS

Some of my earliest memories go back to the days of the travelling people, or tinkers, as we called them then. I had won a prize book for something or other at Garlieston School when I was seven years of age. Already an avid reader, I was fascinated by the main story in the book, a tale about the adventures of a little boy kidnapped by gypsies. This, I decided, was the life for me. When, during the summer holidays that followed, I came upon four caravans of them pulled up in the roadside enclave of a strip of woodland near to our home, I must have thought that they had been sent there by a sympathetic providence. I hung around those caravans during every daylight hour possible, to the scandalization of my mother and the intense amusement of my grandfather, who had been well used to all kinds of travelling folk on his native Isle of Mull.

Travelling folk love children, and I ate and drank things with them and listened to tales from them that would have further scandalized my mother, could she have been eavesdropping on us, for the children of travelling folk know most about the baser facts of life from a very early age. When I arrived at the site one day to find the caravans gone and nothing left to indicate that they had ever been there but the cold ash of their fires and the flattened grass and weeds where their caravans had been parked, I was devastated. I never saw them again, and I was inconsolable for days. I never forgot them, and the brightness of their caravans and their clothes and the music of their tin whistles and mouth organs and the warmth of their hospitality to a wee 'cottar bairn' remain with me to this day.

'They might have taken you away with them,' remarked my mother uneasily. 'No bloody fear of that!' parried my father with true parental affection. 'The tinks have more sense than to try to steal him. They have enough problems of their own to contend with!'

I had another, less pleasant, encounter with the tinkers some years later, when I was about ten years old. I was on summer holiday at the home of my great-aunt Christina MacDonald, in Blairgowrie, Perthshire. I know nothing of the Blairgowrie of today, but it was then an important raspberry-growing area, most of the produce going to the jam factories in Dundee and elsewhere. Raspberry picking in those days was traditionally the work of the travelling people, and each summer they descended on the Blairgowrie fields like clouds of quelea birds descending upon the rice fields of far-off Africa. To those farmers whose stock included largish flocks of poultry, they were just about as welcome as were the queleas to the tribal rice farmers, too. The 'tinks' had a well-established reputation for thieving, and they had a particular predilection for domestic fowl. But they were fast and tireless berry pickers, and the berry farmers were glad to see them.

My great-aunt Teen was one of the latter. She had a raspberry farm on the outskirts of the town. My summer holiday in this particular year coincided with the start of the raspberry season and the arrival of the travelling folk. Teen asked if I would like to have a go at the berries. 'Eat what you want,' she said, 'and when you've had all you can eat, fill your can and I'll pay you the same as I pay the tinks for whatever you bring to the weighing machine.'

It seemed a good deal to me. I could fill myself with rasps and earn some good pocket money into the bargain. I started at the opposite end of one of the rows on which the travellers were working.

The cans were large. When full, they were taken to a weighing centre in the middle of the field where a recorder took down the weight of the can and the name of the picker. The can was then emptied and the picker returned to the rows of canes for another lot. The pickers were paid by weight. It seemed to take forever for me to fill my can, for my fingers were not as fast and as nimble as those of the travellers. Besides, I was in no hurry. I was on vacation, the weather was beautiful, and the rasps were good. It was an idyllic way to spend a holiday.

I had just rounded the end of the row when I stopped dead in my tracks, horror-stricken. Before me was the biggest tinker I had ever seen in my life. Tinkers are supposed to be small, dark folk, but this guy was huge. He looked as enormous as the Finn McCool of legend and his face was hidden by rufous hair. But it was not his size or forbidding appearance that paralyzed me: it was what he was doing. He was calmly urinating into his can of rasps. He looked up and saw me standing open-mouthed before him, but his only reaction was to smile the most menacing smile I have ever seen on anyone, his jagged, tobacco-stained teeth grimacing at me through the tangle of hair on his face. I turned and fled helter-skelter up the field to seek out my great-aunt Teen.

Teen listened to my excited stammers in some amusement. When I had finished, she said : 'Dinna fash yourself, Donnie boy. I ken all about what they do. It's a auld trick. They do their water in the can to increase the weight. When the rasps are a wee bitty dry, they soak in the moisture. That's why I pay the tinks a wee bit less than I pay the other fowks.'

I was staggered, probably as much by my aristocratic aunt's philosophical approach to the foul deed I had witnessed as by the actual doing of it. 'But these rasps go to the jam factory, Aunt Teen!' I stuttered. 'Och well,' she replied smilingly, 'they're a' steam-boiled anyway, so no harm comes of what they do.'

It was on the tip of my tongue to retort that even steam-boiled tinker's pee had little appeal to me but I decided not to bother. I have never been much of a fighter of lost causes. But I have to admit here and now that I have never felt quite the same about raspberry jam since that day, whatever its brand name and however attractively packaged it may have been.

There were no raspberry fields of any size around Galloway for the travellers to work in, and indeed travelling families were thin on the ground then compared to the large numbers to be found in the more northerly counties such as Angus, Perth and Aberdeen. The few that existed took occasional seasonal work on the farms. I had little contact with them on those work sites, but I do have one rich memory of a potato field in Galloway during the hot summer of 1945. I was 15 years of age at the time, and a 14-year-old slip of an Antrim tinker lassie nearly broke my back.

Perhaps an explanation would be in order here before the more prurient of readers gets too excited. Potato picking, or tattie howkin', as it was more generally called, was indubitably one of the more unpleasant tasks I have ever been asked to perform on a farm. The long rows of potato shaws were opened up by a tractor trailing behind it a sort of plough with a horizontal blade which cut underneath the buried potatoes and turfed them out onto the surface. Two pre-selected partners crouched one on each side of their drill picking up the potatoes thus unearthed and depositing them in his or her bucket or basket. Speed was of the essence, for the tractor, having opened up the drills for all the other workers in the field, would immediately return to open up your next drill. Woe betide you if you had still not finished picking up all the potatoes on your last section, for you were letting the side down and your partner, having finished her own lot, would be inevitably forced to help you finish yours.

I had worked at most jobs on the farm at one time or another, but potato picking was a new one on me. Nor had I worked for this particular farmer before. Indeed, I barely knew him, but he had once before witnessed me from a far-off eminence retrieving a shot pheasant from a bog just inside the boundary of his farm, and though it transpired that he had complained loud and long to the local police about the rights and wrongs of ownership of edible wildlife on other people's property, nothing could be done about it, to his festering annoyance. At the time he espied me we had each of us been roughly equidistant from our respective homes and I, being younger and much fleeter of foot than he, had been able to get home and hide the evidence long before he had been able to reach a telephone. Besides, by the time he had tracked down the local lawman, the latter was in the middle of a bowls tournament on the village green and, like Francis Drake on a similarly important occasion, he refused to be distracted from his bowling until the contest was over and done with and he had had his celebratory couple of jars with the lads in the pub. It is possible, therefore, that the farmer had this incident to the forefront of his mind when he partnered me with wee Ella McGrory of Ballynahinch, County Antrim, for she had been boasting to all and sundry that she was the fastest picker of potatoes in all Ireland.

I do not doubt her claim. Indeed, I would have been quite prepared by the end of that terrible first day with her to believe her had she claimed to have held the world record in potato picking. That girl could move. Almost at once she had me trailing in her wake, gasping like a beached grampus. I had never worked so hard in all my life and by the time I got home that night my spinal cord had altered shape in quite dramatic fashion and the sound of my vertebrae rubbing dryly against each other would have set the teeth of Oul' Nick himself on edge.

And she could talk too, that little Irish tinker girl. She talked. And she talked. And she talked. Her hands flew with the speed of light over her section as she gathered up the spuds, like a magpie gobbling up its last feed of the day before darkness descended. Her tongue wagged incessantly. Her stories were of the most ribald kind, too, and she was not a bit shy about revealing to me in graphic detail accounts of her conquests among her potato-picking partners in the lush green fields of Ulster. One thing I can say for sure is that if even half of her stories were true, the Ulster boys must have been hardier souls than I, for romance was very far from my mind while trying to keep pace with Miss Ella McGrory in the tattie fields of Wigtownshire.

*   *   *

The tinkers of Scotland go back a long way. A late-12th-century legal document mentions a 'Tinkler James', and some scholars speculate that the tinkers may have been descendants of itinerant tinsmiths and ironsmiths. It has also been said that the name itself is derived from the tinkling sound made by their pots and pans as their carts travelled along the roads.

Scotland has not often been kind to the tinkers, which may explain why they now prefer to call themselves 'travellers'. The word tinker, tinkler or just plain tink was all too often used in a derogatory way. Their way of life, being constantly on the move, made them a race apart and answerable to no authority. The horrors of Culloden and the Highland Clearances saw many outsiders join their ranks, but the genuine travellers of my youth still made a very clear distinction between themselves and the much despised tramps and other social outcasts. Their language or 'cant', to give it its correct name, was a fascinating and complex mixture of Old Scots, Gaelic and Romany, with some smatterings of local dialect thrown in for good measure, and they could switch from code to code at will, emphasising the Scots, Gaelic or Romany as circumstances demanded, a most useful method of secret communication with one's fellow miscreants when being questioned for thieving or poaching.

The travellers could undertake all sorts of seasonal work on whatever farms happened to be nearest them, from the usual early-spring chores of turnip thinning to the autumn harvesting. The men repaired pots and pans and made spoons of cow-horn, baskets from supple bogland saugh and clothes pegs of ash and lime-tree for their women to sell. Many went into the scrap-iron business and, along the River Tay especially, others fished for freshwater pearls.

The women were consummate psychologists and could tell at a glance the sort of fortune it would be most appropriate to read from a teacup to best please the enquirer and thus receive the most lucrative reward. Begging was developed into such an art form by them that it was almost a pleasure to hand over one's hard-earned cash. There was none of the crudity about it that one encounters on the streets of our cities today. Storytelling and ballad singing had always been one of the great traditions of this remarkably resilient race of people, and there were individuals among them who were excellent pipers. I have never heard music sweeter than that which I heard wafting across a glen in the Creetown hills many years ago from a lone tinker playing his bagpipes in some far-off, hidden corrie. In the soft air of that summer evening even the glorious rhapsodies of the larks seemed for once to be subdued and inadequate as the haunting beauty of that unknown pibroch echoed through the hills.

The travellers of Galloway were generally of a much less itinerant nature than those of Scotland's north-east. Most had a base from which they operated and I sometimes got the feeling that, with some of them at least, they plied their respective trades more because it was in their blood to do so than because they needed the few pennies they got from whatever they happened to be selling. I remember a marvellous old lady who would drop by our way on occasion, selling bits and pieces of this and that. My mother would never fail to invite her into the kitchen for tea and scones. The old lady was a wonderful raconteur in true traveller style. She even looked the image of the traditional gypsy; a most regal looking lady with swarthy features, piercing black eyes and a hooked nose, always swathed in shawls and long colourful dresses on even the hottest day of summer. Nor was she short of a bob or two, for she would entertain us with stories of her periodic visits to relatives in the United States of America. One wonders to what extent the bootlaces she sold at the back doors of Machars' cottages really contributed to her fares for those transatlantic trips.

Among the more 'settled' of those wayfaring pedlars was 'Bud' McCulloch, who lived with his wife and two daughters in a tiny, condemned farm cottage at the top of the Kirkinner Brae. Bud was more of a hawker than a true tinker. Summer and winter, rain or shine, he could be seen with his pony and little cart ambling along the narrow byways of the Machars selling firewood and general bric-a-brac to the villagers on his way. He probably looked after his pony better than he looked after himself and his family: it is recorded that a doctor, called to his house to treat one of the family for some ailment or other, opened the wrong door while inside the cottage to find himself, literally, in nose-to-nose confrontation with a shaggy and rather wild-eyed pony. 'Small country cottages,' remarked Wigtown's flamboyant and normally unflappable Dr Lillicoe soon afterwards while recovering from his shock in the nearest hostelry, 'are not best equipped for the harbouring of horses as lodgers on a permanent basis.'

Of the actual tramping fraternity, however, the best known of the 'milestone inspectors' in my day was undoubtedly Snib Scott. Snib was very tall and straight of back, with a huge black beard and shaggy black eyebrows. Glittering black eyes peered out from this facial fungus at a largely cold and uncaring world. Stories about him were legion. He was as cunning as a hill fox and the very mention of the word 'work' was enough to make him physically ill.

Snib was the supreme cadger. There was one farmhouse at which he called, begging for something to eat. The housewife told him that she would be quite prepared to give him soup and scones if he chopped up a supply of firewood to see her through the first few months of winter. Snib eyed the colossal pile of blocks and the weighty looking axe stuck in the chopping block with considerable alarm. 'Missis,' he said at last, 'when a man's belly is empty, he hasnae the strength tae work.' The housewife, being new to Galloway and therefore not yet being aware of the tramp's reputation, took the hint. Two plates of broth and about ten thick cheese scones later she indicated the axe and the firewood heap to Snib. Snib burped contentedly. 'Missis,' he said drowsily, 'when a man's belly is fou', he has nae need tae work.' And off he marched, straight-backed as ever, down the road in the direction of a snug little brackeny copse which he knew would take care of his more immediate need.

Another much-related story about Snib – which must surely be completely apocryphal, but which one would like to think should be true – was that he had come scrounging at one large farmhouse on the day of the annual Young Farmers' Ball at the McMillan Hall in Newton Stewart. A group of very playful young farmers were gathered at this particular farmhouse to discuss the forthcoming event and to try to think up some ploy to liven up the proceedings. Snib, so the story goes, was stuffed with food and plied with enough malt whisky to make him reasonably amenable to the part he was being asked to play in the night's activities. The gift of a £10 note helped banish any doubts he might have had, even to the extent of allowing himself to be subjected to the horrors of a good clean-up. The haircut and removal of all his facial hair he accepted with a sort of grumbling equanimity, but it took a large injection of best malt and the combined strength of his hosts to force a naked Snib, cursing luridly, into a bath of hot, soapy water. An hour or so later, deloused and smelling like an advert for some exotic French perfume, Snib was clothed in an evening suit, white shirt and black tie. His fingernails and toenails were neatly clipped and from somewhere a pair of black shoes were found to cover his large and horny tramping feet. Snib, teeth brushed a sparking white and hair neatly brilliantined down, was totally unrecognizable from the evil-smelling, perambulating flea-circus of old.

The pranksters introduced him at that night's function as a rich visiting farmer from over Dumfries way and, so the popular tale would have us believe, farmers' daughters from far and near vied with each other for the privilege of dancing with this debonair and handsome stranger.

A week later Snib was back on the road, doing what he did best and enjoyed most, cadging from gullible wives, his night of enforced revelry among the High and the Mighty already a thing of the past with him. Indeed, were it not for the four bottles of Johnnie Walker he had packed in his rucksack as a memento while the house was asleep the morning after, it might have been nothing but a bad dream to him.

*   *   *

Things have changed considerably in the past half-century. Like everything else in today's society, those colourful travellers of old have been neutralized, absorbed into the grey culture of modern living. They have been shoved into drab council houses with drab surroundings that have nothing in common with the crisp sweetness of the countryside so beloved of their forebears, where the only sound to greet their awakening each morning was the melodic music of blackbird, song thrush and skylark. Tents and caravans are things of the past. Their children have been integrated with 'normal' children and the old cultures are being encouraged to disappear. The travellers are no longer travellers and their children would be appalled were they asked to skin a rabbit. The only culture worth recognizing is the culture of the hamburger and the slot machine. It is, after all, a requirement of those who lead us that we should all be the same. We must all blend together until, like Orwell's pigs, we have blended to such an extent that none can tell the one from the other.

But I have had a mischievous thought as I write this, and it is a thought which I shall dredge up every now and then to comfort me each time depression threatens me in my twilight years. Might there, sometime in the distant future, be a chance that within the pantries of the House of Commons a descendant of one of those marvellous tinkers of the past will be employed? And might it be just too much to hope that, unable to resist any longer that long-quelled streak of mischief inherited from those distant wanderers, he will perform some perfectly unspeakable act in the House of Commons' raspberry jam?

Chapter 12
GENTLEMEN OF THE SHADOWS

It had its beginnings in Wigtownshire, but I was far away from Galloway when my love affair with poaching came to an abrupt end. Endings – especially abrupt endings – are often more interesting than beginnings, so perhaps this one can best be described by quoting from a story I wrote for the fishing magazine *Waterlog* some time ago:

> They called him 'The Otter'. He must have had a real name, but I never knew it. He was one of that hardy breed known euphemistically as 'night fishers', and his beat covered some of the most scenic areas of central Argyll.
>
> The Otter was a poacher of the old school. He drifted through the night like a ghost, always on his own and rarely seen even by the most vigilant of watchers. He had never been caught, although water bailiffs and gamekeepers would brag over their pints that they had 'nearly caught' him on occasion, embellishing their accounts with extraordinary tales of derring-do and wild pursuit. It was all harmless fantasy and few believed them, but what was accepted by friend and foe alike was that the Otter was a man of principle. Not for him the barbarism of poisons or explosives or foul-hooking. The net and the leister were his stock in trade.
>
> I think there was a touch of the John McNab about the Otter. There must have been occasions when he sold some of his

catch, for most poachers do, but, if ever he did so, the recipients were uncommonly discreet about it. What was much talked about was his generosity to the less fortunate in life. Old people and those with large families to feed could rely on finding the occasional salmon hanging in their garden sheds when the going got really rough. It all added to the legend and, from a practical point of view, it was his insurance cover against the possibility of betrayal.

I met him only once when he was in his prime, and even then it was only the briefest of encounters. I was a forestry student, billeted in a large house deep in the mountains of Argyll. Students the world over are perpetually hungry and we had more cause to be hungry than most: porridge, chocolate-spread sandwiches, and a noxious, bright-yellow custard was our staple fare on most days. It was a situation that would have precipitated violent disturbances at Barlinnie Prison, and it was one that called for a certain amount of radical thinking.

I had been an enthusiastic poacher in my youth, but the responsibility that came with being a forestry student and the possibility of the start of a good career after my studies were over had made me decide to retire from the black art while the going was good. However, this was a whole new ball game, and death through malnutrition seemed an odd way for a reformed poacher to go while the rivers and hill burns around us were teeming with salmon and sea trout...

The grey light of dawn was filtering through the thickness of the mist and I was lying on the river bank, watching the silver darlings milling around below me in the peaty waters. I already had a good fish beside me and I was just thinking it was time to be off home when he touched me with the toe of his boot. My heart almost seized up on the spot and my head snapped round to gaze into the darkest and keenest eyes I had ever seen in my life. 'Watch yersel', son,' he hissed, 'the bloody bailiff is on the prowl.'

Then he was gone into the mist.

I had met the famous Otter, and I still remember the thrill it gave me. With the idealistic romanticism of youth, it was, for me, like being able to boast that I had met the Scarlet Pimpernel.

But night fishers as a rule dislike unscheduled encounters. One such ended my own poaching career almost a year later. It was a night of glorious moonlight, with the air still balmy from the heat of the past day. I had caught my quota and I was shouldering my bag when I heard voices close to hand. I melted into the willows. Then came a sound that curdled my blood: the soft 'ruff' of a dog answering his master. I took off instantly at high speed, heading for the hills.

A gap in the clump of tall whins that covered part of the adjacent field beckoned and I shot through this like a ferreted rabbit. It was a fateful decision, and the outcome of it remains etched in my memory to this day.

In a little clearing inside the whins a young couple were inextricably entwined in what poets, being poets, choose to call the tender turbulence of love. I suppose because it was a warmish night, the lovers had considered it expedient to divest themselves of every last stitch of their clothing. So engrossed were they in their own affairs that they neither saw nor heard me, and such was my velocity that it was impossible to evade them, though I did my best in the circumstances. My desperate attempt to hurdle them might even have succeeded had not the masculine half of the ardent duo – mad, passionate fool that he was – raised his hindquarters suddenly and in most unseemly fashion. The heel of my gumboot caught him fair and square on the rump, doing God knows what damage to the poor girl under him, and I flew base over apex into the whins beyond them. A split second later, the dog arrived on the scene.

Bright moonlight, which can do so much for one's libido when one is gazing into the eyes of love, can have quite the opposite effect on one's system when strange dogs enter the equation. This dog, probably a docile enough animal were one to encounter it in daylight, was transformed on this fulgent night into a huge, slavering brute of a thing, chillingly reminiscent of that hellish mastiff in Conan Doyle's most famous story. It paused momentarily, baleful yellow glare taking in the strange goings on before it, then it went straight into action.

To this day, I do not know whether the hound saw me or not. If it did, the intelligent creature obviously dismissed me as being of no consequence. It sprang upon the unfortunate couple, biting and chomping with an indiscriminate fervour that did adequate justice to its unprepossessing appearance. Love cannot blossom in such unsettling conditions, and the little clearing was now a screaming, cursing, snarling, whirling tangle of frantic white bodies and enraged black mastiff. Seldom, if ever, can those tranquil glens have experienced such a hullabaloo as that which rent the atmosphere on that beautiful night of half a century ago.

Looking back on it all now, I suppose that cavillers might quibble that chivalry demanded I should stay around to offer some form of succour to the innocent victims. The sad fact is that I did no such thing. Long before the dog's owner arrived, I had slipped off through the whins and into the wooded shadows of the surrounding slopes...

I think that most country-born-and-bred boys are, at heart, poachers, and this was certainly true of the Galloway of my youth. Most of us dabbled in it and those that hadn't had at least thought about it. It was one of the last great adventures left to experience in a land that was becoming increasingly tame and domesticated.

I never knew a girl or a woman poacher. This was a man's world. Man was the provider; woman did the cooking of whatever he brought home for her. Today, Tesco is the provider, the microwave does the cooking, and if you asked the average girl to cook a rabbit for you she would think you had been at the magic mushrooms again. Mind you, if a girl did cook a rabbit for her partner these days, he would be quite convinced she was trying to get rid of him. But 60 years ago in rural Galloway the ability to spirit a hare from the bog and a fish from the water was of vital importance to a great many families, especially when a week's wages for the Head of the House – as was the case in the MacIntosh household – usually amounted to little more than a few pounds.

Some of us started our poaching careers earlier than others. It usually depended upon how enthusiastic a boy's father happened to be about the whole business. I could have been no more than six years of age when I snared my first rabbit. I have a clear memory of it now. My father had been given permission to hang snares on the fence that ran along the railway line which cut through the Pouton Farm, and he took me along with him each morning when he went out to check their contents. Rabbits were in abundance and the railway banks were riddled with their burrows. After checking, the snares had to be lifted – cattle and sheep had a peculiar habit of chewing at the wires and had been known to get their tongues ensnared in the nooses – and they were re-set each evening at dusk. Although the railway ran close to the Big House and rabbits were even more prolific in that locality, the proprietrix would not allow us to set snares any closer than half a mile from her home: she had many free-ranging chickens and guinea-fowl and she was highly protective of them.

I had found a snare in our garden shed and I had hung it on the railway fence at the point nearest to our cottage – which also happened to be the point nearest to the Big House. To my astonishment – and considerable excitement – when I checked it the following morning, it contained a large, fat rabbit. It had been snared by the neck and the poor creature was very much alive, though obviously exhausted by its struggles to break free during the night. It made no attempt to escape as I approached it. I was now very much impaled on the horns of a dilemma of my own making, for I was too young to have the strength to break its neck cleanly and end its suffering, nor could I bring myself to commit the ultimate atrocity of beating it over the head with a stone. I could not even trail it home on the end of the snare for fear of probable retribution for having taken the snare from the shed in the first place without permission, and for having set it in forbidden territory.

I looked at the rabbit and the rabbit looked right back at me. It seemed to be thinking – to echo a phrase which was to become popular during a later era – 'You stupid boy!' Cautiously, I reached out and stroked its back. It flinched, but it did not struggle. With utmost care, I slackened the noose around its neck and edged it over the animal's ears and head. It was a very relieved bunny indeed that bolted in a blur of grey into the undergrowth. Come to think of it, it was a pretty relieved little boy who wandered back up the farm track to the house in the early morning sunshine, his snare safely tucked away inside his pocket.

Things were to improve for me, though, if not for Galloway's rabbit population. Under the Old Man's tutelage, we boys became adept at snaring. He showed us how and when to set snares; the difference between setting snares for rabbits and setting snares for hares; the heights at which to set our snares according to the peculiarities of particular 'runs' and the creatures for which we were setting them; how to set each snare according to whether the run was a 'fast' or a 'slow' one; the little kink to put on the loop of a snare to keep it from 'stringing out' on a windy night; the sort of nights on which snaring would be most effective and those on which you would be wasting your time.

Snaring is without doubt the most risky of all types of poaching, for snares have to be set at dusk and checked early the following morning. Should the set snares have been noted by the resident gamekeeper in the interim, the poacher is in deep trouble. Gamekeepers as a rule are a vindictive race, and few things give them greater pleasure than to sit concealed in dripping wet undergrowth with large and equally malevolent dogs by their side waiting for poachers to appear when all decent, God-fearing people are fast asleep in bed. I know of one whose wife told me that on the very first morning after her marriage she woke up to find the other half of her bed empty, her husband – convinced that no one in his right mind would ever think that he would put his job before his marital pleasures on his honeymoon night – having slipped out with his gun and dog to prove the doubters wrong and to see if he could put one over Aul' Sleekit Bob by catching him at large with a ferret in his hand in the plantation up on the hill.

That says it all, really. The aspiring poacher would do well to remember this cautionary tale, for there is a moral in it somewhere. The more peaceful the scene before you at the crack of dawn when you are about to check your snares, the more likely it will be that somewhere among that innocent clump of whins on the opposite side of the field, or buried inside the saughs and the nettles by the burn bank, lies The Enemy. You would therefore be well advised to stroll innocently through the field first, paying not a blind bit of notice to all those snares you have set the night before and nonchalantly humming that catchy little air from Petrovich Mussorgsky's Khovanshchina, which we all know so well and love so dearly. But let your eyes unobtrusively dart about you as you walk, looking for any sign that all is not well – cows staring long and hard at a particular corner of the field; a crow veering sharply as it flies over some bushes; a wheatear chack-chack-chacking anxiously as it flits back and forth in the vicinity of the stone dyke obscuring your view. Little things like that will indicate to you that You Are Not Alone.

It is well worthwhile erring on the side of caution, for if you do get caught, even if it happens to be your first appearance in court, it is no use stating that you removed the rabbit from the snare because you are a member of the Animal Liberation Front and were merely trying to give the poor wee mite its freedom. Nor will it do you the slightest good to protest that you are a visitor from one of the greater cities of England on his first visit to Galloway and you thought the snares were hoops placed there by the landowner as part of some quaint, rural, Scottish croquet-style tournament. The magistrate will have heard these all before, and in any case he (if that is the case) is more than likely to be a landowner himself who has suffered grievously from the activities of felons like yourself and will probably have had his tame pheasant chicks released from their pens and scattered all over Galloway from Portpatrick to the Shinnel Water by Animal Lib nutters more times than you have had hot breakfasts. If you manage to end up with a long stretch in a cushy place like Penninghame Open Prison, don't complain. Indeed, consider yourself jolly lucky. Barlinnie is where he would really like to have sent you.

For the poacher, the gun is much safer: a quick shot, a quick run to pick up what you have shot, and then so quick an exit that you are gone almost before the echo of the shot has died away. The man with the gun who observes those basic rules is a very difficult man to catch.

It was the gun that was to be the start of our higher education in the craft of poaching. It stood in a corner of our back room. It stood there, untouched, all spring and summer, for those are the seasons of giving birth and for the rearing of young. Spring and summer are for the fishing, when the trout are fat and the salmon and the sea trout are on the run upriver. But on late-autumn evenings, when the moon was right and the teal and the mallard were winging their ways to the meres and the stubble, the gun would come into its own.

The gun was old. Very old. It had seen service in many parts of Scotland before it ended up here in Galloway. Indeed, I seem to recall hearing that it had been the property of my grandfather on the Isle of Mull at the turn of the century before being handed down to my father. It was a double-barrelled 12-bore shotgun, the old-fashioned kind with hammers, and, even to those who knew nothing of such matters, this gun looked the part. There was nothing showy about this weapon, but one instinctively knew at a glance that this gun was efficient and that it had been used by people who knew what they were doing. Just as one knew that the pearl-handled gaudiness of the revolvers worn by the screen cowboys had nothing in common with the sinister black smoothness of the weapons carried by the real-life Earps and Mastersons of the Old West, so too would the knowledgeable person have recognized this gun as being a professional's gun, a poacher's gun. It was a gun that I always thought looked oddly out of place in the full glare of the sun, for there was such a darkly functional look about it. It was a gun made for the shadows, just as its owners had been men of the shadows. And like the men who had once owned it, it too had had a hard life. Its black barrels had been shortened, not by design, in the way that some poachers were in the habit of shortening theirs, but by accident. My grandfather, I was told, had slipped on some rocks on the Gribun shore on Mull while wildfowling, breaking the stock and denting the ends of the barrels. Now, shiny brass strips held the dark wooden stock together, the only bright part of its whole nondescript length. The barrels had become dangerously thin through constant use over the decades, but it was a gun that was still being used most effectively through the middle years of the 20th century.

By the time my brother and I had become teenagers the Old Man had taught us how to use it, safely and effectively. Always, the emphasis was on safety and effectiveness. Empty the gun before you climb walls or go through fences, and before you come within range of roads and buildings. Never point a gun, empty or loaded, in the direction of anyone or anything you have no intention of shooting. Always keep the hammers down in the 'safe' position until you are just about to shoot. At all times within the house, the gun must be empty and all ammunition stowed away safely and out of sight. Shoot only when you are sure of killing what you are aiming at – cartridges were highly expensive items and, while the bourgeoisie could afford to blast away at impossible targets like there was no tomorrow, each cartridge had to count with the Old Man. Shoot only at sitting targets. Birds rocketing high overhead at the speed of light with a force nine gale fluffing up their tail feathers were strictly for sportsmen. And the Old Man was no sportsman. He couldn't afford the luxury of being one. Besides, I believe that he genuinely hated the idea of wounding a creature to the extent that it would crawl off to die somewhere in agony. Shooting was a necessity for him in order to feed his growing family, and when it no longer became a necessity, he stopped shooting.

Astonishingly, neither my brother nor I were ever made to pay for our misdeeds – indeed, our younger brother Neil joined the other side by becoming a gamekeeper, a post which he was to occupy with the Forestry Commission for the next 34 years. But I had become rather active in my poaching activities and perhaps a trifle too well-known for my own good. As a result, the local bobby had seen fit to place upon my head a curse of such intense bitterness that he had only just stopped short of pasting up notices for my body to be delivered, dead or alive, to Garlieston Police Station.

Once only do I recall having come close to receiving my just desserts, and this only came about because of an act of sheer folly on my part. I had been out shooting duck with my close friend and companion, Jock Blain, along the Eggerness shore, an exercise to which we believed ourselves legally entitled as we were between the high-water and the low-water marks at all times. We had parked our bicycles far out on the main Garlieston – Kirkinner road and, as we had already shot a couple of nice mallard, we were on the verge of calling it a day when a roe deer stepped out of nowhere in front of us. Acting more from instinct than from good sense, I dropped him with a single shot.

The shot was still echoing around the bay when it dawned upon me what awful complications were now involved. We were a couple of miles of pretty rugged walking from our bicycles, and they were at least four miles from our home by the nearest route. We had two heavy guns, two large mallard drakes, two distant bicycles and – now – a colossal roe deer to lug along with us.

We stood in silence eyeing the corpse. Jock lit a cigarette. Then he hissed: 'Look yonder!' My eyes followed the direction of his gaze. Far over, just beyond the shoreline, and sited before a pocket of rough woodland, stood the Innerwell Fisheries house. Beside it, the figure of a man was gazing in our direction. He was too far away for us to be able to see him properly, but it was patently obvious that we were being spied upon through binoculars. Seeing that we were watching him, the figure turned and darted into the house.

'We'd better get our backsides out of here,' remarked Jock grimly. 'Whoever that was, you can bet your boots that he has gone to phone the polis.'

'But we shot this legally ...' I began to protest.

'With your reputation,' interrupted the ever-practical Jock, 'nothing is legal!'

It would be tedious to go into detail as to how we got home with the beast that night. Suffice to say that we arrived at three o'clock in the morning and that we walked every inch of the way. I knew the country like I knew the back of my hand and we followed tracks through field and marsh and forest all the way home, avoiding the main road, and thus – I was to learn later – eluding a police block at the northern junction of the Sorbie/Kirkinner/Garlieston road, and a late-night visit to my home by one of the only two police cars operating in the Machars at that time. 'Your mother offered them tea, but they couldn't wait, thank Christ,' commented my father thankfully as we were hastily burying the hide, head and hooves of the deer in the moonlit fields well away from the house. 'They asked for you. They wouldn't say what they were after, but I didn't think they were here to sell raffle tickets at one o'clock in the morning!'

*   *   *

The 'poachers' we read of from time to time in the newspapers today are not poachers at all. They travel in packs, like wolves. And they are noisy people, like the society in which they are reared. They come in cars and trucks from their city ghettos, armed to the teeth with automatic weapons and explosives to destroy our wildlife en masse. Nor do they hesitate to poison great stretches of river to get what they want. They are greedy to an extreme. One for the pot is of no use at all to them, for they are selling their spoils for great personal gain. Enough is never enough for them.

By contrast, the old timer was a loner. He would occasionally ask a close personal friend to accompany him if he was going for a night out on the long-net, but that was only because he could not operate the long-net effectively on his own. Most of the time, he preferred his own company. The poacher of old was a quiet man. He never advertised his presence, because it was not in his interest to do so. He walked in the shadows always, on the shadowy side of the dry-stane dyke or the hedge, or he slipped quietly and unobtrusively through the shadows of the trees along the side of the wood. He blended with the shadows. Even at his favourite local, he would rarely be found seeking company at the bar. More often than not, he would be seen sitting on his own in the shadows of the far corner, his pint on the table before him, rolling his cigarette carefully and methodically, seemingly oblivious to all around him. But he was never oblivious to what went on around him. His cunning old eyes would be flitting from side to side, taking in every movement, every gesture, and his old ears would be aquiver, like the ears of the hare clapped down tight in its form among the rashes of the bog, alert to every sound.

The old-time poacher rarely talked about his exploits, even through drink. It was simply not in his best interests to do so. He left such boasting to others, others who were much younger and infinitely less talented than he. He looked and he listened, and he used what he saw and heard to his own advantage. He was rarely a churchgoer, even in his declining years, when we are all supposed to be taking a keen interest in what the afterlife may have in store for us. I remember one quoting these lines to me long ago:

> Solomon and King David
> Led merry, merry lives,
> With many, many concubines
> And many, many wives;
> But when they reached to old age
> And had many, many qualms –
> Solomon wrote the Proverbs
> And King David wrote the Psalms.

Such a swift and radical transformation would have been out of character for the old-time poacher. He was a simple man, but he was too honest to change like that. There was no hypocrisy about him. Because of rheumatism and arthritis and all the other infirmities of age that tended to afflict people of his lifestyle with particular severity, he often had to adjust his ways quite a bit when he was no longer able to get out and about as he once did. He had to adapt his needs to a more orthodox and civilised type of life. But the call of the shadows would remain with him right to the end.

Let me conclude this chapter then, if I may, with the sequel to the *Waterlog* story with which it began:

I paid a sentimental visit recently to the place in which I had spent my youth as a forestry student in the mountains of Argyll. The beauty of the place was undiminished and the whins through which I had bolted all those years ago were still there. A dipper still worked the river, but the waters somehow seemed a little lifeless to me. Not one fish of any consequence was visible, and the few trout I saw would hardly have served as an appetiser for the old grey heron hunched disconsolately over the river bank.

My old stamping grounds had been turned into a public garden, with hordes of visitors pouring through the gates on a daily basis. The accents owed more to upbringings in Glasgow and the English Home Counties than to the Highlands of Scotland. Not one of those I met looked capable of handling a leister.

On the penultimate day of my visit, I tracked down my quarry. He was sitting in what had now become his favourite watering hole. I bought him a pint and a dram and I joined him.

The Otter looked much as I remembered him from that brief encounter of long ago; older, of course, but still trim of physique and Romany-brown of face. He was the fittest looking octogenarian I had seen in many a long year.

It took several of the more expensive malts to convince him that my intentions were strictly honourable. Soon we were chatting away about old times on the river.

'I'm sure you still manage a fish or two for yourself when you need them?' I hinted slyly. He looked at me as though I were mentally impoverished. 'Gettin' fish,' he replied with quiet reproof, 'has never been a problem for the Otter.'

I told him that I was due to return to England soon and would like to take a salmon with me. 'Do you think you could...umm...help?' I enquired hesitantly. The old man downed his whisky in one gulp and raised his empty glass ostentatiously before me.

'Easy,' he replied confidently. 'You leave it to me.'

I went to the bar and ordered a large Oban. I brought it back to my companion. He motioned wordlessly at his empty beer glass. I went back to the bar and returned with another pint. He drank gratefully.

'Give me the money,' he said, 'an' I'll get ye a good salmon.'

'Money?'

'Aye,' said the Otter. 'The fish farm at Cairndhu. That's where I buy mine these days.'

Chapter 13
THE MIDNIGHT GROCER

The dingy old van was parked at the junction of the country lane that ran through the estate grounds. Sitting behind the wheel and eating his midday pie was the Midnight Grocer. It was his favourite parking spot, especially at this time of the year when the weather was fine. The sky and the woods and the hedgerows were restless with life. The first swallows had arrived, streams of them darting hither and thither, twittering excitedly as they sought invisible insects away up there on the edge of the firmament. Linnets flitted low over the golden whins, searching for suitable nesting sites within their spiky seclusion, and somewhere on a nearby treetop could be heard the monotonous, repetitive call of the tiny chiffchaff, celebrating his return from his winter vacation on distant balmy shores.

Wood pigeons abounded. They cruised over the fields and hedges, their swift-winged winter flight temporarily abandoned as they flapped lazily and aimlessly from point to point, occasionally soaring up and over the road to land in the trees around the edge of the wood with a pistol-shot cracking of wings. They sat there in full view, unafraid, displaying proudly, chests gleaming lavender-blue in the sunshine, croo-croo-crooing endlessly to the world while their partners crouched on frail nests somewhere deep inside the spruce thickets beyond them.

Nests! The Midnight Grocer was a thinker. He pondered now on the strange ways of living things. Why, he wondered, should the bigger birds all be so careless in the construction of their nests, while the small ones crafted theirs with such loving care? Rooks sat on bundles of twigs high up on their windy eminencies, often on the same nest year after year, doing nothing much more to the last year's ruins than add a few sticks to it and shit on it. Pigeons were even worse. A few dead twigs laid haphazardly, one on top of the other, was good enough for this bird; an incredibly fragile platform barely wide enough or strong enough, one would have thought, to hold the two eggs she laid, never mind the weight of herself sitting on them.

Compare those, he thought, with the nest of the chaffinch. Such a neat, compact little cup of mosses and silvery lichens and fine grasses and downy feathers, all intricately woven and interwoven and stitched together so beautifully that you felt on your first sight of one that angels must have had a hand in the making of it, and so comfortable did it look on the inside that you were convinced that the same angels must have been thinking of the baby Jesus while they were lining it.

The Midnight Grocer had an eye for the beauties of nature. He was probably also the most happy-go-lucky person in all of Galloway. It was just as well, for he had never had a lot going for him from the very beginning. An attack of poliomyelitis in early childhood had left him with a limp and a slightly withered hand, and his parents had left him not too long after that. Now, at the age of 36, he was a consumptive chain-smoker with a cough so harsh and racking that it gave everyone within hearing distance chest-ache just to listen to it. He had no relatives that he knew of, but he had long ago been taken under the roof of two elderly spinsters who owned the village grocery whose van he now drove.

It was a symbiotic relationship. He needed them, and they needed him. They were like two older sisters to him. They cooked his meals and they washed his clothes. They sewed for him and they knitted for him. They provided him with his own little bedroom in their house. In return, he worked incredibly long hours in their shop and in their grocery van which he drove around the rural areas for them twice a week. The money they gave him was barely worth the taking, but he was a man of modest needs. He had no hobbies, apart from smoking. He did not drink, and the only interest he had ever shown in the opposite sex had been in blethering to them.

It was from his van duties that he had gained his nickname. Like most nicknames acquired in Galloway, it had originally been applied as a humorously scurrilous epithet, and there was no disputing the fact that there was a certain justification in this one. His beat covered a very wide area indeed, and the Midnight Grocer did have a tendency to arrive very late in the day at the homes of some of his more distant customers. This was due almost entirely to the fact that he felt compelled to stop every so often to admire the view and engage his penchant for idle chitchat with just about anyone he happened to meet en route.

Breakdowns, too, were frequent. His van, like its driver, had had a rough life. It was, in fact, one of the most terrible little vans ever to disgrace the highways and byways of Galloway. It stank to high heaven of diesel and paraffin, and it was as draughty as a sheep fank. It rattled and clattered on its way along road and track, making as much noise as a World War I tank, while belching poisonous blue gases from its rear end. Nor was it blessed with heating of any sort, other than that created by the engine, and on winter nights when the wind came screaming over the land the cold pierced his cadaverous frame like a skewer.

But the Midnight Grocer had never been heard to complain. His was the cheeriest of dispositions. Despite the wretchedness of his existence and the long hours and constant pain from the thing that was eating at his insides, the smile rarely left his face. There were, as a result, plenty of customers around those outlying farms who would wait up late at night to buy things, whether they actually needed them or not. His customers liked him and they felt sorry for him, and he could always be sure of a plate of soup somewhere at the end of his day before he began the long journey home...

He finished his tea and screwed the lid back on his flask. He turned round in his seat and looked into the back of the van. He smiled contentedly. Most people in their right minds would have reckoned that he didn't have much to smile about. Whatever the Midnight Grocer's good points, orderliness was not one of them. That which now gave him such apparent pleasure would have given most shopkeepers a fit of the horrors. His mobile shop was a shambles. It looked as though some malevolent poltergeist had been running riot inside it.

But then, that was how it always looked. It was his van, and his shambles, and he would smile benignly at any complainant. There was never, ever, the slightest attempt made at stacking things tidily before he set off on his rounds. Everything seemed to have been thrown in higgledy-piggledy and piled in heaps around the sides of the van. Tins of meat, pilchards, Heinz soups, tea, Bisto, packets of margarine, lard, dried eggs, matches, cigarettes, jars of cod liver oil, syrup of figs, vegetable extract, bars of soap, bundles of candles, drums of paraffin, bags of flour. Throughout all this conglomeration lurked tangles of cod line already armed with large and vicious hooks, just waiting to impale careless fingers.

The centre of the van was piled high with an incredible assortment of weekly newspapers and magazines in various stages of disintegration – *Galloway Gazette, Picture Post, People's Friend, Red Star Weekly, The Dandy* and *The Beano* comics, even an *Oban Times* and a *Perthshire People's Journal* for the Highland family who lived out on the little back road that ran between the village of Sorbie and the Garlieston to Whithorn road. The papers that found themselves at the top of this heap had, inevitably, the Midnight Grocer's footprints stamped indelibly on them, along with a liberal coating of some horridly glutinous chocolate-brown substance.

So far as anyone could recall, the van had never been cleaned out since its original purchase many years before. Indeed, local gossip had it that the mummified remains of a pair of rabbits – given to the grocer one Christmas by a local poacher – had been found in the spring of the following year under a cairn of food tins, and even then they were only discovered by the merest of chances.

But the Midnight Grocer cared little what anyone thought. The van was his kingdom, and only his employers could take his kingdom away from him.

He gave one last lingering look, then settled himself down behind the wheel. He lit a cigarette, then put his van into gear. He edged it out onto the road.

He began to sing:

Ae fond kiss, and then we sever —
Ae fareweel, and then — for ever
Deep in heart-wrung tears I'll pledge thee!
Warring sighs and groans I'll wage thee!

He drew hard on his Woodbine. The rolling Galloway countryside spread out before him. Here and there on the slopes on each side of the road he could see gangs of workers busy weeding the turnips. He drew again on his cigarette. A spasm of coughing overtook him and he barked harshly, painfully. He opened the van window and spat thickly out into the clean Galloway air. He breathed in and out deeply, in and out, in and out, his chest wheezing like a broken-down melodeon. He began to sing again:

Had we never lov'd sae kindly —
Had we never lov'd sae blindly —
Never met — or never parted,
We had ne'er been broken-hearted!

Another fit of coughing seized him. He fumbled on the seat beside him for his cigarette packet. Far in front of him a lone figure trudging along the side of the road caught his eye. He thought about stopping to offer the traveller a lift, then changed his mind when he got nearer and recognised him. Snib Scott, the tramp. Just the time of year for old Snib to be back on his patrols, remembered the grocer. At the beginning of every winter he disappeared, hibernating, some said, in a hostel of sorts around Stranraer, and at the first hint of spring he would be tramping the old haunts again, sleeping in woods and barns and behind dykes until the winds of November began to bite again.

The grocer lifted his hand in greeting as the van passed the tramp. The greeting was not returned. Snib had never been the most sociable of people, even when begging for food. He strode along with that long, mile-consuming gait of his, his dilapidated 1918 army greatcoat tied around his waist with binder twine and his battered felt hat pulled down to his ears. His face was covered with a tangle of long grizzled hair, a jungle from which two dark, badger-like eyes peered warily out at a hostile world.

The Midnight Grocer's hand strayed unconsciously to his own considerable mop of hair. He scratched himself thoughtfully. On the one and only occasion on which he had picked up old Snib he had lived to regret it: Snib's beard was a complete wildlife paradise of tiny creatures and it had taken a lot of carbolic soap and much painful scraping with a currycomb before the last Snib migrant had been removed from his own woolly patch...

I had been fulminating somewhat bitterly about the vicissitudes of life when the Midnight Grocer's van chugged into view. It was evening, and the day, which had been so beautiful, had turned cold and nasty, with big black rain-clouds gathering fast from the west. I had been cycling home when I had run over some broken glass and the resultant two punctures had left me with no choice but to walk home. I had quite a few miles to go, and it was obvious I was going to get wet.

'Sling your bike in the back,' called the Midnight Grocer cheerily, 'and I'll give you a lift a wee bit down the road.'

I shut the door behind me. The engine instantly gave up the ghost. The Midnight Grocer gave me the starting handle. I got out. It had begun to rain, spots as big as half-crowns splashing on the bonnet of the van. I cranked away for five minutes, sweating and cursing, to no avail. I was also getting rather wet. I got back inside the van. The rain came down in torrents and it gave every appearance of doing so for the rest of the night. The Midnight Grocer began to sing 'The Bonnie Wells o' Wearie'. He had a pleasant enough light tenor voice, but I was in no mood to appreciate it. I gazed sourly out the window, wondering what to do. I did not fancy spending a night in the van but neither did I fancy walking six miles home in this downpour.

'Did ye hear about the Weedow McCardle?' asked the Midnight Grocer suddenly.

'No,' I replied resignedly. 'Tell me.' The grocer was an absolute repository of gossip about everything that went on within his round, and, often, points far beyond it.

'Well,' he began, 'ye ken her son John?'

'Aye,' I said, 'I ken him fine.' A likeable youth, but an awful rascal. He was 17 years of age, very good-looking, and as libidinous as a billy-goat.

'Well,' continued the Midnight Grocer, 'the other night he came hame lookin' a wee bitty worried. "Mither," he said, "sit doon. I've a confession tae mak' tae ye. Ye ken that wee Jeanie McGregor doon the road? Weel, ah've made her pregnant." The poor old weedow nearly had a hert attack. "Oh my goodness, son," she wailed. "Whatever will poor wee Ella Bell do? I thought ye were goin' strong wi' her?" "I still am, mither" her son replied, "an' that's the next thing I have tae tell ye – she's pregnant tae!" '

The Midnight Grocer lit another Woodbine. He began to cough again. Darkness was slowly settling down over the rain-drenched fields around us. 'Would ye like something tae eat, Donal'?' he enquired. 'I'm getting' quite peckish masel'.' He reached behind him and fumbled among the accumulated rubbish. He fished out a paper bag and handed me a pie from it. He took one for himself and began to munch happily at it. I looked at mine. Even in the gloom it looked barely edible. It was of a most unappetising grey hue and there were spots of mould on the crust. I scraped them off and peeled back the top layer of pastry. The meat, like the pastry, was grey. I bit into it and chewed. Even the taste was grey. I felt something that was neither meat nor pastry rolling about on my tongue. Part of it got wedged between my teeth. I gaffed it with my forefinger and looked at it. It was a clump of unidentifiable hair. I opened the window and slung it out. I ate the rest of the pie, carefully chewing before swallowing in case I encountered something else not intended for human consumption.Something made a rustling sound in the back of the van. I glanced over my shoulder. In the dim light I could see movement among a pile of papers over in the far corner. 'Rats!' I exclaimed in horror. 'You've got rats in your bloody van, man!' The Midnight Grocer laughed. 'Nah, Donal',' he said, 'that's no' rats! That's Jasper!'

Jasper. His cat. As old and arthritic and flea-bitten as old Snib, the tramp.

'What on earth is Jasper doing in your van?' I queried.

'Well,' replied the Midnight Grocer, 'I did have a plague of mice a wee while back, so I let Jasper sleep in the van for a couple of nights tae get rid of them. He liked the comfort of the van that much that I hadn't the heart to move him.'

He started to sing again. There had been no sign of life on the road since we had met up a couple of hours before. I thought again about the prospect of having to spend a whole night in this disgusting van in the company of the Midnight Grocer and his equally disgusting cat. I decided that I would rather face the elements. I opened the van door. 'Wait here,' I said, 'and I'll walk to the nearest farm and see if I can find someone who can start your van.'

I pulled the collar of my coat up around my neck and trudged up the hill into the black night and the pouring rain...

*   *   *

It was to be another three weeks before I saw the Midnight Grocer again. He did not look his usual cheerful self. I asked him what was bothering him. He told me that Jasper was dead. He had opened the van one morning and found the cat's body, and a large glass sweetie jar lying shattered beside him.

'Stone dead, he was,' the Midnight Grocer told me mournfully. 'Poor Jasper! I don't know what finished him. Old age, maybe. Or maybe the jar fell from the top shelf onto him.'

He lit a cigarette, drew on it and exhaled, coughing. The thin blue smoke hung in a cloud around his head. He mused reflectively: 'It couldn't have been the pie he was eatin' at the time he dee'd, surely? I'd only had them a few weeks and they were okay when we et them.'

My mind went back to that pie and I thought about that clump of hair I had found inside it. Suddenly, I didn't feel too good.

Chapter 14
THE WORTHIES

One of the greatest of Galloway's characters was born in Balmaclellan in 1712. Christened 'Robert Paterson', in his late 20s he became smitten by an obsession that was to make him renowned throughout the Lowlands as 'Old Mortality'.

Around 1740, so the story goes, a raggle-taggle band of Highlanders passed near to his home. Paterson, rather unwisely, hurled epithets at them, declaring that the Lord would sort them out for 'supporting the heresies of Rome' – a phrase familiar to those of us today who have heard that charismatic Reverend, Ian Paisley, at his stentorian best. The Highlanders, having just been on the receiving end of a trouncing from the forces of King George II, were in no mood to take rubbish from anyone. When they had finished belaying him with sticks they looted his home and took him off with them on an unscheduled countryside ramble far off into the moors around the Wether Hill before dumping him, terrified, naked and sore, among the bracken to find his own way back home.

His experience with the Highlanders did nothing to endear him to their cause. Almost at once, he joined a religious sect called 'The Cameronians', travelling to their conventicles throughout Galloway. Gravestones became an obsession with him, particularly those of the Covenanters, who had suffered such persecution for their beliefs. He became obsessed by the thought that the inscriptions on their headstones would fade and that future generations would thus know nothing of the struggle of those brave and remarkable people. He began a one-man crusade, cleaning the headstones, deepening the inscriptions with his stone-chisel, adding words of his own, and even – in places where no memorial at all existed – making and erecting headstones himself.

As with many fanatical crusaders, he tended to pay more attention to the needs of the dead than to the more pressing ones of the living. Especially to those of the living who were dependant on him. His movements became more and more erratic and the periods he spent away from his Balmaclellan home became more and more prolonged until, finally, he stopped coming back altogether, leaving his wife and five children to fend for themselves. Until his death in 1800, he continued to drift from one churchyard to the next, mounted on his old grey mare and never accepting any payment other than the hospitality offered to him by the people he encountered in his travels.

Sir Walter Scott met him once, and in his historical novel *Old Mortality*, he wrote:

> An old man was seated upon the monument of the slaughtered Presbyterians, and busily employed in deepening, with his chisel, the letters of the inscription, which, announcing in scriptural language the promised blessings of futurity to be the lot of the slain, anathematised the murderers with corresponding violence.

Old Mortality was a character, a worthy of the villages. He was by no means the first ever to be found in Galloway nor, hopefully, will his like be allowed to become extinct, though the signs are not favourable at the time of writing.

My dictionary defines 'character' as 'amusing or eccentric person' and 'worthy' as 'eminent or distinguished person, often used in a facetious way'. In the Galloway of my youth, the two were indistinguishable. The character tended more likely, perhaps, to have been the one who did things on occasion, while the worthy seemed to do little more than sit on the mill brig or on a bench in the town square exchanging bon mots with his compatriots. But the two were generally linked by that endearing – and essential – touch of eccentricity that set them apart from the hoi polloi. It was a characteristic that made them instantly recognisable, even before they had opened their mouths. But, once they had opened their mouths, they were quite unmistakable. Around a century ago, Alex A Cuthbert wrote in *The Gallovidian* about his childhood in Garlieston:

> I seem at times to hover on the outskirts of the group of villagers who used to loiter about the bridge over the mill-lade and to be listening to their discussion on the poor laws, free trade, non-intrusion, or the merits of sermons which they have heard in the village chapel, or at Sorbie, or at Whithorn.
>
> I hear one of the group giving an account of the sermon to which he had listened the previous day. The subject of discourse had been the miracle of turning the water into wine, and the preacher had explained that the wines used in Palestine were not so potent as some better known beverages of modern times – that unlike the whisky made at Bladnoch, these wines were the produce of the fermented juice of the grape – that they varied in strength, and that when the more potent varieties were required for daily consumpt, they were generally diluted with water. And I think I overhear Jamie McMillan, in his deep voice and in slow measured tones, deploring the minister's indiscretion in making any such explanations, and saying – 'when the minister cam' to this bit it just made me sweat, for there'll no be an auld wife in the country noo but'll tak' to the mixin' an' say she has Scriptur' for't.'

Those characters of old were never short of an appropriate – or inappropriate – word to suit the occasion. A preacher known to me had been posted to the parish of Old Luce in Wigtownshire. It was not a posting to which he had been looking forward very much; preachers are not always the models of Christian charity and forgiveness that we mere sinners of their flocks automatically assume them to be, and some minor dispute which this particular pastor had had with the congregation here many years previously had been allowed to escalate in his mind until it had become a grievance of some considerable magnitude. Their Moment of Redemption came when he was asked to address the good ladies of the local WRI. He began his talk with the immortal words:

'You've no idea how much pleasure it gives me to be standing here before you Old Luce ladies ...'

One of my own very special favourites from my early teenage years, though, was old Jeck Aird. Jeck was a farm hand, and he was very much the old soldier, having served in World War I. He was a marvellous character, always happiest when he had an audience of youngsters to enthral with his tales of gruelling marches under the hot sun in faraway places. Jeck was of true military stock, in fact, for he had had a father and an uncle involved in Britain's – ultimately – victorious siege of 'Sebastardpol', and he had that marvellous ability which all true storytellers have of being able to transport the listener right back to the grime and the sweat and the blood and the thunder of battle as one sat there by the edge of some tranquil Galloway cornfield listening to him. He was working on a farm near Garlieston when his call-up papers for World War II arrived at his home several miles away. His wife walked over the fields to where he was busy harvesting to deliver them to him. Jeck, in the middle of forking sheaves of corn onto the stack, immediately stuck his fork into one of the remaining sheaves, jumped down from the cart, and set off at a brisk and soldierly pace over the fields, his wife scurrying frantically and forlornly in his wake. There was to be no denying this old warrior his second chance in 25 years to gather yet more material for his stories, courtesy, this time, of Adolf Hitler.

Jock Ross was another who could tell a tale or two when 'in the trum'. Jock was not a true Gallovidian – he had come from the Highlands originally – but he had for many years been employed as a gamekeeper on the Castlewigg Estates near Whithorn. I had spoken to him on a few occasions, but I have to confess that I did not know him too well. He was of my father's generation, and the two of them would meet quite regularly in one of the Whithorn pubs to exchange reminiscences, with the better of Jock's stories being related to we youngsters when the Old Man returned from his night out.

Jock Ross was from a renowned piping family and he was to eventually teach my brother George to play the bagpipes. One of his tales concerned a simple crofter who hailed from a very remote part of the Hebrides and who had never been away from his native island. However, his fame as a piper had spread to such an extent that he found himself being awarded the highest accolade it was possible for any piper to achieve. He was invited to play before Her Imperial Majesty Queen Victoria at Buckingham Palace. In due course his train arrived at London and he was met by one of the palace flunkeys and billeted in a luxurious suite at the Ritz, from which, during the wee small hours of his very first night, he found himself unceremoniously evicted.

News of the disgrace filtered through to his home island with astonishing rapidity, and all who knew him were understandably puzzled as to how such a mild and reasonably abstemious person as Dougal the Piper could have made himself such a pariah insofar as the Ritz management and clientele were concerned. When he eventually returned home, they were all agog.

'Och well now, I don't really know myself what gives with these English at aal, at aal,' said the old man, reaching thankfully for his first dram. 'Everything was going chust sublime until they threw me out. There wass I in my room that night, minding my own business and quietly playing my bagpipes...'

There were many worthies throughout Galloway, and all of them had a story to tell, given the right circumstances...and the right amount of libation when the long day's toil was over. I often wondered how blacksmiths always appeared to live forever despite the incredibly long and hard hours they worked and the appalling conditions in which they laboured. They were a constant attraction, too, to all and sundry, whether at work or at the bar of the village pub, for they were full of acerbic wit and they were consummate storytellers. Tommy Woods was still hammering away on his Sorbie anvil until he was nearly 90 years of age, as fine an advert for hard work and harder drink as you were ever likely to find in your life. He had been a good runner in his youth and, when asked in much later life if he could still run, he would reply: 'Aye, ah can still rin a'richt, but ah dinnae cover the grun' sae fast!'

Tommy went to a ploughing match away over in the Borders country on one occasion with a friend. On the way back home through Galloway, they ran into thick fog, so he persuaded his passenger to sit on the bonnet of the car to 'gie me "hup!" and "hi!" till ah got hame'.

Jimmy McAtee had always been a great favourite of mine. He, too, lived to a ripe old age and he had a huge family. Jimmy took odd jobs here and there, picking up such money as would allow him to go on the randan for a day or two, then, money finished, back at his place of work he would suddenly appear, 'sober but no' a bit wiser', as he would put it himself.

He was a lovely old character, and great fun to be with. I felt privileged to be considered his friend. His bon mots were the stuff of legend. On one occasion, when told of a young, newly-married lady who was being so indulged by her doting husband that she was now the proud possessor of a dozen pairs of shoes, Jimmy was unimpressed. 'Twal' pair o' shin,' he commented scornfully, 'an' only yin pair o' feet tae pit in them!'

He was scathing about another relationship, but for a quite different reason. A rather pale and willowy fellow from far-off London's literati was about to become married to the village belle, an extremely lively and pretty girl. Jimmy was not confident that theirs would be a long and happy affair. 'Gie them a fortnicht!' he would prophesy enigmatically. He was right. Ten days only after the nuptials, they had parted. Jimmy's comment perhaps said it all: 'Hoo can ye dae ocht whun ye hae nocht tae dae ocht wi'?'

He visited some relatives on one occasion at their farmhouse in the huntin', shootin' and fishin' country of darkest England. The house was one of those vast, old, timbered buildings so typical of that part of the world, and it was already beginning to succumb to the wear and tear of the centuries. Experts with much knowledge on the subject of ancient buildings were gathered in the living room to offer their varying opinions as to what they considered the old house needed to render it shipshape once again. There was much learned discussion about the deleterious effects of such agencies as brown-rot, dry-rot, wet-rot, string-rot, furniture beetles and death-watch beetles, and the merits of kiln-drying versus air-drying versus dehumidification. Jimmy just sat back in his chair, happily drinking and smoking, but contributing not one word to the conversation.

Finally the lady of the house, feeling that she had better bring Aul' Jimmy into the conversation before all her Scotch evaporated, asked him: 'Have you got any opinion on the subject, James?'

All eyes switched to the sage and the chatter was stilled, to be replaced by that hushed and respectful silence the Persians of old must have adopted when about to get another earful of wisdom from their prophet Omar Khayyam.

The old man sucked at his pipe, a great snottery, gurgling sound, and tamped down the black, oily tobacco with a horny forefinger, keeping up the suspense like the consummate showman that he was. When the verdict came, it was delivered with the finality of a bullet to the heart:

'Lassie, yer fuckin' aul' hoose is din!'

*   *   *

My relationship with my brother George was always destined to be of a fragile nature. But there was no questioning the fact that, from the day he was born to the day that he died, he was a character of the highest order. His was the most engaging of personalities, and he was loved by every old dear who ever encountered him, despite –

or perhaps because of – his propensity to be always on the lookout for an opportunity to shock. As a child, parodies of popular nursery rhymes were a favourite ploy of his, and 'Jack and Jill' types of verses never came out of his mouth quite as originally written. More often, gaggles of twittering dowagers would hear him declaim (to their shock and discomfiture, pretended or otherwise):

> 'Jack and Jill
> Went up the hill
> To fetch a pail of water,
> Jill came down
> With half-a-crown
> And it wasn't for drawing water.'

And the things he could do with 'Little Miss Muffet' has no place in this – or any other – book.

In later life he would quote the following sadly prophetic lines to anyone who cared to listen:

> 'My candle burns at both its ends,
> It will not last the night;
> But let me tell you now, my friends –
> It gives a lovely light.'

I last saw him in the bar of the Castlewigg Hotel, on the road between Whithorn and Sorbie. I had been having a drink with my father when suddenly there he was beside us. Neither my father nor I had seen him for some time; indeed, it had been very many years since I had last seen him, for I had been working in Africa and Canada in the interim. Geordie, ever the entrepreneur, almost immediately tried to interest me in a scheme which had obviously been cooking in his fertile mind for some time:

'Donald, I've hit on a great idea that'll make us both a ton of money.'

'Oh yeah?' I said warily, for I had heard Geordie's money-making schemes all too often before.

'Aye,' he said, 'I'm going to build a chain of brothels right across the Southern Uplands.'

I choked on my drink. 'WHAT??'

'That's right,' he said calmly, 'whorehouses, from Dunbar to Stranraer. Never was a part of the world more in need of them.'

I looked at the man. He was deadly serious.

'You're loopy!' I said.

'Nah, man,' he said, obviously hurt, 'I mean it. Just think of all these politicians down there in London, looking for their wee bit on the side and they're too feart now with all this Christine Keeler scandal hanging over them. They'll pay any amount of money to find a discreet hidey-hole far away from London. And where else could be more discreet than Galloway?'

'And how do you propose to acquire the funds to start all this?' I enquired incredulously.

'I have my contacts,' he replied mysteriously.

I studied him long and hard. I believed him. Geordie would find the money if he had to, one way or another. Usually another.

'And where do I fit into your scheme of things?' I asked in some curiosity.

'You're a forester,' he replied smoothly, 'And, after all, discretion is the name of the game. Your job would be to plant fast-growing conifers around the individual chalets to ensure privacy.'

'And you would be doing…?'

'I would be the personnel manager, interviewing all staff,' he replied smugly.

'So,' I said, 'while I am out planting jaggy trees in the wind and the rain and the mud you would be inside, nice and cosy?'

'Interviewing staff,' he repeated, and he didn't even have the grace to blush. 'But,' he hurried on, 'you would be well paid for your discomfort. And you would have shares in the company.'

'I once read,' remarked the Old Man sourly as we walked

together out to the car, leaving Geordie behind at the bar to tap up another prospective customer, 'That the MacIntoshes had a clan curse hanging over them, but little did I realise that one day I would become the father of it.'

*   *   *

King George II, who was on the throne at the time of Old Mortality's wanderings, would have appreciated my brother's practical approach to life. Indeed, he would probably have been head of the queue on opening night. When his dying queen urged him to marry again after she was gone, the monarch replied lovingly: 'Non, j'aurai des maîtresses.' (No, I shall have mistresses.) Her Majesty's reply is reputed to have been: 'Ah! Mon Dieu! çela n'empêche pas.' (Good Lord, that doesn't prevent it.)

It is not easy to imagine His Majesty, King of Great Britain and Ireland and Elector of Hanover, sitting on the 'brig over the mill-lade' at Garlieston. But, had he been able to do so, he would have got on right royally with the local worthies once he had mastered their dialect.

That monarch was a character, and the people of Galloway have always loved characters.

Chapter 15
THE SPORTING LIFE

Sportsmanship did not die – as some of us of certain vintage would have the younger generation believe – with the advent of our modern era of shamateurism. Skulduggery in sport was with us from the very beginning. Even ancient Greece, from which we might have expected better things, was by no means immune from it. The comic dramatist Aristophanes wrote around 400 BC that such was desire to win all things at whatever cost, if his own mother were to try to pass him in a chariot race, he would not have had the slightest hesitation in shoving the blade of his sword straight through the spokes of her near wheel.

So much for the code of the Olympics.

It is doubtful if Wee Winkie, at the tender age of eight, would have been too familiar with the works of Aristophanes. If he had ever heard the name mentioned he would probably have assumed it to be that of one of the Italian family who ran the ice-cream shop up in Whithorn. But Aristophanes and Winkie had this much in common: they were full of fun but they were also winners, and woe betide anyone who stood in their way.

The highlight of the Garlieston Primary School sports day was undoubtedly the three-legged race (boys aged eight and under). Much fancied for the event during that fateful summer of 1938 were Andy Turner and myself. It was not that either of us, individually, was all that much faster than our peers in a straight race, although it was certainly true that each of us had that slender physique that gave athletes such as

Jesse Owens and Harold Abrahams the edge over bulkier opponents when the chips were down. It would also not be wandering into the realms of braggadocio to say that each of us, given the proper motivation, was capable of a fair turn of speed, usually when being pursued for some misdemeanour or other by adults armed with staves. But even top sprinters are not necessarily good three-legged racers. This fact has been proven time and again. There is a knack about this noble sport that is gifted only to God's chosen few. In a three-legged race it is absolutely vital that there should be a telepathic understanding between the partners, a complete gelling of minds and limbs from the moment that the handkerchief binds your right ankle to his left one and you take your place among the other competitors at the starting line. One false step, one leg movement that is not synchronous with his, and the race is over before it has properly started.

My partner and I had this absolute coordination of mind and movement and we had proved it time and again in practice. Had our rather severe headmistress Jenny Whiteright been the sort to enjoy a flutter now and then and had she allowed the tote to set up shop at the edge of our sports field, the gambling moguls of Newton Stewart and Stranraer would have had to close the book on us at a very early stage of the proceedings. At this event and in our age class, my partner and I were quite simply, The Greatest.

Our status as odds-on favourites was rapidly justified. With ten yards to go we were flying, out in front of the pack and with the others gasping in our slipstream. It was at this point that we committed that fatal error so common among even top practitioners in athletics today: we succumbed to arrogant over-confidence. In other words, we eased up before we hit the tape. And it was at this point that we fell victim to what would forever afterwards be known in Galloway school sports circles as the Aristophanes Effect.

It rankles with me even to this day. Our shackled ankles were hooked from behind with an expertise that would have done justice to a professional all-in wrestler. Our world became an instant blur of whirling limbs and startled yelps as my partner and I executed simultaneous but quite uncoordinated double somersaults, to land in an inextricable macedoine of arms and legs that would not have looked out of place in the pages of the *Kama Sutra*.

Several yards beyond where we lay enmeshed and stunned on the hallowed turf of the Garlieston football field, Wee Winkie and his partner hit the tape in triumph, and I had learned a valuable lesson about the depths to which my fellow human beings were prepared to stoop in order to win a coloured celluloid windmill attached to 12 inches of bamboo stick marked 'Made in Germany'.

Winkie and I became great friends in later life and, to be fair to him, it has to be conceded that the delightful sense of mischief that he never lost from the day he was born to the day that he died was at least as much a part of his character as the winning wiles of his childhood. But my experience back then in the three-legged race was not, sadly, an isolated case. Similarly dark deeds were being perpetrated in the name of sport at schools all over Galloway. In order to secure the best possible advantage for their progeny in forthcoming egg and spoon races, I have seen decent, God-fearing mothers do things on behalf of their children that would have had Robert Maxwell stirring uneasily in his grave, had that old rascal been dead and buried at that time. It was on such a day at a village in the heart of Galloway that a sack liberally sprinkled with itching powder was issued to the betting favourite in the girls under-12 sack race. Long before she had reached the halfway mark she had left the others to fight it out among themselves as she undertook a series of simian-like full veronicas all over the park, frantically endeavouring to shuck the sacking from her tortured loins, heedless of the fact that her fellow competitors had finished the race and were now huddled together gazing at her gyrations in awe and some considerable alarm.

But fortunately such heinous activities appeared, in most cases, to be but a passing phase. By the time the little minors had become majors in village society and, as a consequence, parental influence over them had begun to wane, the inherent sporting decency of the Gallovidian youngster took control. Sport became sport, and summer athletics were a much anticipated time of the year all over rural Galloway.

Most towns and villages had their own special carnival week, the highlight being the culminating sports day. Among the oldest of these were the Glenluce and Port William sports. The latter were held on the football field high above the town, while the former were held on a flat and (often) boggy piece of ground surrounded by trees alongside the burn. On cloudy days the Glenluce midges were simply voracious. I remember on one occasion playing for a Dunragit forestry team in the final of the five-a-side tournament there and the midges hung as thick as locusts over the field. Clad only in football shirts and shorts and stockings, we were practically eaten alive. But at least we were only on the field for the 15 minutes it took us to complete the game; God knows how the pipers managed out there in their kilts playing for the Highland dancers for the bulk of the afternoon. My brother used to maintain that he had never seen a sober piper in his life, so perhaps therein lies the answer: maybe the midge-repelling properties of Bladnoch's famous malt whisky have never received the credit they deserve.

Each part of Galloway had its own particular hero or heroes on the athletics field. Louis Donaldson from 'The Isle' was one, and as he was the fortunate possessor of those swashbuckling, piratical features guaranteed to make the hearts of the young and the should-have-mair-sense ages flutter like bats coming home to roost in a Sussex belfry, numbers of female spectators increased quite dramatically wherever this talented athlete happened to be performing.

My own two heroes were the brothers Tam and Billy Kelly. They hailed from Macharstewart, a farm out in the middle of the Indian Territories somewhere between Sorbie and 'The Whaup'. Tam was the good-looker. He had the physique of a Sean Connery, the stamina of an Alpine ox, and the lungs of a Sherpa. He would have run non-stop from Wigtown to Dumfries had the occasion demanded. But for sheer unbridled excitement, none could match the blistering pace of Billy when he was haring up the home straight in his chosen race.

Billy was quite unlike Tam in every respect. He was built like a greyhound, and indeed his nostrils seemed to quiver like those of Mick the Miller as he waited for the trap to be sprung at the start of a race. His specialities were the mile and the half-mile and, in my era, he was supreme at both these events. I do not recall ever having seen him beaten, despite the often outrageous handicaps to which he would be subjected in races when his fame began to spread around Galloway and beyond.

Sports days were always fun, no matter where they were held. Often, the smaller the village the more fun they were. One of my more abiding memories is of a tiny place in the Galloway hinterland. I had been enjoying a leisurely drive through the moors and had stopped for a chat with Aul' Sanny, the local blacksmith, whom I had not seen for a number of years. The smiddy was closed and the whole village seemed to be closed, too, for the single street was devoid of any sign of human life. A notice on the smiddy door stated briefly: 'Gone to sports'. Eventually and with some difficulty, I located the sports field, an uneven piece of pastureland about a mile up a rough and winding track from the village. In contrast to the village, I found the field to be a seething mass of humanity. It was, indeed, the annual sports day.

I wandered round the field until I tracked down my quarry. Aul' Sanny was a lanky, wizened leprechaun of a man in his late-70s, as bright-eyed as a jackdaw and as lively as a sparrow. He was even livelier today, for it was his birthday and he had been celebrating right gloriously since early morning. He stood before me now, guzzling from a half-bottle of whisky.

An important looking fellow with a megaphone marched past, bellowing something into it. Aul' Sanny handed me his bottle. 'Haud that for a meenit, Donal',' he beseeched me, 'while I get ready for this race.'

'Race?'

'Aye,' he said, 'The aul' men's race. Every year for the past ten years I've run in it, an' every year I've won it. This year the prize is up fae ten bob tae twal' shullin's an' sixpence, so I've been in trainin'.'

I eyed what was left of the whisky. 'Aye, Sanny,' I said, 'I can see that.'

Sanny untied the laces of his hobnailed boots. He took them off, then he stuck his half-bottle into one of them. He removed his false teeth and secreted them in the toe of the other boot. 'Watch that nae bugger snaffles them or the whusky, Donal',' he cautioned. 'Ye cannae trust naebuddy these days.' He then divested himself of his jacket, his waistcoat, his shirt and his moleskin trousers in that order and laid them on top of his boots. We who had been standing around him edged away hastily. His semmit was a grimy smiddy-grey in colour and it was as full of holes as a colander. His long johns were positively revolting. They were of a sort of awful ochre scumble, except around the seat where the ochre darkened dramatically into a sinister shade akin to molasses. They had obviously seen neither soap and water nor the light of day in a long time, and they stank of stale urine, horse-hoof scrapings, and other things far too disgusting to mention to my intended audience.

'You're surely not proposing to run like that?' I exclaimed, shocked. But Aul' Sanny was not listening. He was already striding determinedly to the starting line.

It was no contest. Aul' Sanny had been a good sprinter in his youth and a lifetime at the forge had kept him in good shape despite his addiction to John Barleycorn. He streaked up the field like an elderly cheetah, his wedding tackle walloping about outside the aperture at the front of his long johns, and he hit the tape several lengths ahead of his nearest rival. It was obvious to all who witnessed the event that Aul' Sanny was – to employ a modern euphemism – particularly well-endowed, and it is said that for weeks afterwards not a word of sense could be got out of any of the village maidens, for they were all walking about in a dwalm with glazed eyes and wistful little smiles on their faces. Even a lot of the married women got crotchety all of a sudden with their menfolk for no apparent reason...

One always expected the unexpected in village sports, and that, to a great extent, was their attraction. Even in village sports there had to be some degree of organisation involved in the scheduling of events and so on, but there was never any sense of the tight scheduling that was necessary at the bigger events in the main towns. Everything was so much more casual, and there was no chance of bureaucratic intrusion into one's anticipation of the unexpected. In village sports there was the additional advantage that everyone knew everybody, including all those who were out in the arena making dam' fools of themselves. It was a day of fun and laughter for spectators and competitors alike.

Sports days are still very much a part of the Galloway I knew in my youth, I am glad to say, and in no place is the excitement and the fun and the laughter generated by those events more in evidence than at the village of Parton in Kirkcudbright.

It was while he was rummaging through a collection of old farmyard implements for scrap metal in the late 1970s that Mungo Bryson of Parton came across an old rusted 'gird 'n cleek'. Childhood memories came flooding back to him of those innocent days long before 'the telly', when the greatest pleasure in life for a child was to run barefoot with his 'gird'. The gird was an iron hoop about three feet in diameter, and the driving and guiding instrument, the 'cleek', was an iron hook on the end of a long handle. Children took their own girds to school each day and parked them alongside the school railings just as today's generation park their bicycles. In the first half of the 20th century the passion to own one's own gird 'n cleek was as strong as the desire is today to have one's own mountain bike. It cost a bit less than the mountain bike, too.

With the vague idea of trying to see if those childhood days could be brought back, Mungo Bryson cleaned up his find and persuaded the local blacksmith, Joe Corrie, to produce a few more sets. When these were given an airing in Parton the event created much excitement among the youngsters, who had never seen their likes before. The enterprising Mungo spotted the potential and soon the girds were joined by other – virtually forgotten – games and pastimes from long ago. In no time at all there was an informal gathering of villagers and friends in a field by the shores of Loch Ken to try out their skills. Parton's unique 'Alternative Games Day' was born.

And 'The Parton Games', as they are now more commonly

called, are certainly unique. Here is where they hold the Gird 'n Cleek World Championships, and here is where they feature such other eye-openers as 'spinnin' the peerie', 'tossin' the sheaf' and 'hurlin' the curlin' stane'. Snail racing is popular with the gambling element, with the shell of each little chap painted in its owner's colours. There are many other old favourites, too, including the slow bike race and Balmaclellan skittles. But my all-time favourite has just got to be 'flingin' the herd's bunnet'.

I have never flung a herd's bunnet in my life, nor do I ever expect to. But it sounds just the right sport for me. The name has such a leisurely ring to it. This must surely be a sport that requires no more mental or physical effort than a fluid arm action and an idea of how to make the best use of whatever prevailing winds there are. A dextrous flick of the wrist and, given the right conditions, your herd's bunnet could be floating down the middle of Loch Ken in no more time than it takes to write this, with the herd to whom it belonged trying in vain to persuade his dog to swim out and retrieve it. It would, I imagine, be a deeply satisfying experience.

The day will come – but not too soon, one hopes – when I shall have to depart this mortal coil. When I do, I could wish for nothing better than to be allowed through the pearly gates on the day on which they are having their annual sports on the heavenly pastures. Should I be so lucky, I am sure that I shall find that the entire proceedings will be a carbon copy of Parton's marvellous alternative games. In the promised land, one should expect to find such gentle pleasures, presided over, no doubt, by Himself with the long white beard, while the Virgin Mary presents the myrrh and the frankincense to the lucky winners.

But there is one thing I can tell you here and now: if I find that the winner at flingin' the heavenly herd's bunnet is Wee Winkie, it's myself that will be checking the skip of the cap to ensure that it has not been loaded with lead shot for maximum velocity.

There are some of us who just can't help it, Virgin Mary or no Virgin Mary.

Chapter 16
FOOTBALL CRAZY

'He's fitba' crazy,
He's gone clean mad,
The fitba' game has robbed him o'
The wee bit sense he had...'

This may be the era of multiple-choice entertainment, but the word 'bored' is one that is heard with ever-increasing frequency from the lips of our progeny, from the tiniest of infants to the largest and most truculent of teenagers. Despite the fact that the apparently bottomless pockets of indulgent parents seem able to bring evermore sophisticated – and therefore evermore expensive – toys and computer games into receptive young hands on demand, and the pleasures of Bacchus become more and more freely available at an earlier and earlier age, it is all to no avail. Ennui spreads like a creeping paralysis throughout the youth of this once vibrant land. 'I am bored!' is the mournful ululation that echoes from coast to coast, and by Jove the poor little things certainly manage to look the part for much of the time.

It was not always thus. Certainly not in Wigtownshire. In the Wigtownshire of half a century ago, no one had time to be bored. For children as well as for adults, there was always plenty to do. This was particularly so in rural areas, away from the comparative civilisation of the 'big' towns such as Newton Stewart and Stranraer. The child who was so indiscreet as to voice aloud in the presence of adults his discontent at a life that placed so much free time upon him, just had to be either masochistic or mentally deficient. The television could not be switched on to give harassed parents respite from this grizzling, for the simple reason that this was well before the era of television in the county. So work of a (usually) unpleasant nature would instantly be found for the complainant, regardless of age. There was never any shortage of things to do around the home, because this was also – for many country homes – pre-electricity and pre-running-water days. Paraffin had to be collected from the village store (often several miles away), lamps had to be filled, water had to be carried from the well or the outdoor pump, firewood had to be sawn into blocks and then chopped up to keep the home fires burning, and, from a very early age, girls had to learn to help with the baking, the cooking, the ironing and washing of clothes and the day-to-day cleaning requirements of the house. And so on, virtually ad infinitum.

Offspring reared in homes blessed with an outdoor privy had to be particularly circumspect about their complaining: incurring the wrath of parents in those homes could quite easily result not only in the usual good beating but – far, far worse – being condemned for the foreseeable future to the task of carrying ordure for disposal from the lavatory, a threat guaranteed to instil obedience even in the wildest of wild spirits. A chance meeting with one's friends while hurrying to some secret disposal destination with a couple of buckets full to the brim with toilet ejectamentae just did not bear thinking about.

Although we children did not appreciate it at the time, being fully and constructively occupied was no bad thing. It was a necessary grounding for the hardness of the workaday adult life that was to follow. Keeping oneself occupied was especially essential during the winter months. In the summer one could get out of the house, but the winter was a long and dreary affair and children were confined indoors for most of it.

There was not a lot of incentive for adults to go out at this time of the year, either, after the long day's toil was over, for the Wigtownshire winter climate could never be confused with that of Ibiza. The former tends to lean rather more towards precipitation than the latter, and no amount of candyfloss from the Scottish Tourist Board can camouflage that fact. A weekly visit to the pub for a pint and a game of darts was about the optimum in social activity for most men, and even then it often meant cycling two or three miles over exposed moorland tracks in driving sleet and rain to their adopted hostelries, clad in the quite inadequate raingear of the day.

For the more active teenagers, there were the weekly village youth club sessions, and these could be well patronised or not, depending mainly on the popularity, charisma and inventiveness of the person or persons running them, while the women had what the men often unkindly referred to as 'the bliddy Rural'. The Women's Rural Institute was probably what kept a lot of country women sane, for theirs was the toughest job of all. Looking after the home in those days was a full-time occupation, and this weekly escape must have been a much-looked-forward-to event for them. Part of the attraction was undoubtedly the fact that the in-fighting at some of the 'bliddy Rurals' could be as intense and as bitter (and, therefore, as entertaining) as at any political gathering at Westminster. Committee elections were often savagely contested, and those who won competitions such as 'Best Knitted Socks' and 'Best Clootie Dumpling' could be sure that, while they might secretly bask for a long time in the glow that would result from the accolades to their triumphs in the 'WRI Activities' columns of the *Galloway Gazette*, somewhere out there in the sticks the inevitable javelins would be getting sharpened, and, just as inevitably, out of the darkness they would come whistling towards the hapless victims. And they would continue to do so for quite some time after that issue of the newspaper had ceased to be of interest to anyone but the lucky winners.

Winter just had to be tholed. Wigtown Man was a phlegmatic man. He just stuck it out and waited. Winter was simply a transitory period between better times, and with the passing of the months the better times got nearer and the anticipation of them mounted visibly. Particularly so with the male of the species. Under the dark, wet pall that hung over the land during much of the winter, Wigtown Man would – like the hibernating bear of Canada's north-west – be seen out and about only when absolutely necessary. But, with the approach of spring one could almost feel the stirring of new life in the atmosphere. And this stirring had less to do with the burgeoning buds and the blossoming of the daffodils and of young love than with a sport that was participated in with the utmost enthusiasm by the young and the not-so-young, by the competent and the incompetent, and even by those whose normal idea of exercise was lifting a pint jug from bar top to mouth.

The 'simmer fitba' was about to begin.

Winter football did exist in Wigtownshire, but it never commanded anything like the same level of excitement generated by the summer variety in those bygone years. The weather was just too foul, particularly for the spectators. A few hardy souls, fortified by their favourite anti-freeze in the nearest pub before the game, would turn out to cheer on their local heroes, but games would rarely be anything other than sparsely attended. In addition, while the summer season would see every available football field swarming with youths clogging a ball around, winter football was regarded by most as being strictly for the elite few. The half-dozen or so teams that took part each year in the 'Winter League' had their own small and exclusive coterie of players whose experience and expertise allowed no place at all for the inchoate enthusiast of the summer months. And, to be honest, few summer footballers had much hankering to be part of the winter scene. Like the swallows, they had their season, and when that season was over they slipped quietly back to the anonymity from whence they had issued forth a few short months before.

Winter football may have been for the elite and summer football for the masses, but there was a joyous abandon about the latter that was totally absent from winter football. The weather may have had a lot to do with it, of course; it took a very special sort of person to gain much pleasure out of running about on sodden pitches in mid-February while the wind was blowing sleet over the land in sheets, and it took an even more special type of person to stand on a bitter-cold sideline for 90 minutes watching the spectacle.

But with the spring came sunshine, fitful though it could be at times. Suddenly, it seemed as though every spare strip of pasture in the ancient county, from Drummore in the west to Garlieston in the east and from Newton Stewart in the north to Whithorn in the south, echoed to the healthy clatter of steel-shod boots interspersed with much strong language and occasional roars of agony, as burly sons of the soil locked horns in near-mortal combat. This was the start of the summer football season, and it also signalled the rebirth of what was euphemistically referred to as the 'Practice Match'.

For the Practice Match, there were two near essentials – a pair of learigs and the mindless courage of a Gurkha.

Perhaps, for the uninitiated, the learig should be explained. This was a boot commonly worn by the ploughmen of that era. But this was no ordinary boot. This boot was not made; it was constructed, and probably by the same shipwrights who built the all-iron dreadnoughts of old. With its epidermis of stiff, thick leather (stripped – one was tempted to conjecture – straight from the bodies of embittered old bulls and hammered into rough shape by some foundryman's apprentice), a foundation bristling with studs, and a sharp wrought-iron prow pointing upward at a 45 degree angle to the rest of the boot, the learig was a most formidable and fearsome piece of equipment. A man going berserk while wearing a pair of those would have cleared the toughest pub in Glasgow in ten seconds flat. Had the learig been available to the Bonnie Prince and his clansmen on their long march south of Hadrian's Wall, it is almost certain that Gaelic would be the language spoken in London's fair city to this day. The Practice Match aficionado felt positively naked without this armament, and the air fairly crackled with sparks when he sailed into action with them and steel clashed with steel on the field of battle.

These matches were not for the purist. For a start, it was rare indeed for teams to consist of the standard eleven players. Everyone turning up was expected to take part. As the days lengthened hay and harvest necessities would take their due toll, so you could have a low, of say, four-a-side when times were really busy, to a general melee involving anything up to 40 warriors during slack periods.

Two strong men of more or less equal ability selected their sides on an 'eeksy-peeksy' basis, the toss of a coin deciding who should have the first – and often vital – choice. Stamina, strength, and freedom from any visible contagious diseases were the main criteria in selection. Where there was an uneven number to choose from, the one left at the end – the one whom no one wanted – would find himself appointed referee, whether he liked it or not. If numbers were even, and thus there was no one left over to take on the whistler's task, 'refereeing' would become the responsibility of the two captains, each taking care of the application of the laws of the game (as interpreted by him) in 'his' half of the field. Every endeavour would be made to avoid this situation; sheer anarchy would inevitably result and bitter would be the recriminations between hitherto close friends for weeks afterwards.

About the only foul not tolerated was the handball. Just about everything else was considered legal. I still retain a vivid memory of a time when, at the tender age of 15, I found myself dragooned into taking part in one of those matches. Our team captain had instructed me to closely mark the very much older and extremely tricky opposing winger. I was not making too good a job of it, and finally I was exhorted by the exasperated captain: 'Never mind the bliddy ba', Donal'. Jeest kick that bugger up in the air. An' whun he comes doon, kick him up again. An' keep kickin' him until the bugger stops movin'.' It was a piece of advice that stood me in good stead in many a Practice Match thereafter.

As the offside rule was never applied in those Practice Matches, goal scoring could be prolific. Poachers abounded in goal areas, the sturdiest and best shod hanging around the opposing keeper like carrion crows. Only the brave and the very foolish dared venture into this hell's kitchen.

These matches had no time limit and could often last until it was so dark that players at one end of the field could see only the fleeting silhouettes of those at the far end. (I remember one match ending 26 goals to 25, the deciding goal being scored as a sickle moon was rising over the bay beyond.) As there was, of course, no such thing as football strips and each player wore his daily working togs with nothing to distinguish him from his opponent, conditions for the unwary became distinctly hazardous as the shades of night began to settle over the field. A 15-stone belligerent thundering down on you out of the gloom had all the lethal potential of a runaway rhinoceros. It says much for the hardiness of the countrymen of that era that bad injuries were so few and far between.

It was rumoured that a cricketing visitor from the Home Counties of England happened upon a Practice Match one glorious summer evening while he was out walking his dog. Being a newcomer to the area and therefore quite unaware of his potential peril, he stood at the edge of the field to watch. It is possible that his survival instincts were somewhat impaired by his astonishment at what he was witnessing, for he stood rooted to the spot when the action surged in his direction. In a trice, he found himself an unwitting and terror-stricken participant in his first-ever Practice Match for what would turn out to be the longest 20 seconds of his life. Unscrambling himself frantically, miraculously unscathed, from the whirling tangle of bodies, he sheltered behind a tree for the remainder of the game, his dog shivering at his feet. No doubt he would have returned to his gentler playing fields south of the Border, much the wiser for his experience and with many a tale to tell over his 'G and T' in his club.

A much more civilised variant of the Practice Match was the 'Jumble Fives'. So far as I can gather, this would appear to have been the invention of the Cloys, a remarkable family of brothers who worked on the farm of Millisle, near Garlieston. Five in number, the Cloy brothers were all good players themselves. They were also good organisers. They brought order to the Practice Match mentality in their little neck of the woods. They persuaded the farmer to let them have periodic use of a level strip of pasture land between the Garlieston to Sorbie road and the Millisle burn. It was an ideal setting for what was to follow. Those wishing to take part in the Jumble Fives paid a gate fee (I forget what this was – probably about sixpence) to be allowed to take part. Names of intending participants were taken as soon as they paid the fee, and all names were drawn from a hat at a specified time. The first five names drawn would play the next five, and so on, in a knock-out competition, the gate receipts being shared by the finalists at the end of the evening's play. Contestants came from far and wide to take part, and these ranged from callow youths with little or no knowledge of the game to experienced players from the winter league fraternity looking for a bit of a laugh and the possibility of some beer money. Good players therefore mingled with the learig brigade, for in the Jumble Fives it lay with the luck of the draw as to whom you might find yourself playing alongside. It was great fun, and, as the Cloys saw to it that the games were properly refereed by old players who knew what they were doing, the risk of injury was kept to an acceptable minimum.

The burn could be a bit of a snag, particularly if it was in spate. On one or two occasions the ball, travelling at a fair rate of knots down the centre of it and followed along the bank by half a hundred luridly cursing footballers, had bobbed well on its way to the Solway Firth before it could be fished out. Once, too, in the field across the other side of the burn a cantankerous old bull took temporary charge of the ball before someone with a sheepdog managed to retrieve it.

The Jumble Fives ended as suddenly as they had begun. I do not know to this day the cause of their demise, but I suspect it may have been because the indefatigable Cloys left the area and there was simply no one else left with the same interest in organising them. But whatever it was, I never pass that strip of pasture in bus or car today without looking out of the window and remembering…

But the pièce de résistance at this time of the year was the summer league. This was what everyone had been waiting for. All the other events were mere sideshows. All over Galloway, from Stranraer to Dumfries, one would find a league of some sort operating through the summer months. This was the time of the year when the villages of Galloway came into their own. The winter league was mainly for the town teams such as Annan, Kirkcudbright (St Cuthbert Wanderers), Newton Stewart, Dalbeattie and Stranraer. But the summer football was for the wee places, and how they revelled in it! Nearly every village, no matter how small, had its own team, and local support for those teams was of the highest order. Dances would be held in village halls to subsidise the teams, and those halls would be packed to capacity, while the village shopkeepers, small business people and the surrounding farmers would be unstinting in their generosity.

The matches themselves were most keenly contested, often on

pitches that would have given the eminent gentlemen of FIFA haemorrhoids. Playing surfaces varied considerably, but of one thing you could be very sure – each one had its own idiosyncrasy. Fields on coastal fringes were occasionally so boggy as to have large patches of rush grass growing on them, and even – so help me – marsh marigolds. Up in the moorland villages around New Galloway, peat was the common factor. Footballers playing on those surfaces invariably ended their games looking dead ringers for Kentucky Minstrels, plastered as they were from head to foot with black mud. Spring tides played periodic havoc with the Garlieston pitch, though in fairness it has to be said that many who played on it reckoned that the soft, springy carpet of sea grass with which it was covered made it the easiest surface in all of Wigtownshire on which to play.

At Glenluce, the pitch had what looked at a casual glance to be a one-in-three gradient, the slope running north to south from the main Stranraer road to the edge of the Ladyburn Glen at the bottom. To float a ball into the goalmouth at the bottom end required but the gentlest of punts from the goalkeeper at the top end, such was the steepness of the pitch. Conversely, playing up the hill in the teeth of a northerly wind meant the employment of strictly defensive tactics, as hopes of getting the ball anywhere near the opposing penalty area were virtually zero.

Over at Port William the pitch was excellent and level. It was also on the summit of a veritable mountain. One had to be fit to negotiate that precipitous ascent to the top and still endeavour to kick a ball around for 90 minutes on the plateau. In addition, what might have been a gentle breeze at the bottom of the hill would often turn out, 'way up there, to be a howling gale roaring in over the deep from Newfoundland.

They bred them tough as whalers in that outport.

A surface much favoured by defensive Goliaths was one on which cattle had been grazing immediately prior to the match. The end product of the domestic cow gave terrific impetus to those wonderful, long sliding tackles so much in vogue then. As players were quite often responsible for ensuring that their own football gear was washed after games, bitter must have been the thoughts of many a hard-pressed wife and mother as she scrubbed this green, stinking gunge from the clobber in the kitchen sink o'nights.

Deep pools of water in which the ball floated like a cork when it landed; great, flat slabs of best Creetown granite on the surface where the thin layer of turf had eroded away through constant foot traffic; crops of hay growing six inches high over the playing surfaces – I've seen them all on Galloway pitches. But somehow, the imperfections merely added to the fun that both players and spectators always got from those summertime football matches. And usually, it was all for free.

As might be expected, there were characters a-plenty in most of those village teams and stories about them abounded. A village policeman stationed over Kirkcudbright way who had no mean opinion of his own abilities (he had, so popular rumour would have it, been a trialist for either Heart of Midlothian or Hibernian before his move to Galloway) found himself playing at centre-half on a very muddy pitch in opposition to a very chatty centre-forward from a visiting Wigtownshire team in a friendly match. The lawman was having a singularly unproductive evening; his opponent running rings around him. The greasy pitch did not help his defensive skills, either, and he found himself more often flat on his back on the ground than in a vertical position. It did not help matters one little bit that his loquacious opponent lost no opportunity in telling him where he had gone wrong after each failed tackle. Towards the end the policeman was reduced to undignified – and equally unsuccessful – attempts to put his bête noire out of action with vicious swings that would have earned him an instant red card in our present, more enlightened times. Probably the brawl that followed his last scything tackle simply resulted from sheer frustration as his opponent skipped lightly over his flailing legs yet again. Or perhaps not. Maybe it had something to do with his opponent's words of consolation as the latter helped him up out of the mud with a friendly little pat on the head: 'Never mind, son, I'm sure you must be a better polisman than you are a fitba' player...'

One real character from those summer league days was Jimmy

Robb, now alas, no longer with us. Jimmy was short but tough, and he was a very nippy and effective forward. His was the most engaging of personalities, but he brooked no nonsense from anyone, especially on the football field. During one memorable game he was opposed by a player from a visiting team, yet another player whose undoubted footballing skills were only equalled by his extremely high regard for himself. Like Jimmy, this player had rather a short fuse, and a great deal of niggling took place between the two of them whenever their flight paths crossed during the course of the game. The inevitable explosion came late in the match when Jimmy's opponent took the feet from him as he was on the verge of scoring. Jimmy picked himself up and dropped his assailant with as neat a left hook as you are ever likely to see. Let me tell it now in Jimmy's own words, as he was to tell it many times in many pubs for many years after it had happened:

'Ah hut him, so ah did, an' he went doon, so he did, an' he got up, so he did, an' ah hut him again, so ah did, an' he went doon again, so he did, an' he got up again, so he did, an' ah hut him again, so ah did, an' he went doon again, so he did…'

The more Jimmy had to drink when he was telling the story, the more blows his opponent received on that fateful evening. By closing time on a good night the poor fellow would have been up and down like a yo-yo, and it seemed to most of us in the admiring audience that much of the game's scheduled 90 minutes must have been taken up by his unfortunate opponent being 'hut' by Jimmy and going 'doon' then – rather foolishly, to our minds – getting up again for more of the same medicine.

*   *   *

On my last visit to Wigtownshire I passed by one or two of those old footballing haunts. I did not do so out of sentiment or with any intention of seeing what changes had taken place, or whether I could recognise anything from my past around them. One of the benefits of being a 'senior citizen' is that one has long since learned that things change and that memories are best kept as memories, for reality invariably disappoints. As Wigtownshire's own John McNeillie wrote in one of his books under the pseudonym 'Ian Niall':

'When you go over that hill for the last time, never look back. And take your shadow with you.'

Well, here I was back, shadow and all, and I saw nothing in my travels that might have caused me to alter my convictions or my opinion that there was truth in Ian Niall's rather gloomy cautionary words. As I passed along the Sorbie road I noticed a herd of cows grazing placidly where once the learigs had clattered in the still summer air around Millisle. There was nothing at all to remind me that a football pitch had ever existed there. The whole of that period might only have been a fantasy born in an ageing memory. Even the burn looked placid, barely capable of carrying a stray football anywhere.

At Garlieston one of the ugliest sewage plants I had ever seen in my life occupied the site of the old football field, a field that had once been home to a team that had even won the summer league during one memorable year, a team superbly marshalled by the rock-firm defensive talents of big Jock Thomson and Davie McKeand, a team whose forward line had been graced by the silken skills of the effervescent 'Beeman', Hughie Howatson.

Progress is necessary to survival in this day and age, and we tumble over each other in our eagerness to prove just how progressive we are as we hurtle into the millennium. Human waste has to go somewhere, and the day of the privy and the bucket has long gone, thank God.

But surely a sewage plant is rather a sad memorial to a summer league so fondly remembered by we old-timers who had watched its hugely entertaining games from the sidelines, who had played in them, and who had lived through that era and derived so much clean and innocent pleasure from it all?

Mother, hand me my learigs. I have some unfinished business with this progressive society.

Chapter 17
THE LUM CAT

The bay shimmered in the evening sun. (Which was, at that time of year, an event worthy of a paragraph or two in the *Galloway Gazette*, if not the *Guinness Book of Records*.) The broad expanse of water that stretched from Burrow Head to the Mull of Galloway was a pellucid blue-green mantle of molten glass, casting images of such startling clarity that the Mochrum scart, swift-winging its way low over the bay, nearly had a heart attack when it glanced down and saw itself reflected – for probably the first time in its life – on the surface of the water.

Across the bay to the west a long thin streak of pastel shades ran from north to south along the horizon, neatly separating the blue lucidity of sea and sky with its irregular patchwork of faded dun and celadon and greige hues. This was that narrow promontory of Wigtownshire known as the Rhinns, for once in a while free from the gales that blasted across it from the grey Atlantic for far too much of the year. At the extremity of this strip of land, on what is the most southerly point in all of Scotland, the Mull lighthouse stood proud and clear against a cloudless, azure sky.

On the Machars side of the bay, conditions were no less agreeable. All over the fells the dead, brown cover of last year's crop of bracken was being replaced with quite dramatic suddenness by a delicate wash of lime-green from the upsurge of the new growth, and even the loden hues of the miserable strips of plantings that were ranged in military formation around the farms facing the sea seemed to have taken on a new sparkle. So, too, had the cottage. Tucked snugly in at the foot of the hill, the wee house with its newly whitewashed walls glittered and danced in a heat wave more in keeping with the Costa del Sol than the Machars of Wigtownshire.

The long, dreich winter was over at last and the cottage had been on the receiving end of a thorough spring-cleaning. Anyone requiring further evidence of this could have satisfied curiosity by walking in through the open back door. Brand-new wallpaper of a sort of hibiscus pattern adorned the living room walls, linoleum of a rather bilious pea-green hue concealed, for the present at least, the joints between the stone flags of the floor, and sheets of aquamarine oilcloth covered the kitchen and living-room tables. Doors whose dreary brown scumble had hitherto merely served to complement the general dinginess of their surroundings, now positively glowed with their bottle-green coating of Carson's Enamel Paint, courtesy of Cousin Dougie, the boatman down in the Isle. Curtains of a delicate white lace, the result of a recent shopping trip to Stranraer, hung limply from the front windows. The atmosphere, inside and out, was saturated with a penetrating mixture of whitewash, black-lead, Brasso and paint odours.

Around the cool tranquillity of the hearth the family were dispersed, tired but satisfied with their efforts. Sprawled in his armchair, like a beast washed up from the deep, lay the Head of the House, the newspaper over his face fluffling up and down in time to his snores. The Old Woman knitted a hairy sock in the chair opposite, while the Bairns on the floor were peacefully engrossed in a game of snakes and ladders.

On the hearth in front of them lay Cat. A white, grotesquely fat creature of uncertain antiquity, Cat had drifted in from the cold a dozen or so years ago looking for lodgings and, taking an immediate fancy to what he saw, had stayed on, doing nothing at all over the years to earn his keep. He was probably the least inquisitive, and certainly the laziest, cat in existence. The mouse and vole population in the area could wax and wane as it liked and Atlantic storms flay the house until it shook, but Cat cared naught for what went on in the outside world. He ventured outside the door of his adopted home only when forced to by the call of nature, and his only real interests in life were eating and sleeping.

Cat slept now…

*   *   *

There was a lilt to his step and a song on his lips as Boy wended his way home over the moor. The fishing had been good, the lark trilled his endless paean of joy in the clear blue yonder, and already the little heart's-ease was sprinkling the land with her delicate blue-white-and-gold mosaic. The unforgettable fragrance of bog-myrtle hung heavy in the air and Boy was at peace with the world. Besides, he was reflecting, the Old Woman's annual madness of spring-cleaning (he had exorcised himself from the house the moment the subject had been brought up) should, with any luck at all, be over and done with by now.

Past experience, nevertheless, had taught him never to take anything for granted, so it was with the caution of a seasoned shirker that he approached the cottage. He offloaded his fishing gear in the garden shed, removed his heavy sea boots quietly at the back door of the house, and padded noiselessly through the kitchen in his stocking-soles to reconnoitre.

His optimism was justified. The tableau of domestic harmony in the living room would have gladdened the heart of a Wee Free minister. Silent as a ghost, he edged his way back into the kitchen.

It is probable that an older and wiser youth would have left well alone. To a stripling of some 13 mischievous summers, however, this was an opportunity of a lifetime. Not a soul had witnessed his arrival and he now looked around him for a means of announcing it in style. His roving eye settled on the kitchen table. There lay the answer to every playful boy's prayers – a large shopping bag made of heavy-duty brown paper. He did not hesitate. Picking it up, he went out into the garden. It took, I suppose, less time than it takes to write this to blow it up to its fullest capacity, and probably not much more time to tiptoe back inside and raise it high over his head. An instant later it crashed down on the kitchen table with the full force of his wiry young arms.

The resultant explosion seemed to rock the little cottage to its very foundations and the racket reverberated around the four walls like a clap of thunder.

Individual reactions to unexpected detonations within the confines of small farm cottages tend to vary somewhat, dependant on the relative fragility of the individual nervous systems involved. But one thing is guaranteed: the reaction is always instantaneous, and such was the case here. The Old Woman dropped her knitting with a startled squawk. The Bairns shrieked in mezzosoprano unison. The Old Man sprang sharply upright, newspaper flying, eyes staring wildly, his mouth opening and closing wordlessly like a spent kelt.

Cat shot up the lum.

What might be termed a pregnant silence followed. It was a silence broken only by a certain amount of heavy breathing on the part of the Old Man, and frantic scrabbling sounds from the dark recesses of the chimney as Cat endeavoured to secure a more comfortable roosting spot on the narrow ledge high within. That he was not being entirely successful in his efforts was apparent from the ominous wafts of soot that began to drift down on the hearth, and from his plainly audible gurrs of discontent.

Perhaps predictably, the first move of any practical significance came from the Old Man. 'We'd better be getting that dam't cat out of there before it brings down more soot,' he growled worriedly. Getting down on his hands and knees on the hearth, he peered up into the inky darkness. An instant later he recoiled with a ferocious Galloway oath as a tarry cloud enveloped him, lending more than a hint of the Kentucky minstrel to his distillery features and Viking moustache.

For the next half-hour, the position could best be described as stalemate. Neither vicious threats nor the considerable blandishments of the whole family could budge Cat from his firm conviction that, dark and drear though his immediate future might seem at this moment, it sure beat to a frazzle returning to a world full of maniacs armed to the teeth with hand grenades. Even a saucerful of milk placed on the hearth below him failed to elicit any better response than another shower of soot and a high-pitched whining snarl.

By this time, the Old Man had had enough. 'There's only one way to get the bastard down out of there – bring the chimney-cleaning things out of the shed,' he ordered. 'And for God's sake hurry!' he roared, as more of the black stuff billowed down.

Cleaning the large, airy chimneys of those days was a technically simple but physically trying process. First, the fireplace aperture had to be covered with a sack to catch as much as possible of the soot. A heavy weight was then attached to the end of a long piece of rope and a good stout branch of whin or heather affixed to the rope a short distance up from the weight. This contraption was then dunked up and down the chimney from above. As there were rarely proper ladders to be found around these old cottages, climbing up on the roof with all this gear required not only a good head for heights but also a fair amount of agility, and it was an exercise generally considered to be the responsibility of the Head of the House, when sober. And so it was here.

An old potato bag was found and fixed around the fireplace in the hope of bagging both Cat and soot before damage to the living room decor became irreparable. With strict instructions to all to remain on guard until Cat hit the sack and could instantly be whisked outside, a quietly swearing Old Man looped the rope, coil upon coil, carefully over his shoulder. Picking up the weight attached to the end and pausing only to shrivel Boy with a venomous glare, he marched round to the end of the house to begin his arduous ascent.

Ten minutes and a pair of skinned knees later the Old Man stood poised on the roof by the chimney stack, wheezing bronchially. Slowly and steadily he hauled the weight up beside him and held it over the chimney pot. Then, paying out the rope very gradually for fear of causing damage to the inside wall of the chimney, he breathed a silent benediction and sent the chunk of iron clattering and bumping down in the darkness.

The impasse below was broken in splendid fashion: Cat exploded through the ancient hessian like a cannonball.

Since vanishing from their ken, a considerable transformation had taken place in the household sloth. That he was much exercised mentally was very apparent, but even more remarkable was the change in his coiffure. Whereas the glossy white pelage of youth had admittedly dulled somewhat of late to be replaced by the yellow tingeing of age, now Cat was as black as a Nubian slave. In addition, he exhibited a turn of speed quite unsuspected by all, an athletic mobility that would have done credit to a creature of the African plains.

Like a black comet he whizzed round the living room, followed by a trail of viscous soot. His three complete circuits were interrupted only by a couple of valiant attempts to climb the wallpaper and by a brief but vigorous contretemps with each of the doors, to which Carson's Enamel Paint made tenacious – albeit ultimately unsuccessful – attempts to ensnare him in its glutinous bottle-green grip. Boy, fearful of the wrath to come but unable to tear himself away from the scene of his crime, was intrigued to note that Cat even made it some distance up one of the lace curtains before it shredded under his weight.

The living room was a complete shambles. Wallpaper hung in strips and there was soot everywhere. A thin black mist of the stuff drifted slowly upward, turning daylight into premature dusk and the pristine white of the ceiling to a sort of blotchy elephant-grey. Clumps of cat hair clung to the doors with the adhesive finality that cat hair tends to exhibit at times like these, while to the hibiscus motif of the walls Cat had added some involuntary green and black stippling of his own, creating patterns that might have been conjured by Van Gogh had he been in a suitably satanic mood. Nor had Cat confined his attentions to the wallpaper. In his manic convolutions he had succeeded in applying his indelible artistry to the new linoleum, the oilcloth on the living-room table, the snakes and ladders board on the floor, the smaller and less agile of the Bairns beside it, and even the remaining lace curtain on the window.

To the occupants of the living-room, Cat looked like a bad dream. The family, rivetted to the spot in a mixture of shock and sheer undiluted horror, resembled a team of miners at the end of a particularly gruelling shift at the coalface. Seldom, if ever, can 14 pounds of hitherto inanimate flesh have created so much havoc over such a limited period of time.

Fortunately for everyone's sanity, especially that of the star of the show, the party was about over. Cat's frantic yellow gaze lit upon the open back door and he was gone through it like a streak, heading for the blessed peace of the wild and empty moorland behind the house. Not far behind him, and also moving at speed, was Boy.

*   *   *

Cat survived a further two years, but he was never quite the same again. His nerves seemed to bother him a lot. He followed Boy's every move with the keenest interest, and it required only the slightest rustle of paper in his vicinity to spark off a series of loud and menacing growls and much spasmodic twitching of the limbs.

Come to think of it, precisely the same could have been said of the Old Man.

Chapter 18

BULLETS AND THE PADDY

I was fortunate enough to have worked in Newfoundland for a few years in the latter part of the 1960s. Newfoundland is quite a large island and it suffered greatly from the effects of the last Ice Age, most of its soil having been scoured away from its surface by the glaciers, leaving nothing but bare rock sticking out of the sea. Today, it is covered by a thin layer of acidic, peaty soil which supports, for the most part, great stretches of moorland covered in blaeberries and even greater stretches of natural spruce forest. Fishing and paper-pulp are its only notable industries and the climate, especially in winter, can be rugged, to say the least.

Newfoundland does not attract the jet set. There is a starkness about the land that tends to be off-putting to the stranger. But I loved it, and especially I loved its people. Where I worked, most of the inhabitants were descendants of Irish who had settled there at the time of the potato famine in the mid-19th century. Because the island had always been the forgotten part of the British Empire and, until recent times, even Canada had wanted nothing to do with it, their accents had remained unchanged through the generations. You could almost have identified the part of rural Ireland that the Newfoundlanders' ancestors had come from by their brogues, even though few of the people themselves had ever crossed the Atlantic to visit the land of their forefathers. Their cultural links with the 'Old Country' remained, too. A night with a fishing family in some remote Newfoundland outport with the wind shaking the walls of the wooden cabin and the melodeon and the jew's-harp in full swing and a bottle or two of Newfoundland's infamous black rum – called, appropriately 'Screech' – on the table before you, and you had a night to remember until the day you died. And, when the tunes and the songs dried up, there was always the storytelling.

Newfoundlanders were much like the Gallovidians of old. They were great storytellers. Like the Gallovidians, too, their lives were rarely easy ones. But they have always been a happy-go-lucky race, prepared to make the best of their God-given lot. Like the early days in Galloway (and until the construction of the trans-Canada highway across the island) transportation between coastal towns and villages was mainly by sea when the weather was favourable. Interior roads were just impassable muddy tracks for most of the year.

There was one other thing that the people of Newfoundland had in common with those of Galloway. Just as the Gallovidians had their own train service (before a minor lackey of London's far-off government received a generous emolument for wiping it off the map with one stroke of his uncaring pen) so too did the Newfoundlanders before it suffered an identical fate. Being a nation renowned for their caustic wit, the Newfoundlanders named their train 'The Newfie Bullet'.

The line ran from Port aux Basques, on Newfoundland's west coast, to the island's capital St John's in the far east. During its tortuous 570-mile journey the train had to traverse some very forbidding territory indeed, from windswept caribou tundra to impenetrable boreal forest interspersed with bottomless muskeg. It was never a train in much of a hurry – it was old, and, in any case, this was part of the world where the element of hurry in any deed tended to be viewed with the gravest of suspicion.

To be fair, there were distractions en route that might have taxed the explanatory ingenuity of – even – British Rail. During the fall, lust-maddened bull-moose would often challenge its right of way, with – it has to be admitted – a quite embarrassing degree of success. Then again, when the barrens were ablaze with succulent berries, it was only right that passengers should be allowed to disembark and fill their cans and baskets with them. Winter would inevitably block the line with huge snowdrifts, but these would generally take no more than a day or two to clear since the train would always be carrying an ample supply of shovels against just such a contingency. In spring and summer the streams and lakes along the railway line would be alive with trout and char and salmon, just waiting to be caught … Need I go on? Every Newfoundlander, man and woman, is a born fisher.

There was an old story – widely believed when I was there – about a lady who had boarded the train at Port aux Basques for St John's. Some 300 miles into her journey she asked the attendant how much longer it was going to take them to reach the city. 'God knows,' replied the honest fellow with that engaging frankness one has come to associate with railwaymen the world over. 'But,' he continued, casting a critical eye on the lady's obviously advanced state of pregnancy, 'Why did you come on such a long journey when you knew you were in that condition?'

'Sure,' she replied indignantly, 'I wasn't pregnant at all when I boarded this bliddy thing at Port aux Basques.'

*   *   *

Once upon a time the Machars of Wigtownshire had its own 'Bullet'. It is true that its right of way was never challenged – so far as I am aware – by bull-moose, lust-maddened or otherwise, and it is true that the only berries I ever recall seeing by the side of the line were the occasional clusters of wormy brambles, too sour looking for even the blackbirds to bother with. Both the Cree and the Bladnoch rivers were within easy reach of the railway line, but it was a well-documented fact that all the salmon travelling up those waters were owned by well-heeled gentlemen of leisure and no Machars man or boy worth his salt would have dreamt of removing from those rivers that which clearly did not belong to him. There are some things which are just beyond the pale.

So there was never any real excuse for making unscheduled stops on this line. That is not to say, however, that unscheduled stops did not occur from time to time …

The Machars Bullet was born in grand style. On the 8th of September 1871 the town hall at Newton Stewart was packed to capacity for a:

Public Meeting of Gentlemen Favourable to the Extension of Railway Communication from Newton Stewart by Wigtown to Whithorn.

Chairman of the meeting was Lord Garlies, heir to the Earl of Galloway. The proposed route had been surveyed some 18 years previously, but, in the time-honoured tradition of bureaucracy the world over, nothing at all had happened in the interim. Now, things really began to move. The railway, it was decided, would travel in a more or less direct line from Newton Stewart south to the county town of Wigtown, then with a slight south-westerly deviation to serve the villages of Kirkinner, Whauphill and Sorbie. However, Lord Garlies – in observation of the true aristocrat's tradition of 'not in my back yard' – insisted that, one mile short of the seaside village of Garliestown (named after him initially, and later to be renamed 'Garlieston') the line should swing south in order to avoid contaminating his family's estate lands. The station of Millisle came into being at this point, with a small and discreet branch line being opened to connect it with Garlieston. By June 1877, the whole line from Newton Stewart to the terminal at Whithorn had been constructed, a total of 19 miles, one furlong and 8¹/₂ chains.

Although this chapter is not intended as a synopsis of the history of this particular section of the Wigtownshire Railways, as it was then called, it is interesting to note how costs escalate in the course of a century. The Aberdonian businessman who eventually found himself being awarded the contract was paid £47,357 5s 9d for the 13 miles and 20 chains stretch from Newton Stewart to Sorbie, and this included some very difficult rock cutting and a large and costly viaduct over the Bladnoch River. Today that sum would probably be just about enough to cover the monthly salary of the chairman of British Rail. A London contractor offered to supply flat-bottomed rails at £94 5s 3d per mile, while the venerable firm of R & W Callander of Minnigaff agreed to supply larch sleepers 9 feet by 9 inches by 4¹/₂ inches at 3/6d each.

Business was brisk from the beginning, both in goods and in passenger services. Cattle and sheep had to be transported to and from the Newton Stewart market each weekend, and there was much import traffic via the Garlieston harbour. Garlieston also had its own special passenger traffic: twice each year the Isle of Man steamer ran excursions from Garlieston to Douglas and back and these were very popular, special trains running to connect with the steamer from Stranraer, Dumfries and even from as far away as Carlisle.

The Newton Stewart to Whithorn line was a scenic one, especially during the spring and summer months. I should know. I travelled it often enough. Indeed, for three years I travelled it virtually every day from Sorbie Station to my school in Newton Stewart. Newton Stewart, the point at which the Whithorn line met the main London – Dumfries – Stranraer line, was a most pretty station, with tall trees alive with rooks on the bank to the north between the station and the Newton Stewart to Glenluce road. To the south of the station at this point were rolling green fields dotted with whins as far as the eye could see.

Heading south to Wigtown were the heather-clad flats of the Moss O'Cree with, beyond them, the silvery blue sliver of the Solway and the Cree estuary. On the other side of the water the hills of Kirkcudbright were a shimmering smoky blue on hot days, becoming a lowering, thunderous slate-grey the moment rain threatened.

Occasionally small herds of Belted Galloway cattle could be seen grazing peacefully, the distinctive black and white bands on their flanks making them look oddly out of place here in South-west Scotland, despite their name, as though they more properly belonged to some African veldt. Black and rufous hued bullocks were everywhere, and shaggy lowland sheep seemed to be atop every knowe. Mostly it was green fields that the train travelled through, although here and there a spinney of trees would be seen in the distance as it rattled on its way. The line ran alongside the wartime aerodrome of Baldoon, a training base for the RAF, and lumbering Ansons and Lysanders and droning little queen bees towing drogues could often be seen high overhead as they went through their paces.

It was a very busy line in those wartime years. Apart from the civilian traffic there were special trains full of servicemen going hither and thither, often airmen heading for Baldoon, or new batches of English soldiers going to gunnery school at Burrowhead near to the Isle of Whithorn. A train packed with American soldiers pulled up at Newton Stewart station on one occasion as we were waiting for the Bullet to take us home. One of our classmates was a kilt wearer and he was an instant attraction with the Yanks, who persuaded him to perform a sort of manic Highland Fling for them on the platform. They showered him with chewing gum and chocolate bars, and we who were lucky enough to share his compartment ate right royally that evening on the way home.

Contingents of Norwegian soldiers sometimes found themselves as guests of the Machars Bullet, much to their amusement. One of them told me that they had a train just like it where he came from on the fringe of the Arctic Circle but, while our Bullet, being used to civilization, ran on coal, the Norwegian Bullet ran on sticks and peat and reindeer droppings. (He surely had to be joking about the reindeer droppings?)

There were others, decidedly less welcome than the Americans and the Norwegians, who arrived for onward transportation one day at Newton Stewart station. We were crossing the railway bridge, making our way to the Bullet's platform, when our nostrils were assailed by a most horrendous odour. It got stronger and more potent as we went down the steps, becoming almost suffocating in its intensity as we walked up the platform. We soon discovered the source: awaiting the Stranraer to London train were two dozen large and very dead goats. They were quite unlike any goats we had ever seen before, being covered with very long hair and having looks of such extreme ferocity that not even the glaze of death could eradicate it from their cold yellow eyes. 'Wild goats fae the Cairnsmore hills,' explained the porter. 'Gaun tae feed the London folks.'

A Catholic member of our group crossed himself hastily. The rest of us turned shades varying from light green to yellow. I don't know how much truth there was in the porter's statement, but we certainly believed it then. Life, it seemed to us even at that tender age, was full of injustices. Not only did we have Hitler plastering the long-suffering citizens of London with his bombs, but we Scots were adding insult to injury and death by feeding them with meat that we would have certainly hesitated to give to our sheepdogs.

We were a pretty motley gang of young hooligans, we who travelled on the Machars Bullet. Our school was the Douglas Ewart High School in Newton Stewart, and our ages ranged from about 11 to 17. Each age group kept separate from the others, with each occupying its 'own' compartment on the train. Our compartment arrangements were on a strictly unisexual basis, too: boys only with boys and girls with girls. This was not a rule of the railway – it was our rule. In that day and age we boys would not have been seen dead with a member of the opposite sex, not in any situation in which we would have been liable to be seen by our peers, anyway. There was definitely no fraternization, no tender little romances, within the confines of the Machars Bullet insofar as we were concerned. This was one of the very few things about us that our parents never had to worry about. I verily believe that, were a girl to be so brazen as to enter our compartment as the train was about to leave Newton Stewart station, when we had recovered from our shock, she would have been in danger of being hurled out through the window and into the clean fresh air of Galloway before the train had properly got up steam for its journey. And had a boy inadvertently found himself in a compartment full of girls, he would have probably died of shame long before he had reached his destination.

For all that, we were a pretty wild bunch and we got up to some pretty rough shenanigans once the train got moving. I am ashamed to recall them now. Luggage racks were for swinging from, like our hero Tarzan did in the pictures, and seats were turned into wrestling arenas and miniature rugby fields, school caps being used as substitute rugby balls. But I am glad to say that we never deliberately vandalized anything, broke anything, slashed seat covers. We would never even have thought of it. Such forms of hooliganism were to be for future generations in other parts.

The Health and Hygiene Mafia of today would have had a field day about the Bullet's lack of facilities. Many of the compartments were isolated from the rest of the carriage, with neither toilet facilities nor any way of getting to a toilet in emergency. There were no corridors. Once you were in your compartment, that was your lot until you reached your destination. Fortunately, youngsters usually have good plugs on their bladders and our journeys were not overly long, but I dread to think what might have been the end result had anyone suffered from a sudden attack of Montezuma's Revenge. As it was, I do have a recollection of one lad who found himself being caught short on the longish stretch between Newton Stewart and Wigtown one miserable winter's evening – a stretch made even longer by an interminable delay when the bullet had to stop for something or other just outside Newton Stewart station. The poor boy was in agony, so the compartment window was hastily opened, the sufferer stood up on the seat, and he obeyed Mother Nature's command out of the window and into the pure clear air of Galloway. On reflection, one hoped that if anyone happened to be looking out of his or her window on the downwind side at the time the boy was relieving himself, the experience would have been attributed to an unseasonably warm Wigtownshire shower.

The Machars Bullet may not have been the fastest train in Scotland, but there was no doubt that it was a pretty reliable old thing. The occasional snowdrift blocking a cutting might hold up its progress for an hour or two on winter evenings, and twice I remember sheep refusing to get off the track near to Whauphill. But it took more than leaves on the line or the wrong sort of snowflakes to block its progress. There was nothing namby-pamby about it. Like the Gallovidians who travelled on it, it was rugged and it took a lot to stop it. Eventually, it got you to where you wanted to go. Your greatest danger on the Bullet – apart from little boys peeing in your face – was in being blinded by flying cinders from the engine's smoke stack when you had the window open, or in having your legs and private parts welded to the seat by the occasional geyser of steam erupting from the radiators situated underneath you. The Bullet provided a most necessary service for the people of the Machars. And no service was more important than the Bullet's link with 'The Paddy'.

The Paddy was the London – Stranraer Irish Mail train. It called at a number of stations as it wended its way through Galloway, and, because of this, this part of its journey from London was easily the most tedious. But, in sharp contrast to the Bullet, it was practically jet-propelled. It stopped for nothing as it hurtled on its way between stations. A flock of sheep straying onto the Paddy's track would have been instantly converted into mutton before any single one of them could utter a startled bleat. It stopped at stations on its way only for as long as was absolutely necessary and not one moment more.

One of its obligatory stops was at the tiny station of Dunragit, near Stranraer. Dunragit, oddly enough, was considered quite an important station, for it was at this junction that passengers wishing to catch the Glasgow train disembarked. One could only wonder at the thoughts of strangers from the distant city when they found themselves turfed out into a winter blizzard in the middle of the night in this rather desolate outpost seemingly in the back of beyond.

One story (probably apocryphal) about this station, told to me many years ago, concerned the station porter at the time. A bitterly cold night saw him on duty, waiting for the arrival of the Paddy from London. The old man, knowing that the pubs would all be closed by the time he knocked off work, had taken the precaution of purchasing a half bottle of whisky before he came on duty. He had not intended to broach it before he clocked off for the night, to be fair to him, but the caul' was fair deeleteerious, so it was, and the oul' arthuritis was giving him gyp, so what's a man to do? But perhaps if he had been stone cold sober at the time and his feet more steady, this story need never have been told …

The Paddy duly arrived. The porter began his platform duty call: 'Change here for Girvan, Ayr and Glasgow. Change here for Girvan, Ayr and Glasgow. Change here for Girvan, Ayr and Glasgow …' as he marched up the platform. He never completed his sentence in the manner intended, for his feet slipped on the icy platform. As he tried wildly to regain his balance, the bottle slipped from his pocket, smashing to pieces on the platform, and the final call the startled passengers from

London heard was: 'Change here for... Hell, damnation and buggery.'

Both the Paddy and the Machars Bullet fell victim to the Westminster axe. The Bullet went first, on a suitably wet, dismal Saturday night on the 23rd of September 1950. The Paddy went about a decade later. The tracks fell silent, and everything around them seemed to fall silent, too. Not long afterwards, the tracks were removed for scrap metal. With them went a large part of the greatness that was Galloway.

*   *   *

A few years ago I walked part of the route on which the Machars Bullet used to travel with such panache. It was wildly overgrown. In a cutting not far from the site of the old Whauphill station I came upon a most beautiful sight: a sprawling crab-apple tree surrounded and partly entwined by a vast dogrose bush. I sat for a time on the opposite bank, just looking at the spectacle.

It was a lovely late-spring day. Both the crab and the rose were in full bloom, their delicate pink and white blossoms making a magnificent show in the early morning sunshine. A movement in the crab tree caught my eye and I crossed over.

In the fork of a branch I discovered a cosy little nest of interwoven lichens and leaves containing two eggs of the most exquisite pale blue with faded-pink dots. A goldfinch nest. It was so well concealed among the crab blossoms that only one who knew what he or she was looking for could have found it. I edged my way cautiously back out of the tangle of dogrose and stood on the track. The male bird appeared out of nowhere, perching on top of the tree, peering anxiously at me, his scarlet head moving from side to side and his wing-flashes a glory of rich gold against the pink of the blossom around him and the blue of the sky beyond.

He began to sing. I walked off slowly down the old track on which the Machars Bullet had carried us so often those long years before, and the liquid sweetness of his song was with me long after we were out of sight of each other.

191

Chapter 19
DOING PORRIDGE IN
AFRICA AND GALLOWAY

We were a somewhat motley collection, we who had found ourselves gathered together at this meeting in the staff quarters of the Monrovia University in Liberia. Our hosts were two African professors who worked in the university, and our gathering consisted of – reading in a clockwise direction from where I sat – an ex-cowboy from the Great Plains of northern Alberta, two Irish nuns, an African priest, an Irish priest, a Lebanese timber magnate of considerable wealth and charm, a New Zealand accountant, the Syrian owner of a chain of brothels, and yours truly, an itinerant forester. It was not that I had any business being among them myself, for I had only dropped in en passant for a beer and a chat with my friend Amos, one of the professors. But, before I could make my excuses and depart – for I am no lover of meetings or gatherings of strangers – I had found myself inextricably enmeshed in this one.

It did not take me long to figure out that this meeting held promise of being much more interesting than most. Not only did the subject matter intrigue me, but so did the incongruity of the venue and the mishmash of occupational and national diversity of those present. Somehow, one does not expect to drop in at the home of a learned African professor in the heart of tropical Africa and find oneself expected to contribute to a discussion on Robert Burns in the company of cowboys and nuns and bordel proprietors. At least, I didn't. Arrangements for the forthcoming Burns Night at the local branch of

West Africa's very active Caledonian Society were being discussed, and every single one present except myself appeared to be on the committee.

I looked around the group as the preliminary drinks were being dispensed. The priests had stout, the nuns had tea, Amos and his colleague were on Scotch whisky, and the cowboy confiscated the bottle of bourbon and set it down beside him. Both the Syrian and the man from Lebanon had cola, while I opted for a bottle of the local lager. 'Are there any Scots on your committee?' I asked curiously. 'Two,' replied Amos, 'But they couldn't come tonight. Playing in a bridge tournament.'

I had already been aware that Amos had graduated in Edinburgh, and it transpired that his colleague Sam had also graduated there. Both, I discovered, were not only Burns enthusiasts but they were quite fanatical about all things Scottish. Sam had spent much time around the Castle Douglas area, even returning to his native land with a wife from Moffat. She, it turned out, was one of the absentees.

The meeting got under way. Sam's wife, it transpired, had volunteered to make the haggis, for most of the ingredients could be purchased in local expatriate stores. For any minor item that could not be obtained in this way, she reckoned that an adequate substitute could be got from the local markets without causing the Great Bard to turn in his grave. The Syrian had offered to supply the sheep, and he said that he would be happy to do the slaughtering. I could well believe him, for he was the most evil looking brigand I had seen in many a long day's march. He looked as though he would equally happily have slit his grandmother's throat for ten Syrian piastres.

'What is a haggis?' asked Sister Felicity timidly. 'And how do you make it?' Sister Felicity was a new arrival from Galway, a prettily delicate looking young thing with large, soulful eyes.

Amos was well prepared for such questions. From the floor behind his chair he produced a large, well-worn book entitled 'Scottish Country Fare'. He leafed through the pages and settled back in his chair.

'Clean a sheep's pluck thoroughly,' he intoned with relish. 'Make incisions in the heart and liver to allow the blood to flow out, and parboil them, letting the windpipe lie over the side of the pot to permit the phlegm and blood to disgorge from the lungs…'

'Jesus, Mary and Joseph!' whispered Sister Felicity, turning pale green.

'…Boil the heart, liver and lungs for half an hour,' continued Amos remorselessly, 'Then take them out and trim away any skin and diseased or black looking bits, then mince along with a pound of suet. Peel and scald six onions, then chop them up and mix them with the mince. Toast some oatmeal by the fire until it is light brown and dry. Spread the mince on a board and cover it lightly with the oatmeal. Season with a lot of pepper, salt and some marjoram.

'Have a large sheep's stomach ready, with all the contents cleaned out of it. And' he added helpfully, 'Be quite sure that the stomach is thoroughly cleaned out. African sheep are chock-a-block with hookworm and tapeworm, and African tapeworms can reach up to 20 metres in length.' (I felt that this latter piece of information, while interesting, no doubt, to those who wished to make a study of flatworms, could easily have been omitted from the discourse without prejudice to the main theme.)

'Stuff the mince in the bag,' Amos went on, 'And pour half a pint of beef gravy or broth of some sort in along with it. Don't fill the bag too full − give chance for the meat to swell. Then sew the whole thing up with cat gut. Let the bag boil for two to three hours, pricking it when it swells to capacity to prevent it from bursting…'

Somewhere about the time of the tapeworm information, the two nuns had left the room hurriedly and we could hear them murmuring to each other through in the kitchen. For the greater part of Amos's reading the cowboy's mouth had been hanging open. Now he reached for the bourbon bottle, poured himself a large shot, and gulped it down. He gazed in my direction with a mixture of awe and revulsion. 'Do you mean to tell me,' he asked incredulously, 'That these Scats actually eat that shit?'

'Buddy,' retorted Amos coldly, 'I am chairman of this branch, and I am therefore an adopted Scot. I eat haggis, and so will you if you want to come to our Burns Night!'

'Why,' I asked Amos after the meeting had ended and everyone else had gone home, 'Are these people on your committee when so few of them even know what a haggis looks like?'

'Oh,' he explained, 'Only Sam, his wife, the doctor and the accountant are on our permanent committee. The others are only on the organizing committee for the Burns Night, and only because they are contributing in one way or another. The cowboy is employed by a large American mining company up north, and they have a very large and modern commissary, of which he is in charge. He has promised to supply the bulk of our food requirements gratis. The Lebanese chap says he will supply all our booze, even though he doesn't drink alcohol himself, and, as you have heard, the Syrian is supplying the sheep.'

'And the missionaries?'

He smiled wryly. 'The priests are only here for the drink and the chat and to make sure no one molests the nuns. The nuns are going to make the scones and the oatcakes and the porridge.'

'PORRIDGE?' I stared at him in disbelief. 'A lot of those who will be attending the Burns Night,' he explained, 'Will be from far out of town. I have offered them accommodation in our staff quarters for what's left of that night. So I have decided to make it an all-Scottish weekend in honour of Rabbie. On the Sunday morning following the Big Night, we will have porridge and scones and oatcakes for breakfast.'

'Dammit!' I breathed. There seemed little else to say.

I refused his generous offer to have me co-opted onto his committee but I did accept his invitation to the forthcoming shindig. Unhappy though I generally am when I find myself in the company of more than four people at any one time, this – my first ever experience of a Burns Night anywhere – might prove entertaining.

And so it proved. I don't know how many native-born Scots were among the crowd of 300 or so who attended that Burns Night in the university auditorium, but I would guess not too many. Just about every other conceivable nationality was there, though, but undoubtedly the African nation was in the majority. The New Zealand accountant piped in the haggis expertly, and Professor Sam, resplendent in the grey, white and black Scott tartan, delivered the traditional address in a broad Kirkcudbright brogue. The haggis was as good as any I have ever had in Scotland, although I must confess here and now that I am not a great haggis fan. The whisky flowed like – well – whisky does at any Burns Night anywhere in the world. One of the Scottish guests had an accordion and he joined the piper on the stage. Drunk and relatively sober alike took to the floor for the obligatory reels. The racket from the revellers almost drowned out the sound of the music.

Just after midnight things began to deteriorate a little. A huge, jet-black figure clad in a kilt of gaudy Barclay tartan suddenly exploded on the scene from God knows where. Wearing nothing else but this garment – as was bullishly and embarrassingly evident as his kilts flew higher and higher with his flailing legs – he thundered through the eightsome reel sets like a stampeding hippo, uttering wild tribal whoops and shrieks and knocking dancers over like ninepins. Within seconds all pretence at organized dancing had vanished and everything had degenerated into a general free-for-all, with men grabbing the women of their choice and demonstrating to all and sundry their own highly individual interpretations of how Scottish reels should be danced. It resembled a scene from Prester John.

It was time for me to leave, I decided. I slipped out of the door into the hot humidity of the African night. I took the path that wended its way from the back of the hall and out through the compound. The moon was at its fullest and the compound was beautifully illuminated with gold and silver. Flame trees were scattered around the compound and they cast shadows that were deep and velvet-soft and soothing. As I strolled along, taking my time, I could hear the pounding beat and the yells of the revellers in the hall behind me, while somewhere far, far in front of me on the edge of the town a lone drummer beat a melancholy tattoo.

The path passed by a large mango tree. On the ground under the tree a couple – obviously escapees like myself from the Burns Night festivities – were making love, oblivious to the mosquitoes. The man was black and the girl was white. I wished them good night courteously as I passed by but they did not reply. Indeed, they neither looked at me nor did they pause in what they were doing.

The sweetly aphrodisiac scents of moon-flower and frangipani followed me all the way to Amos's house, and the fragrance was still with me as I lifted the mosquito net and climbed into bed. As I drifted off to sleep I thought about the lovers and I wondered what the lad from Kyle, the man in whose honour we were all here this night, would have thought of them, black man and white girl, being so disrespectful to his memory as to leave the festivities in order to go and lie together under a mango tree. And then I thought: I know what his approach to that situation would have been. 'We're a' Jock Tamson's bairns' – that's what his first thought would have been. And of another thing everyone who knew him could be sure: given the slightest chance he too would have been right out there in the compound under a mango tree with a girl, rather than sweat it out in the seething, claustrophobic cacophony of that hall.

Sunday morning was quiet. Very quiet. It was around ten o'clock before Amos appeared in the staff dining room, our scheduled breakfast venue. His helpers soon followed in dribs and drabs. The nuns had gone to Mass, but they had prepared everything earlier that morning.

Now, there was one thing that I discovered about myself that weekend which I had never given much thought to before. There are very many things Scottish that export well. Scotland's people do, for a start. The names of her pioneers are to be found all over the world, bequeathed to towns and rivers and mountains and even whole lands. Her whisky certainly exports well, too. But haggis and porridge? Emphatically not, in my humble opinion. At least, not insofar as tropical Africa is concerned. There is, to me, something not quite right about eating haggis or porridge in the sweltering heat of the White Man's Grave. The porridge on offer that morning was strictly of the packet variety – the pallid, watery supermarket kind that can be cooked in three minutes flat and leaves you feeling just as hungry half an hour later – but I could no more have eaten that gruel that morning than I could have eaten live witchetty grubs. The haggis of the night before had been slightly more acceptable, mainly because much alcohol had been consumed before it had been piped onto the table, but surely hot porridge in the quaking heat of an equatorial morning is carrying the Scottish identity a bridge too far?

But, as I sat back and watched the others pretending to enjoy it, I got to thinking about this remarkable cereal that seems to have been keeping the Scottish nation alive since the beginning of civilized time and has nurtured and sustained what must surely be one of the hardier races ever to have set foot on this earth:

'The oat,' remarked Dr Samuel Johnson, a man who never missed the chance of a jibe at those north of Hadrian's Wall, 'Is a grain which in England is generally given to horses, but in Scotland supports the people.'

The most important food crop throughout old Caledonia, from Thurso in the extreme north to Galloway in the far south, was always the oat, and it became established in Scotland as long ago as the Iron Age. Throughout the centuries this humble cereal has owed its popularity with Scottish farmers to the fact that it could thrive in all but the most drastic of climes and in soils that could be considered less than fertile. Its popularity with the hoi-polloi lay in the fact that it produced oatmeal.

There were three grades of oatmeal – fine, coarse and medium ground. Fine oatmeal was used for such things as the making of scones; oatcakes and brose were made from the coarse variety.

Medium ground oatmeal was used in the making of porridge.

There are few who can regard porridge with complete ambivalence. You are either for it or agin it. In my own humble opinion, it is very much an acquired taste. My early childhood reeks of memories of an exasperated grandfather endeavouring to hold me pinned to his knee while he forced great dollops of the lumpy, cloying sludge into my wincing guts. Such things tend to leave their mark on a little fellow.

But one must not carp too much. There are many who actually like the stuff and it is, after all, one of the most Scottish of all meals. And it is easy to make. However, while the actual cooking of porridge created few problems even in the old days, there was, then, an almost mystical ritual that had to be observed in the making, the serving and the eating.

Today you can buy packets of ready-processed oats which require the minimum of preparation to turn them into porridge, but such a simplistic approach to cooking would have been viewed with derisory suspicion by those wonderful old countrywomen of my youth. For a start, real porridge was made with unrefined oatmeal.

The oatmeal was added, ever so slowly and always with the left hand, to boiling water at a ratio of about a third of a cup of meal to half a pint of water per person. While this was being done, the mixture was being stirred slowly and continuously in a clockwise direction with the right hand – it was considered to be unlucky to stir anti-clockwise – until, quite suddenly, the brew would thicken. It was then covered and allowed to simmer for about 15 minutes, during which period salt would be added.

The porridge was then decanted into separate bowls, more salt being added according to the whim of the individual. (Delicate souls from the blunt end of Britain tended to substitute sugar for the Scotsman's obligatory salt, while our transatlantic cousins, ever the innovators, would sometimes adorn theirs with – horror of horrors ! – maple syrup or strawberry jam.) Real old traditionalists would serve individual bowls of milk, into which the diners dipped their spoons of hot porridge before eating.

With the somewhat austere formality so typical of those days, in some country places it was considered to be poor etiquette to eat sitting down: porridge had to be eaten standing up.

While the ubiquitous barrel of salt herring often kept body and soul together in coastal communities, porridge was de rigueur just about everywhere. In many homes it was often the only meal of the day.

For over a hundred years in jails all over Scotland, it was the staple diet. However, even the most virulent critic of porridge would have admitted that the stuff dumped on prisoners' plates half a century ago bore little resemblance to the real McCoy. Indeed, one high spirited acquaintance of mine who had just emerged from a longish spell of incommunicado residence at Glasgow's notorious Barlinnie Prison stated that his sudden conversion to the Jehovah Witness cause had to a great extent been inspired by his wish never to sample prison porridge again.

Many years ago, on bleak November nights when the Sorbie wind was howling down the chimney and warlocks stalked the black spruce woods without, my father would relate to us grim tales of a winter spent in lodgings with a colleague in the hills around Glen Trool. Their landlady was a ferocious old termagant of a rather parsimonious bent. They subsisted solely on the tubercular looking rabbits and hares one tends to find inhabiting those bleak mountain regions. And, of course, porridge. Each weekend she cooked their porridge quota for the week in a massive cauldron. The steaming contents were then poured into a vacant bedroom drawer and allowed to cool. When the mixture had set like putty, she divided the slab into seven roughly equal portions, one for each day of the week.

With the passing of each day the epidermis would gradually thicken, as it tends to do in porridge, so that by the end of the week the remaining sections would have developed a hide like a brontosaurus. The landlady was very proud of her ability to cook porridge and, as her two lodgers were terrified of her, they were obliged to eat this skin along with the rest of the frightful meal in order to avoid offending her. The Old Man would add ghoulishly that their frantic efforts to gulp down this grisly pelt under her watchful supervision must have been reminiscent of the actions of a couple of cormorants endeavouring to swallow a pair of singularly recalcitrant conger eels. To add spice to an already interesting repast, their landlady's somewhat cavalier approach to daily household chores meant that long deceased beetles, moths, earwigs, cockroaches, spiders' webs complete with original occupants, clumps of unidentifiable hair and fluff, and other assorted detritus from the bottom of the drawer would often form a colourful mosaic on the underside of their daily chunk.

Chacun à son goût, indeed!

A flurry of correspondence in Scottish newspapers in the early post-World War II years on this subject carried stories in much the same vein. Indeed, Ayrshire miners who wrote into those papers in droves had equally harrowing tales to relate about thick slices of cold porridge between mouldering crusts of bread forming their sole sustenance at the coalface.

While one should always be prepared to believe everything one reads in the newspapers, of course, especially if they are Scottish, still, all this seemed to me to be too much reminiscent of the string of horror stories that old-timers of whatever generation feed to their offspring to let them know precisely how hard things were in the good old days and how well-off they were nowadays. It was not until many years later that I began to realise that the Old Man's story, while perhaps embroidered a little for effect, may not have been entirely apocryphal:

Prior to my departure for Africa in the early 1950s, I had been posted to a large forestry commission nursery at Dunragit, near Stranraer. We had a very large squad of workers comprising both men and women from the very young to the near-retirement age.

Erchie was very much in the latter category. He had seen active service in World War I. I was sitting beside him at 'piece-time' one bitterly cold winter day when he produced from his lunch box a thick slice of bread. Then he unwrapped a grimy piece of newspaper and took from it an even thicker slab of grey, wobbly something-or-other that looked utterly repellent. He laid this on the slice of bread. From his pocket he then produced a small jar. He opened it and inserted his forefinger. He smeared the yellow gunge he had extracted from the jar with lavish abandon over the grey slab. I watched, fascinated, as he lifted his 'piece' to his mouth.

'What in the name of God,' I enquired, 'Is that you're eating, Erchie?'

'Caul' parritch!' remarked the old man with evident satisfaction. 'Fills yer belly an' sticks tae yer ribs. Ye cannae bate it. Ah've etten it a' ma life.'

'And what is that yellow stuff?' I persisted.

'Hot mustard,' replied Erchie. 'Grand fur a wunters' day. Pits fire in yer belly an' lead in yer pencil. Ye cannae bate it.'

He bit into his 'piece' and chewed contentedly, gobs of yellow

Coleman's mustard sticking to each end of his moustache. 'Ye shud try it, Donal'. It disnae half gie yer sex life a lift!'

I shuddered. Permanent celibacy seemed preferable to me. But one could not help but admire these old-timers. The trenches of Mons and Yprés must have held few terrors for those men of steel, reared as they were on such awful fare.

Chapter 20
SPECTRAL WOODS

Woods cut, again do grow,
Bud doth the rose, and daisy, winter done,
But we, once dead, no more do see the sun.

William Drummond of Hawthornden. (1585-1649)

All my life, I seemed to have been travelling for this moment. This was where my travels had started, on Pouton Farm, near Garlieston, and now I was back. Like the wild hare who, once startled from his form among the rushes, takes off at such a speed you would think he intends to run and run and keep running until he runs right off the face of the earth, so had I left this childhood home, vowing never to return. But the man who is wise to the ways of the hare knows that if he hangs around the spot where he disturbed him for long enough, the foolish creature – impelled by an instinct so abstruse as to be comprehensible only to the god of all hares – will eventually return by some long and circuitous route to his beginnings.

It had taken me rather longer than most hares to return, and my journey had been even more erratic than that of the average Galloway hare. But I had come back and that was the main thing, even though it had taken me all of 60 years to do so. I waded across the burn and sat on an old stump and looked around me, letting my mind drift back over the decades:

Sixty years. It had certainly been all of that, but I could see every nook and dell of that wood as I sat there. *Coille-na-Ròcais.* That's what we had called it then in the tongue of our forefathers. The Crow Wood. I could smell the turpentine scent of the resin that oozed from the hunchbacked pines of its brackeny knowes and I could hear the soporific burbling of cold, clear water running between moss-covered boulders in the burn that flanked it; a low, musical chuckling of water that somehow or other managed to percolate through the strident clamour of the rooks high above us in the tall, bare elms of March.

Few were the daylight hours that we did not spend in the Crow Wood. Summer and winter, rain or shine, we were there at the slightest opportunity. There we saw the first shy primrose of the year peeking timorously out at the world from under the shelf of the burn, and in the snow-laden firs of winter we watched the acrobatics of the tiny siskins as they foraged for microscopic insects. We sheltered behind the dry-stane dyke that bordered the wood on the east when November rains came slashing over the cold bleak fields and, in the long hot days of summer, we basked in the dappled cool of its glades while bumblebees droned among the foxgloves and the happy song of the chaffinch rang out through the treetops.

We had the sort of incredibly detailed knowledge of the Crow Wood that most children have for what they regard as being their own particular patch of territory. We knew every single thing about it. We saw everything there was to be seen, things that the eyes of adults would never have seen, partly, perhaps, because the eyes of adults are too far from the ground to see tiny things, or – more likely – because the eyes of adults are unseeing eyes, for adults are too preoccupied with Things That Matter In Life, like the fitba' results on Saturday and how good the wee wifie next door looks in her nichtgoon and God-I-could-fair-murder-a-pint. Nothing escapes the eyes of children. We saw the delicate faded-blue of the smallest forget-me-not on the burn bank and the dark Prussian-blue of the bugle among the stones by the dyke, while the shiny beaten-gold of the marsh marigold was the first thing we came to look at in the little area of marsh in the centre of the wood each morning.

We had an intimate knowledge of everything that happened in and around the Crow Wood. We knew where the bejewelled flicker of the dragonfly was most likely to be seen on sultry autumn days and we usually saw the old grey heron standing patiently by the burn long before he saw us. We knew where the secretive wren had her chosen nest of moss and brown fern with its six tiny white eggs pin-spotted with pink. We knew, too, where her faithful consort had located each of the other nests he had so painstakingly built for her, only to have them rejected by her as being unsuitable for no other reason than that, being feminine, she was entitled to feminine whimsy. We also knew in which one of those discarded nests he slept at night for warmth. We knew all this, and we knew it because we observed. And we knew all of those things because we loved the Crow Wood.

But we knew the Crow Wood only by day. Never would we have attempted to go near it by night, even had we been allowed to do so. This was a wood where hippogryphs and dryads might well have been found, were we to be so bold as to venture through it when the moon was high overhead and the wind blowing in from the north. It was as vast and mysterious to us then as some Germanic forest from the fables of the Brothers Grimm but, looking back on it now, I don't suppose the Crow Wood amounted to much more than a few acres of fairly ordinary mixed woodland. It was surrounded by rough pastureland bedecked with knowes of whins, a rolling landscape that swept east to the Solway Firth and to the moors of Grennan far to the west.

The wood belonged to the farm on which we lived, but no one ever seemed to bother with it. There were no other children for miles around, so we made full use of it. My being the oldest by a short head ensured that I had the starring role in any of the games we played, and I cannot recall a time when I failed to award myself the distinction of being the Bonnie Prince when the aftermath of Culloden was being enacted within the precincts of the Crow Wood. There were, admittedly, times when I had problems with the other participants in the drama. My two other male leads, while being, in my opinion, ideally cast as the hated enemy, seldom took their roles seriously enough. They tended to be too easily distracted from their prime objective of hunting Jacobites. There are few things designed to upset a bedraggled prince more than the discovery that, while he had been waiting patiently in ambush among the dripping bracken, the Redcoats who were supposed to be hot on his trail were, in fact, happily guddling for sticklebacks in the shallows of the burn, or that the pangs of hunger had driven them out of the wood and on their way over the fields to the comforts of their ain fireside.

I had occasional problems, too, with my partner in this great pursuit after Culloden. It is a commonly held belief that female stars can be temperamental. My sister was no exception. When she was in the mood, no prince could have hoped for a better Flora MacDonald. She was charming, loyal and patient. But only when in the mood. Nettles and bloodsucking insects made her cantankerous. There are few things more unsettling to a prince on the run than to find that the lady who has elected to join him in his hour of need wants to go home to mother because her hair is full of midges and her knickers infested with ticks.

Mostly, though, the Crow Wood was our haven of tranquillity. We never tired of exploring it. We made dens under the tangles of dead bracken that swathed the branches of long-fallen trees, and we gorged ourselves on the clusters of wild, sweet cherries that hung from the old gean tree by the burn. We climbed to the topmost branches of the sprawling chestnut in the centre of the wood – the same tree upon which my grandfather, knowing that he was about to die, would carve his initials a month before he closed his Gaelic bible for the last time and drifted off to the Tir nan Og to which all Hebrideans go when their time on earth is done. We swung like gibbons among its brittle branches, pasting each other with large conkers, and it must have been only by the grace of God that we did not have a catastrophic accident. Only once did one of us have what could be described as a close shave: my brother George lost his grip during some aerial gymnastics, crashing a good 30 feet to the ground amidst a veritable storm of leaves and twigs. He landed, shaken but unstirred, on the thick, soft carpet of moss below.

It was from the southern end that the Crow Wood got its name. Here, the lofty elms jostled with each other in the Atlantic gales, their tough, whippy branches making ideal nest foundations for the large colony of rooks that congregated there each spring. Peak nesting periods were March and April, and during this time we tried to avoid entering that particular section of the wood. Apart from the fact that the racket was deafening, there was the problem of avoiding the steady drizzle of droppings that fell from on high. The greeny-white effluent stank to high heaven and we soon learned that the tolerance of our parents did not extend to our returning home looking and smelling like a bunch of troglodytes who had just emerged from a long spell of hibernation in the bowels of the farmyard midden.

Se we contented ourselves with watching the rooks from the edge of the wood. They quarrelled incessantly and they were terrible thieves, shamelessly filching coveted nesting material from their neighbours whenever the opportunity presented itself. On windy days we would sit with our backs to the perimeter wall, watching as they soared and twisted and tumbled in the wind high over the grey fields, like pieces of charred paper swirling against the backdrop of the scudding clouds.

The Crow Wood was our kingdom. No one ever troubled us there. The only person I ever remember seeing in its vicinity was the shepherd, who would occasionally lean over the wall to chaff with us. Mother had a whistle which she would blow to summon us home for tea, but although – like all country children – we seemed to be in a permanent state of famine, it was usually only with reluctance that we would leave the sanctuary of our kingdom in response to its distant shrilling.

The Crow Wood is no more. It joined the war effort in 1941. Ironically, the man given the task of felling it was my father. From the day he walked into it with his axe to begin work, the Crow Wood was never again mentioned in our house...

I sat by the bank of the burn, watching tiny speckled trout rippling the surface of the dark pool below me. Not a trace of my old Crow Wood remained. There was the odd scrubby hawthorn and tangle of willow and cankered ash around me, to be sure, but of our Crow Wood as we knew it, nothing remained. Nothing. Where once the rose-breasted linnet sang his sweet melody from the bough of the graceful birch and the unforgettable fragrance of meadowsweet hung around the coolness of the Crow Wood's hollows, now only the peewit's lonely cry echoed over an Ozymandian landscape of bare, windswept fields.

The evening mists settled like a shroud around me. But then, with the mists came other sounds, whispering sounds, just a mishmash of sounds, faint and unrecognisable at first, then becoming ever-clearer, more insistent, sepulchral sounds from another, less frenetic age: the sighing of tall trees in the warm winds of long-gone summers, the ghostly tumult of rooks in joyous mayhem among the high tops, and the haunting laughter of children at play in what we had once called our Crow Wood.

And if these sounds were but fantasy, what of it? We Jacobites were ever dreamers. And even old Jacobites are entitled to their dreams.

*   *   *

Both Sorbie and Kirkinner deserve to be better known. They may be tiny villages and rather ordinary looking to the casual visitor, but they are both very much a part of the ancient history of Galloway. In fact Kirkinner has a piece of much more modern history attached to it: here, I was informed, a Miss Britt Ekland had cavorted in the nude during the filming of The Wicker Man. There was, according to my informant, rather a lot of nude alfresco cavorting among the whins during this period, some of it even connected with the film, and sales of binoculars in stores as far distant as Stranraer soared to record heights to cater for the sudden surge of interest in bird watching among the male population of the Machars. I regret to admit that I have seen neither the film nor Miss Ekland, clothed or naked, but I have been asked to assure the lady via the medium of this book that, should she ever find herself in financial distress and looking for a place in which to lay her blonde head o' nights, the good people of Galloway will be only too happy to take care of her. Or at least the male population. To this day there are Galloway pubs where one has only to mention her name to produce the Glazed-Eye Syndrome and sensible conversation goes out the window for the rest of that evening.

Kirkinner was where I had chosen to stay the night for the antepenultimate day of my travels in Galloway, but not to bathe in erotic fantasies about the delectable Miss Ekland, pleasant though that would undoubtedly have been. I had chosen Kirkinner because it was the nearest point to my last port of call.

Kilsture is not a name that springs readily to mind as you pore through the holiday brochures during the long months of winter, trying to decide which part of the world would be drawing the short straw for the pleasure of your company during the forthcoming summer. Indeed, beyond the Machars of Wigtownshire it is doubtful if many people will have heard of it. You will find it on the Ordnance Survey maps, but only if you look hard enough. There, it is shown as a wee splodge of olive located between Sorbie and Kirkinner, and the gentlemen who compile these maps have – with a charming simplicity all too rarely associated with government organisations – labelled it 'The Forest'.

Locally, it is called 'The Forest Mair', and I suppose that that is as good a name for it as any. Nearly 70 years ago my family lived on the edge of the Forest Mair. In fact, it is not too wild a boast that my family has probably had a closer association with this ancient forest than any other during the course of the 20th century. My father worked in its woods in the very early 1930s and – much later on – I worked in them myself. Later still my brother Neil became a gamekeeper there, a post he proudly occupied for the next 34 years. It was perhaps only natural that my travels would eventually take me back there, for I had been responsible, to a certain extent, for the green tinge in that 'wee splodge of olive' on the map. I had planted a lot of trees here in my time, and I was curious to find out whether they had survived our rather cavalier approach to the science of planting. How tall had they grown, if indeed they had grown at all? Or had they been felled to make way for some ghastly modern theme park full of hamburger stalls and plastic amusement arcades? It was time to see for myself.

Kilsture has been around for a long time. Famous figures from Scotland's warring past have amused themselves within its boundaries, mainly by indulging in such masculine pursuits as 'chasing the wild deer and following the roe'. First mentioned in a charter granted by Robert the Bruce, it passed through a number of owners over the centuries before falling into the hands of the Earls of Galloway. During much of this period there was not a great deal growing on it apart from hazel and thorn scrub, the odd clump of native pine, and plenty of bracken and whins. However, around 1790 it was quite extensively planted with more commercially acceptable hardwoods; oak, elm and beech for the drier ground and ash for the black, fertile soil of its damp hollows.

The exigencies of World War I and its aftermath saw most of these trees felled during the early part of the century. Various timber companies came in over the years, extracted what they wanted, and departed. The company that my father worked for was one of those. Indeed, we lived in the old Kilsture house for some years, until the Forestry Commission took over the whole area in 1934. My own recollection of this period is pretty hazy as I was fairly small at the time. But I do have two vivid memories. One of them is that we were never hungry. The Kilsture woods were alive with game and no woodcutter worth his salt would have allowed his family to starve while pheasants roosted nightly in the old thorn tree at the foot of the garden when the snow lay thick on the ground.

The second memory I have of the place from those days is that the house was haunted.

There was no question in the minds of my Hebridean mother and grandfather that there was something unnatural in the house. I needed no convincing at all, but my more pragmatic Perthshire father did not believe in ghosts. Or so he claimed. It's not that any of us actually ever saw anything, so far as I am aware. But sometimes in the blackness of a winter night, when the arctic winds came raging in from the Irish Sea over the flat fields and the grey dykes surrounding Sorbie to rattle the slates on our roof, sometimes when banshees were keening eerily and without pause in the chimney and sending flurries of blue wood smoke swirling back into our living room, sometimes, just sometimes, we could hear it. We could hear it moving up the bare wooden stairs to the attic...CLUMP...CLUMP...CLUMP...CLUMP... Heavy footsteps, slow and deliberate...CLUMP...CLUMP...then a drawn-out squeaking sound as the attic door was pushed open with agonising slowness...footsteps again, over the bare wooden boards of the attic floor, not clumping footsteps this time, but soft, padding, sinister footsteps, such as might have been made by large furry feet belonging to some brutish creature unknown to God or civilised man. Then would come the scrape of a phantom chair being dragged into position over the attic floor (our attic was empty of everything except dust) and – most spine-chilling of all – a very human, very deep and melancholy sigh, followed by the chair legs creaking in protest as though from the weight of SOMETHING – some perfectly unthinkable THING – sitting waiting for us up there in the darkness, with nothing at all, God save us, between us and IT but the frailty of the ceiling boards.

Then we would all huddle a bit closer to the fire, the scepticism of the head of the house waning noticeably as he jockeyed for position with the rest of us. My grandfather would throw another log onto the flames, sending showers of sparks flying up into the black void of the chimney to join the tempest outside. The paraffin lamp on the mantelpiece would be turned up to its highest level and God himself could not have induced any single one of us to leave the safety of that hearth before the light of dawn had banished all nightly spirits to their rightful repose amidst the morning stars.

*   *   *

From the outside, the house looked much the same as I remembered it. It looked much more cheerful, though: the blue whinstone walls had a less faded look about them and the whole façade had been tarted up to meet the demands of modern family living. Two large skylights protruding from the roof showed that the old attic had been converted into bedrooms and the ubiquitous television aerial sprouted from one of the chimney stacks.

The resident forester invited me in for a coffee. He had lived in the house for the past eight years and I found him to be most informative and helpful. Nothing about the interior evoked so much as a flicker of memory within me. It was all so orderly and up-to-date. I did not bother to ask about the ghost, partly for fear of ridicule and partly because of my conviction that it had simply become so disgruntled that it had exorcised itself from the house. There can surely be few things more off-putting to self-respecting ghosts than exposure to microwaves and Australian soap operas.

The Commission still ran the place, the forester told me, and, though there had been some felling, most of what we had planted was still there. The forest, he reckoned, was probably even more of a naturalist's paradise now than in my day. Roe deer and foxes were in abundance and the open nature of the forest created by the mix of tree species had attracted many types of moths and butterflies. These, in turn, had increased the bird population considerably. But the red squirrel had gone, wiped out by disease, and the corncrake – so vociferous in the surrounding fields in my youth – had vanished, a victim of modern farming methods.

I gave thanks and said my good-byes and walked down the track from the house to the main road. It had started to rain steadily. The clouds were low in the sky, with that settled-in look that tells everyone who has ever had anything to do with Galloway that the rain was here to stay a while. I pulled the collar of my coat up under the brim of my hat and trudged on.

The piping call of a bullfinch attracted my attention. I leaned over the roadside dyke and peered up into the tall larch tops, trying to locate it. These were the first trees I had ever planted in my life and I gazed at them, trying to envisage myself as a young lad all these years ago, planting bag slung around my back, sticking trees in the ground for a posterity that, in truth, we youngsters had little interest in. Why should we have had? Posterity was for the birds and the present was for us, the youth.

I climbed over the dyke and went into the trees. They towered far above me, their delicate lime-green fronds hanging heavy with water. I began to whistle, trying to imitate the call of the bullfinch as I had done so often in my youth. To my delight he appeared out of nowhere, settling on a fragile branch above me, cocking his glossy blue-black head inquisitively and piping mellifluously in answer to my calls, the soft pink hue of his breast gleaming richly in the murk.

I followed the line of ancient beech around the perimeter wall, skirting tangles of dogrose and briers as I did so. I had been given the job, back then, of removing all overhanging branches from those old trees so that they would not interfere with the development of those we were planting. To a youth such as myself who would much rather have climbed trees than walk on terra firma like a normal human being, this was an ideal job. The safety-conscious authorities of today would have had apoplexy if they could have seen me then, scrambling high among the branches like an ape, wielding billhook and handsaw, without benefit of rope or safety harness. The trees were very gnarled and wind-battered now, but the lumps of the old calluses from the branches I had cut down were still clearly visible.

The rain had eased somewhat by midday. I sat down on a gentle slope covered in tall, straight poles of silver-barked oak. This had been a mass of whin and blackthorn before we cleared it with axe and billhook ready for planting. Adders had been in abundance here, sunning themselves in the short grass between the thickets. Indeed, Kilsture as a whole had been a haven for these reptiles. The more foolhardy among us took awful chances with them, holding the twisting, furiously hissing reptiles by the tail at arm's length. We deserved to be bitten, but none of us ever were.

It was still spring and the new bracken had only just begun to edge its sappy green shoots through the thickets of last year's growth. The dead, coppery stalks of winter crackled and snapped as I ploughed through them. A few yards in front of me a roe deer, startled by the noise, exploded from the bracken and bounded away on stiff legs, like an African springbok. On a bare hummock some 50 yards away he stopped to look at me, eyes wide and anxious, nose twitching. I moved, and he vanished from my sight forever among the trees.

I leaned on the ancient wooden gate, looking out over the field bordering the forest. It was full of very tall, old whins. Whins live a very long time, and these, I was sure, would be the same whins that I had walked through so often in my youth. The same dry-stane dyke, too, its ancient stones silvery grey from the lichens welded onto them, wended its way drunkenly round the perimeter. A couple of whaups wheeled and dived over a particularly large clump of whins at the far corner of the field, their strange, melancholy cries echoing their displeasure at something they had spotted below them.

Wigtownshire, I reflected not for the first time, was a land of whins. Whins and dykes and whaups and wind and rain. They were all part of the beauty of the place, and it wouldn't be Wigtownshire without them. I recalled Robert Louis Stevenson's words:

> Blows the wind today,
> And the sun and the rain are flying;
> Blows the wind on the moors today and now,
>
> Where about the graves of the martyrs
> The whaups are crying,
> My heart remembers how!

The whaups were still highly agitated. Thinking that perhaps a fox was the source of their annoyance, I let myself through the gate and made my way over the field. Somewhat to our mutual embarrassment, what I succeeded in flushing from the depths of the whins was nothing more alarming than a brace of English, male and female. They had, they claimed, been sheltering from the rain when I disturbed them. Maybe they had, but there was a certain *je ne sais quoi* about them that hinted that they may have been telling me this to save my ancient blushes. Or their own. But they were young, so I readily forgave them in my mind for any mild duplicity.

I spoke to them for a little while. They were on their first visit to Galloway, they said, and they were staying with English relatives who had bought a farm cottage nearby and were renovating it with a view to selling it. This, they informed me, was happening everywhere these days. Old abandoned cottages, no longer required for farmhands in this age of increased mechanisation, were going cheap and being snapped up by speculators from the south.

They were enjoying their holiday despite the rain, they assured me. It was, they said, 'different'. But they did not think they would be back. Tenerife, they informed me wistfully, had more to offer young people. They found the local dialect quite impossible to understand so they made little attempt to fraternise with the natives. The pubs were all right in their old-fashioned way, they said, and they were generally full of people from south of the border anyway. 'Visitors?' I queried. No, not all of them, they said. Many had come up from England to escape the rat race and, liking what they saw, had decided to settle down here. Wigtownshire, with its timeless old-world air of bucolic charm, appealed to the more escapist among them.

They moved off towards the main road, he in the lead and she following demurely behind him. I was sorry to see them go, for I would have liked to have had a longer chat with them. They seemed a nice young couple. I hoped that I had not interrupted something between them among the whins that would have imprinted Galloway upon their memories forever.

Back in the woods I sat by the wee spring tucked in at the foot of the slope. It had been there when I was a boy and it had taken me some time to find it, buried as it was under an accumulation of years of dead bracken. But, once I had cleared this away, I found that water beetles still zigzagged their darting, mercurial trails over the surface, and the water was as pure and cold as it had ever been.

The rain had started up again. I rose and zipped up my coat. The weeping skies were drawing the day to a premature close and we were in for a dirty night. I gazed around me. The opposite slope was covered with oak, still bare of leaf for oak is a cautious tree: it is one of the last to expose tender young foliage to the vagaries of a Scottish spring. I had a vague memory of helping out with the planting of those but they were not what I was looking for. I had something else in mind.

I looked around me uncertainly. Then, at the far northern end of the slope, beyond the oak, I could just see the silhouette of a dense grove of conifers. Norway spruce. The Christmas tree of fable and tradition. Memory was suddenly as clear as the waters of the little spring I had just been drinking from. This was what I had been looking for. I had planted those. Our patient, long-suffering foreman, Neil Drysdale of Bladnoch, impressed by my inchoate enthusiasm, had given me this little plot all to myself to plant. These were MY trees. Every single one of them. I had planted them. Now, here they were, standing tall and proud, 50 feet high and more, beckoning to me. I crossed the hollow and walked swiftly through the oak towards them. Once I reached them, I did not hesitate. I got on my hands and knees and crawled under the denseness of their foliage, curling myself up comfortably on the thick, soft mattress of dry needles under them. Somewhere above me a wood pigeon began to croon throatily.

The patter of rain in the surrounding treetops grew steadier, a soporific accompaniment to the pigeon's hypnotic lullaby. I opened my rucksack and took out a packet of biscuits and a flask. The tea was still hot. Even warmer would be the half-bottle of Bladnoch I was reserving for later that night. It was going to be a long one, and I had no doubt that the ghosts of the past would be keeping me company.

But this time, I had nothing to fear from them. Why should I? I was one of them myself.